CRITICAL ACCLAIM FOR
The Great Pulp Heroes

"Highly recommended! The best book about the pulps that we have seen in years. Don Hutchison pours his love for the old magazines into this fascinating work. This should be on every pulp enthusiast's book shelf."

– ECHOES MAGAZINE

"A fantastic book! Don Hutchison is one of pulpdom's finest writers and researchers. This book is a pleasure to read. Buy it!"

– PULP VAULT MAGAZINE

"Don Hutchison was the first, the very first, to write about the great pulp heroes with grace and wit and intelligence-characteristics which still make his work a delight to read.

– ROBERT SAMPSON,
AUTHOR OF YESTERDAY'S FACES

"*The Great Pulp Heroes* is absolutely the last word when it comes to everything anyone needs to know about such popular culture icons as Doc Savage, Tarzan, The Shadow, Captain Future, and many, many more. It's a real page-turner. The narrative style drew me in, and I hoped it would go on forever."

– RON HANNA,
SECRET SANCTUM MAGAZINE

Don Hutchison is widely recognized as a leading authority on the history of the pulp fiction era. He has published numerous magazine and newspaper articles and two previous books on the subject, including *The Scarlet Riders: Action Packed Mountie Stories from the Fabulous Pulps*. He is the creator and editor of the acclaimed *Northern Frights* anthology series.

ADAPTED FROM MY
"GANGLAND'S DOOM" COVER 1973
FRANKLYN E. HAMILTON. 1990

by

DON HUTCHISON

Mosaic Press
Oakville, ON. - Buffalo, N.Y.

Canadian Cataloguing in Publication Data

Hutchison, Don.
  The great pulp heroes

ISBN 0-88962-585-9

1. Heroes in literature.   2.   American fiction -20th century - History
and criticism.   3.   Popular literature - United States - History and
criticism.   I. Title.

PS374.P63H8   1995   813'.5209351   C95-932067-9

Published by MOSAIC PRESS, P.O. Box 1032, Oakville, Ontario, L6J
5E9, Canada. Offices and warehouse at 1252 Speers Road, Units #1&2,
Oakville, Ontario, L6L 5N9, Canada and Mosaic Press, 85 River Rock
Drive, Suite 202, Buffalo, N.Y., 14207, USA.

Mosaic Press acknowledges the assistance of the Canada Council, the
Ontario Arts Council, the Ontario Ministry of Culture, Tourism and
Recreation and the Dept. of Canadian Heritage, Government of Canada,
for their support of our publishing programme.

FIRST PRINTING, 1996
SECOND PRINTING, 1998

Title logo by Steranko
Cover and book design by Susan Parker

Printed and bound in Canada
ISBN   0-88962-585-9

Distribution

In Canada:
MOSAIC PRESS, 1252 Speers Road, Units #1&2, Oakville, Ontario, L6L 5N9, Canada. P.O. Box 1032, Oakville, Ontario, L6J 5E9

In the United States:
MOSAIC PRESS, 85 River Rock Drive, Suite 202, Buffalo, N.Y., 14207

In the UK and Western Europe:
DRAKE INTERNATIONAL SERVICES, Market House, Market Place, Deddington, Oxford. OX15 OSF

Acknowledgements

The author would like to express his gratitude to Wooda (Nick) Carr, Hugh B. Cave, Fred Cook, Dave Darrigo, Tony Davis, Jack Deveny, Doug Ellis, Philip Jose Farmer, Ron Goulart, John Gunnison, Pete Harris, Rusty Hevelin, Tom Johnson, Chuck Juzek, Will Murray, Mark Pijanka, Jim Steranko, Tony Tollin, Albert Tonik, and Bob Weinberg, with special thanks to Frank Hamilton for his evocative portraits of wordsmiths and wizards. *The Great Pulp Heroes* is dedicated to the memory of Robert Sampson, Ryerson Johnson, and Henry Steeger.

Contents

THE GREAT STORY EXPLOSION

They were gaudy. They were gory. They were glorious. And they were everywhere.

Back in the thirties and forties every newsstand in places big enough to have sidewalks harbored stacks of magazines bearing enamelled covers designed to fly-paper the eyes with circus poster brilliance.

And what titles they had: *South Sea Stories! Black Mask! Adventure! Super Science Stories! Hollywood Detective! Magic Carpet! Doc Savage! Railroad Stories! The Spider! Northwest Romances! Famous Fantastic Mysteries! Jungle Stories! Western Raiders! Zeppelin Stories!*

The roll call is endless. They were called the pulps. By definition they were magazines of popular fiction handling such staples as adventure, action and romance. Between their birth in the first years of this century and their demise in the middle fifties they represented the greatest explosion of mass entertainment by way of the printed word that a thrill-seeking public ever experienced.

Variety was infinite. There were detective pulps, western pulps, science fiction pulps, sports pulps, romance pulps, gang war pulps, horror pulps, spicy mystery pulps, jungle and desert adventure pulps, and The Shadow. There were straight aviation pulps with names like *Dare-Devil Aces* and *Sky Fighters* as well as macabre variants like *G-8 And His Battle Aces*, which routinely ladled out titles like "Squadron of Corpses," "The Headless Staffel," and "Scourge of the Sky Beast." From railroad yarns to pirate stories, from the center of the earth to the farthest reaches of the universe, the gaudy, gory, glorious pulp magazines delivered on their promise: something for everyone.

How to explain the euphoria of the pulps? Perhaps you had to be there. You had to be young--at least in spirit. You had to be poor (most people were). You had to be part of that troubled, more innocent time. For armchair adventurers it was a Golden Age, before television, when imagination and a need for heroes were coupled with a world of vicarious wonders.

It is ironic that the most galvanic era in American popular culture was not that of the two Great Wars but the decade of the Great Depression when the popular arts were fired with creative optimism. Middle and lower class workers--whose fear was that of the breadline--flocked to movies with titles like *Flying Down to Rio*, *A Night at the Opera*, and *Grand Hotel*. And hero-hungry readers anxious to buy an hour's anodyne poured mountains of dimes across newsstand counters to find new worlds of adventure printed on cheap pulp paper sandwiched between eye-searing covers. Whole forests were levelled to supply the insatiable demand for dreams that mere pennies could buy. And the word merchants were there to make sure that demand never exceeded supply.

At a penny a word--sometimes more, but often less--you had to sell a lot of words to make a living. Even so, a few pulp scriveners discovered gold in them thar thrills. In the depths of the Great Depression it was rumored that a fictioneer named Frederick Faust (aka Max Brand) earned $80,000 a year on pulp writing

10¢ MAGAZINE GUIDE
Wholesome Reading 10¢

DOC SAVAGE

This AMAZING ADVENTURER

Breathless . . . hair-raising feats in strange lands among strange peoples. . . . Doc Savage and his scrappy pals always help the helpless.

10¢ Exciting yarns that add a new zest to life. Monthly.

THE Shadow

THE WEIRD CRIME AVENGER

The strange creature in black whose sinister laugh sends shudders down the spine of crookdom.

10¢ TWICE MONTHLY

BILL BARNES

ACE OF CLOUD-LAND

He sweeps across the heavens in his Scarlet Bomber and spoils the best-laid plans of evildoers.

10¢ Monthly

Cowboy Stories

FRONTIER LIFE LIVES AGAIN

Thudding hoofs . . . barking guns . . . cattle camp yarns and tales of mountain treachery.

Monthly

10¢

alone. He wound up living like a Medici in a castle in Italy, surrounded by a retinue of servants.

As the audience for pulp thrills grew, the magazines became an enormous market for would-be wordsmiths as well as familiar names. By the 1920s and 1930s the mass-market pulps were into a Golden Age of creativity, with new and exciting writers commanding armies of devoted fans.

The fantasy pulps developed such names as Robert E. Howard, H.P. Lovecraft and Edgar Rice Burroughs. The detective story was elevated to a fine--and peculiarly American--art form by the gargantuan talents of Dashiell Hammett, Raymond Chandler and Cornell Woolrich. The Western pulps had Max Brand, Walt Coburn and Ernest Haycox among others, and the adventure fiction field boasted too many famous names to enumerate.

Possibly the only fictional category invented by the pulps was that of science fiction. Beginning as early as 1910 adventure titles like *Argosy* and *All-Story Magazine* had featured what they called "scientific romances," stories of lost races and adventure on other planets. But it took a man named Hugo Gernsback to begin a new magazine, *Amazing Stories*, that would deal exclusively with this new breed of story as a genre in itself. Gernsback's discovery led the way to other pulp titles that attracted the early works of Ray Bradbury, Isaac Asimov, and Robert Heinlein.

It was a literary Gold Rush, but for the few who struck pay dirt (Hammett, Burroughs, Erle Stanley Gardner) hundreds of others found the panning tough. In his book *The Pulp Jungle*, author Frank Gruber confided: "There were in existence, at this time, some 150 pulp magazines, solidly established. A vast market for stories. But these were still Depression Days and the competition was fierce. It was a literary jungle and every writer was a tiger. You had to be brash, you had to be tough, you had to claw your way into the jungle and fight for your life every minute you were in it. There were more writers than there were magazines. All were hungry writers."

Storytellers have always existed, of course, from caveman practitioners who spun tales to keep the clan together and the demons at bay, through Dumas and Dickens to twentieth century writers like Edgar Wallace who could, and did, churn out a novel a week and in between find time to dash off a play and a few short stories. But never before and never again did there exist a market for wordsmiths like that of the fabulous pulps. Each month brightly colored covers shrilled the names of hundreds of writers as familiar as household brands. To their fans, they were names that crackled with the thrill of lightning: Carroll John Daly, H. Bedford Jones, Cornell Woolrich, Walt Coburn, Raymond Chandler, Robert E. Howard, A. Merritt, Edmond Hamilton, Hugh B. Cave, Talbot Mundy, Harold Lamb, Johnston McCulley, and legions of others.

While the pulp magazine was a twentieth century publishing sensation, the history of cheap fiction for the masses can be traced as far back as the Industrial Revolution. When more leisure time for workers was combined with universal education and the invention of the steam printing press, a new reading public was created. Inevitably, a new type of literature arose to meet demand--a literature that did not attempt to educate or uplift, but existed simply to entertain. Freed of the patronage of the well educated and the wealthy, it was a literature conceived as a branch of show business, produced for a mass audience that wished to be excited and amused.

What we now call "pulp" fiction was produced as early as the 1840's when publishers decided that one way to lower costs, and thus price, was to use newspaper presses and cheap newsprint paper. A news sheet, doubled to make four pages, made a reasonable book-like format. The product of this discovery was something called the family story paper.

Such story papers as *The Corsair* and the *Yankee Privateer*, although called newspapers and enjoying special newspaper postal rates, were really collections of fiction that ran novels in serial form.

Then came the revolution. In 1860 a firm called Beadle & Adams published a paperbound novel for ten cents, titled *Malaeska: The Indian Wife of The White Hunter*. The dime novel had arrived. Small wonder that the first dime novel was a homespun western, or that the most popular series characters would be frontier icons like Buffalo Bill Cody, Kit Carson, and Jesse James. (The dime novel dream parade also included such fictitious buckaroos as Red River Bill, Deadshot Dave, Young Wild West, and the marvellously alliterative Roaring Ralph Rockwood, the Reckless Ranger).

For the next forty years dime novels (later reduced to a nickel) would pour from the presses by the million. They would be much criticized and reviled; but generations of children gobbled them up because they found that beneath their lurid paper covers were even more lurid stories chock full of blood, bullets, heart-stopping suspense and relentless, frantic action. The dime novel shocker introduced and defined many of the staples of pulp fiction: western stories, war stories, pirate stories, romance stories, detective stories, and even continuing character series.

By the turn of the century the appeal of the dime novel had waned. Its characters, style, and action-oriented plots were soon transferred to the "pulps," so called because a publisher named Frank Munsey had begun to print an all-fiction magazine titled *The Argosy* on cheap pulpwood paper. Munsey had the idea that the story was more important than what it was printed on. He must have guessed correctly because the lowly pulp magazine went on to become the most popular form of reading material in America between World War I and the end of World War II.

Street & Smith, a dime novel giant, began converting paper-covered books into pulp magazines as early as 1903. Eventually, *The Buffalo Bill Weekly* dime novel series was transformed into *Western Story Magazine*, with old Bill held over briefly in a series of new stories. Likewise, that resolute but fictitious detective, Nick Carter, became editor emeritus of the newly-created *Detective Story Magazine*. Other genres--science fiction, love story, horror, war and aviation--soon followed.

What made the pulps different from the weekly story papers and dime novels was that they were true magazines, generous in both size and variety of content. They were an all-permeating atmosphere, a delirious environment of irresistibly lurid covers, dynamic illustrations, worshipful letters and breathless fiction. For only ten cents or a little more--the price of a magazine containing novels, short stories, departments and artwork--a reader could get lost in the violent lives of heroes and heroines as outsize and engrossing as any to be found in the great myths and legends.

As pulp publisher Henry Steeger once explained it: "Pulps were the principal entertainment vehicle for millions of Americans. They were an unflickering, uncolored TV screen upon which the reader could spread the most glorious imagination he possessed. The athletes were stronger, the heroes were nobler, the girls were more beautiful and the palaces were more luxurious than any in existence; they were always there at any time of the day or night on dull, no-gloss paper that was kind to the eyes."

Not surprisingly, the heyday of the pulp heroes was the period of the "dirty thirties." The Great Depression had smashed into America with the ferocity of a hurricane. Unemployment became a way of life, creating a new "leisure class," as hundreds of thousands of rootless scarecrow figures shuffled through breadlines and soup kitchens, wan symbols of hard times. Pulp paper fiction was the cheapest thrill around, and tattered copies of

Detective Fiction Weekly and *Dime Western* were passed from hand to hand or left behind in boxcars and hobo jungles. To most citizens the NRA acronym stood for National Recovery Act, but pulp fiction publishers proudly carried the familiar NRA blue eagle on their covers, stating that it promised "New Reading Appeal."

As the Roaring Twenties roared to their cataclysmic market crash, many North Americans had learned to accept organized crime (created by Prohibition) as "big business," and gangsters as a form of barbaric royalty. But the glorification of gang rule took an abrupt turn in the Great Depression when Americans wakened from their paralysis of fascination and began looking for new heroes who did not reflect the rule of force over ideals. As usual, the pulps were there to supply what the public desired.

Pulp avengers--individuals of strength, speed, brains and stamina--arose to do battle with working class America's perceived enemies: gangsters, bankers, punks, fiends, lawyers, politicians, and threatening foreign hordes. The most famous of these avengers, The Shadow, leaped into the fray in 1931 as the first titular hero of his own magazine. He proved that a magazine built around the exploits of a single character was an idea whose time had come. *The Shadow* took off like a flashfire, causing scores of new "character" titles to pop up on the news-stands, ranging from outright imitations to new departures. There were aviation heroes (*The Lone Eagle* and *Bill Barnes*), masters of disguise (*Secret Agent X* and *The Phantom Detective*), western heroes (*The Rio Kid* and *The Lone Ranger*), adventure heroes (*Doc Savage* and *The Skipper*), and even a science fiction hero (*Captain Future*). Ironically, One of the most famous of all pulp hero creations, Johnston McCulley's Zorro ("the Robin Hood of California") never did have his own title, but he appeared regularly in the magazines from his inception in 1919 right up to the final gasp of the pulps themselves.

Much has been made of the pulp magazines as training grounds for serious "literary" authors ranging from MacKinlay Kantor to Tennessee Williams. The fact is that most of the pulps treasured by collectors today represent an unpretentious, calculatedly disposable literature that was too exciting to be respectable and too much fun to be taken seriously.

The series hero is older than Beowulf and Ulysses. No doubt conceived around the flickering glow of Stone Age campfires, the protracted adventures of heroic champions appeal to the child in all of us--the kid who is willing to have a good story repeated because he wants it never to end. In the tradition of such literary ancestors, the great heroes of the pulps were not conceived as carriers of substantive meaning; they were invented for fans of the preposterous, for connoisseurs of the outrageous--for the child that lurks in all of us.

Say what you will of the great pulp heroes, but they were a beguiling lot. With their narratives yoked to gut emotions, they brought messages of a limitless world of adventure and experience, a great shining universe that was full of color and juice, where heroes were not forced to do homework, mow lawns, go to bed early, or eat up their vegetables. It was all fantasy, of course--heroism rampant with seldom a dull or ugly moment--but it got a lot of readers through some hard times and filled their minds with hope, wonder, and even inspiration.

ON SALE
THE FIRST FRIDAY
OF EACH MONTH

NICK CARTER DETECTIVE MAGAZINE

REG. U. S. PAT. OFF.

Vol. VI   FEBRUARY, 1936   Number 6

"Keep your body, your clothing, and your conscience clean."

THE SHADOW'S SHADOW

Thundering automatics blasting red-tipped flame rumble in the night...answering blasts echo back...final volleys from automatics...silence. Then from the blackness behind automatics moves a deeper blackness--a shadow within a shadow--and disappears into the night. On the chill night air is born a peal of laughter. The triumphant laugh of The Shadow! *"Who knows what evil lurrrrrks in the hearts of men? The Shadow knows! H e h h h h h h h h h - h e h h h h h h h h h - hehhhhhhhh."*

Probably No lines in old-time radio or mystery fiction are as famous as that sonorous question and its echoing triumphant answer. Following his magazine debut in April of 1931 The Shadow led the fight against crime and boredom for almost two decades--on the airwaves, in his own long-lived magazine, and in comics and movies, as well as toys, games and all the other paraphernalia associated with a commercially created folk-myth idol. No wonder he was always laughing.

Of all the mystery men of Pulpland, none was more popular or more influential than The Shadow. For legions of fans he was the uncrowned king of mystery. He was mystery personified.

If one were to ask "Who is/was The Shadow?", a generation of radio buffs would intone, "The Shadow is, in reality, Lamont Cranston, wealthy young man about town who, years ago in the Orient, learned the hypnotic power to cloud men's minds so they could not see him." And another generation of pulp story enthusiasts would reply, "Not so." It seems that pulp readers were privy to more confidential disclosures. In the magazine stories Lamont Cranston was but one of the disguises of the real Shadow who was Kent Allard, an explorer-aviator-adventurer whose identity as the Master of Darkness is known only to two Xinca Indians sworn to eternal secrecy.

Unlike his radio counterpart, the magazine Shadow at no time "clouded men's mind to render himself invisible." Instead, he used a black cloak and black slouch hat to blend into the shadows of night, sometimes hiding in the gloom of an otherwise brightly-lit room. In the glowering cover portraits by George Rozen, his cloak became crimson-lined with a crimson collar covering his mouth (pulp covers needed color!) leaving the "burning eyes" and "hawk-like" visage prominently exposed. Other icons which appeared frequently on those amazing covers included his giant licorice-colored .45 automatics and a fire opal ring.

As another contrast to The Shadow of radio fame--who had only his "friend and companion, the lovely Margo Lane" to assist him--the pulp Shadow was supported by a veritable army of aides. They included Burbank, his mysterious contact man who spent his life at a switchboard; Harry Vincent, who acted as The Shadow's advance man and proxy; Rutledge Mann, an investment broker; Clayde Burke, a reporter on the Classic, who furnished

The Shadow with inside information; Moe Shrevnitz, who transported the Crime Master to battle--in his taxicab; Cliff Marsland and "Hawkeye" who posed as criminals to ferret crimedom's secrets; an expert lockpicker named Tapper; and the giant African, Jericho, whose terrifying physical strength was equalled only by his willingness to fight crime.

Whenever necessary, The Knight of Darkness dispensed with his fighting togs to assume the guise of Lamont Cranston, Henry Arnaud, or "Fritz," the dull-mannered janitor at police headquarters. As wealthy playboy Cranston he maintained a friendship with Police Commissioner Ralph Weston; as Fritz he managed to keep an eye on Weston's right-hand man, Inspector Joe Cardona. Sometimes he appeared as a character named George Clarendon, sometimes as elderly Phineas Twambley, and once as the Rajah of Lengore. In one story, "The North Woods Mystery," The Shadow is revealed as Beaver Luke, an Indian character who is said to be establishing new beaver colonies for the Canadian government.

It can be argued that The Shadow as a character ranks among the great creations of popular fiction. Like Sherlock Holmes and Tarzan, he is greater than all the stories in which he appears, his weird and inexplicable nature appealing to some deep recess in the human psyche. Ironically, the character did not spring from any one man's imagination--deep and shadowy or otherwise--but instead was created by public appeal mated with blind luck.

Foremost amongst the pulp publishers of the 1930s was Street & Smith, the fabled fiction factory. The company sponsored a Thursday night radio program, one of whose functions was to promote their *Detective Story* magazine. The "announcer" on the program was a mysterious character with a sepulchral voice known as The Shadow--purely a radio gimmick to lend an air of mystery to the proceedings. Surprisingly, the wickedly mirthful radio voice caught the public fancy. Acting quickly, the Messrs. Street & Smith decided to rush out something called *The Shadow, A Detective Magazine,* copyrighting the title to protect their new discovery.

In its dime novel days the company had created such fictional marvels as Nick Carter, Buffalo Bill and Frank Merriwell. Street & Smith general manager Henry W. Ralston saw the new title as a way of reintroducing the concept of a single-character hero magazine. He even salvaged a leftover Nick Carter manuscript with the idea of rewriting it to fit the new character. Propitiously, none of his regular writers fancied the task of reworking an antedated private eye into some kind of terminally weird cloaked phantom.

In a move born of possible frustration, the job was eventually farmed out to to a young newspaperman and part-time magician named Walter Brown Gibson, who just happened to drop by the company offices looking for writing assignments. Gibson was asked to turn out a 75,000-word story about a mysterious being called The Shadow. That was it. Nobody told him who The Shadow was because nobody knew.

Since the character did not belong to the writer but to the publisher, Street & Smith insisted that Gibson write the novels using a penname. He utilized the names of two magic dealers, Maxwell Holden and U. F. Grant, to create the inspired pseudonym of Maxwell Grant.

The first story, appropriately titled "The Living Shadow," is not a typical example of pulse-pounding pulp action. Gibson was a journalist, not a fiction writer. Creating the adventures of The Shadow was an assignment that required learning on the job. He took as his model an old Horatio Alger dime novel, using it as a guideline to work out the number of chapters and words to a chapter in order to fashion it to the correct length. Nowhere in the book is the identity of The Shadow revealed; Gibson had not decided upon it at the time. The Shadow is merely a mysterious figure whose voice is heard on the radio, sometimes passing on coded clues to his operatives. This was before the dramatized radio series

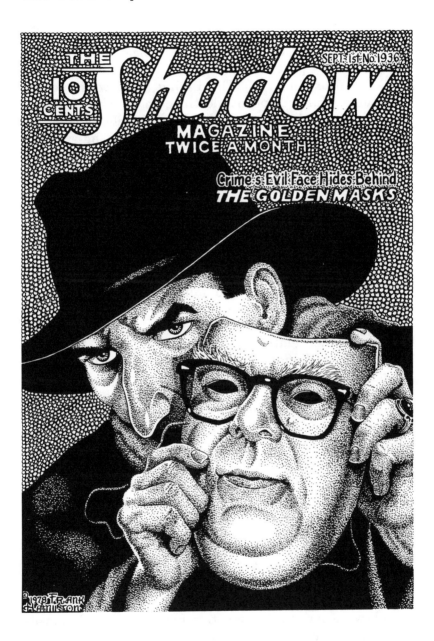

Walter Gibson and Friend

began and refers of course to the "voice" heard on the *Detective Story* program.

The proxy hero of "The Living Shadow" is young, handsome, Harry Vincent--destined to be The Shadow's top agent. As the story opens, the melancholic Harry is about to commit suicide by leaping off a fog-swathed bridge. He is snatched to safety by Gibson's sinister-looking protagonist who, in turn, demands a life of servitude. "Your life is no longer your own," the cloaked stranger warns him. "I shall improve it...But I shall risk it, too. Perhaps I shall lose it, because I have lost lives, just as I have saved them. This is my promise: life, with enjoyment, with danger, with excitement...Life, above all, with honor. But if I give it, I demand obedience. Absolute obedience." In the years to follow, on more than one occasion, Harry must have wished he had jumped.

Almost to everyone's surprise, the first issue sold out. A second one, featuring "The Eyes of the Shadow," introduced millionaire Lamont Cranston, a member of New York's exclusive Cobalt Club. It is strongly suggested that Cranston may be the true identity of the mysterious Shadow. But only an issue later, in "The Shadow Laughs," Cranston is disqualified in the role by the *real* Shadow, who convinces the globe-trotting playboy to leave the country so that The Shadow can impersonate him in comfort. They alone share the secret, with the possible exception of Burbank, The Shadow's chair-bound contact man.

These first three stories are intricate, episodic narratives, brimming with atmosphere and clotted with incidental characters. What they lacked was the delirious action so beloved by pulp fans. This was partly because Gibson was blissfully ignorant of pulp stereotypes--his models were mainstream mystery novels of an earlier era-- and partly because of an editorial vision that saw The Shadow as a living symbol for all that was mysterious and puzzling. As mystery enthusiast Chris Steinbrunner once explained, "Menacing figures dressed in black had long been popular characters in mystery stories, films and plays...Gibson took this terrible dread shape that had hitherto been the hero's nemesis and made it the hero. The Shadow was both the force for good and lurker in the darkness."

One of the places the cloaked phantom lurked was in his own New Jersey mansion, conveniently located close to New York City crime lords. His plush manse had a tower room outfitted as a wireless station from which he and contact man Burbank communicated with his army of dedicated aides. He had his own plane stationed at a nearby hangar and even an autogiro, a prototype of the present-day helicopter, which could whisk him to perilous rooftop encounters.

When he wasn't using Moe Shrevnitz's souped-up cab, The Shadow was ferried around in an imported limousine driven by Cranston's imperturbable chauffeur, Stanley. The back seat of the limousine was witness to numerous magical transformations as the pseudo Cranston slipped into something more comfortable:

> *A low, soft laugh came from the hidden lips of Lamont Cranston. The man half raised himself in the back seat. Something black enmeshed him; the folds of a somber garment fluttered toward the floor. Then the pallid face of Cranston disappeared as the shadow of a hat brim settled upon it. Invisible hands raised clinking objects from the suitcase. All was blackness in the rear of the limousine. A transformation had taken place, though even Stanley had not realized it. Lamont Cranston had become The Shadow!*

Good old dense Stanley. He never did twig to the fact that he served two masters.

Sometimes The Shadow repaired to his sanctum--a blue-lit grotto in the Manhattan badlands. The eerie isolation of the mystic sanctum undoubtedly helped relieve pent-up tension; it was here that the clandestine crime fighter spent endless hours chortling to the four walls and/or writing cryptic messages to himself in invisible ink. It was all very strange; but nobody ever accused The Shadow of being mister average guy.

The Shadow was mystery piled upon mystery. Even his face was something of an enigma. In one novel it is suggested that his true face is absolutely featureless. In another, "The Shadow's Shadow" (Feb. 1, 1933), master criminal Felix Zubian stares into the countenance of The Shadow--not the disguised features of Lamont Cranston or Henry Arnaud-- and he recoils in horror.

What did The Shadow *really* look like? Only The Shadow knew.

Readers must have adored the mysterioso shenanigans. Within months *The Shadow* went from quarterly to monthly, and within a year or two was selling more than 300,000 copies per issue. Gibson signed yet another contract. The magazine would appear twice a month; he was to produce twenty-four adventures per year, one 60,000-word novel every two weeks for as long as the popularity of The Shadow continued. That figure totalled more than 1,440,000 words per year.

The circulation soared. By living, thinking, even dreaming the life of The Shadow, Gibson was to chronicle the Master Avenger's activities for a hectic eighteen years. Keeping two dozen yarns ahead of publication he sometimes turned out a fresh book in from four to six days, often working all night to meet self-imposed deadlines.

Behind a typewriter, he was as superhuman as his own creation. He worked on a battery of machines. When one began to "get tired," he'd move on to another, and then a third. He worked in a continuous flow, actually living the life of The Shadow as he typed, until his fingers began to swell or the tips became bloody.

"By living, thinking, even dreaming the story in one continued process," Gibson revealed, "ideas came faster and faster. Sometimes the typewriter keys would fly so fast that I wondered if my fingers could keep up with them. And at the finish of the story I often had to take a few days off as my fingertips were too sore to begin work on the next book."

An irrepressible raconteur brimming with energy, Walter Gibson was uniquely qualified to serve as The Shadow's personal biographer. While still a boy he had taken to puzzles and sleight-of-hand, and thought seriously of making magic his life's work. Instead he became a reporter for the now-defunct *Philadelphia North American* and later moved on to the Ledger Syndicate where he wrote Sunday features and, with his "Puzzle a Day" column, helped to make the crossword puzzle a national craze. A friend and confidante of this century's greatest magicians--Houdini, Thurston, Blackstone--Gibson ghosted books for all of them as well as devising many of their illusions.

"Magic and Mystery," Gibson once wrote, "are so closely interwoven that it is hard to tell where one leaves off and the other begins."

Magic and Mystery. Mystery and Magic. These were the polarities of Gibson's existence; and they would become the secret of the special qualities that would raise The Shadow beyond the level of a mere pulp character.

While The Shadow was the first pulp hero to be awarded his own magazine, it should be noted in fairness that he reflected a long line of phantom avengers and dual-identity mystery men, some dating as far back as the previous century. These included such early characters as Fantomas, the Scarlet Pimpernel, Arsene Lupin, and the pulps' own Zorro, the cloaked "Robin Hood of California."

One acknowledged inspiration for The Shadow was that of Jimmie Dale, alias The Gray Seal. Jimmie Dale was the hero of a series of books (and pulp serials) written after the end of World War I by a Canadian writer named Frank L. Packard. They are out of print now and are likely to remain so, but they formed a template that Walter Gibson and many of his imitators would follow.

Nearly two decades before the advent of the first pulp hero magazine Packard wrote of a hero who stalked the night in a black mask and slouch hat to aid the helpless and to bring criminals to justice. Like The Shadow, many of the Gray Seal's adventures occurred in a Chinatown setting--a sinister, pulp-style Chinatown where tong wars were declared, ghastly murders hatched, and where a man's life was worth the price of a little opium--or even less.

Although Jimmie Dale owned a luxurious Riverside Drive mansion and belonged to the exclusive St. James Club (surely a model for Lamont Cranston's Cobalt Club), as The Gray Seal he maintained an underworld "Sanctuary," deep in the heart of the east side Bad Lands, where no questions were asked so long as the rent was paid. The Sanctuary was where he kept his disguises, a change of clothes and weapons, and from which he emerged in his disguise as Larry The Bat, a stooped, gaunt underworld figure.

Disguise was also to be a way of life for the jolly illusionist who created and chronicled the adventures of The Shadow under the invented name of Maxwell Grant. As the fame of his character grew, Walter Gibson's anonymity must have proved frustrating. He began to inject characters with monickers like Blister Wagon, Wilton Barges, Lewis G. Barton and Granite Bowles--all anagrams of his real name.

Under any name, Gibson's work brimmed with invention and novelty. Thanks to him, The Shadow did not remain fixed or static in character--and neither did his adventures. The two were always in a state of flux, as mercurial and energetic as the man who pounded them out in a creative fever. Most of the early exploits involved proxy heroes, with The Shadow remaining off-stage as a nebulous figure of Gothic mystery, almost omniscient. As Gibson--and his readers--became familiar with the character, the image solidified into that of a sinister magician-wraith, confounding evil-doers with a bag of tricks ranging from wall-hugging suction cups to finger-snapping explosive powders.

None of this was accidental. Gibson, Henry Ralston, and Shadow editor John Nanovic held regular story conferences, guiding The Shadow's destiny with the care and consideration of loving parents. The "think tank" approach helped Gibson keep the series fresh and ever changing. Unlike many of the pulp hero magazines, one issue of The Shadow is not a carbon copy of another.

What made Gibson's contribution to the form unique was the combination of a magician's flair for misdirection and illusion with a journalist's respect for facts and accuracy. Gibson always stressed that no matter how fanciful his yarns might become, the descriptions of people, places and things were accurate in essential details. Despite his mind-numbing work schedule the reporter in him took the time to check on guns, gems, cults, wills, spies, ghosts, morgues and all sorts of deadly devices that The Shadow might encounter. He briefed himself on unusual localities and strange legends that would intrigue readers.

"I always tried to keep the stories informative," Gibson said. "You pick up any of The Shadows and you read about something happening on the Limited between

New York and Savannah, why you'll find it's running
exactly according to the timetable of 1936 or whenever the
story was written."

Because of the speed with which he had to work,
combined with his lively interest in all things, many of the
characters and details of The Shadow novels are like an
ongoing record of Walter Gibson's life and enthusiasms.
Almost everything was grist for his story mill.

As the author travelled, so did his creation. Gibson
built a cabin in Maine and began to spend winters in
Florida. Both locations became Shadow locales. "The
London Crimes" and "Castle of Doom" were set in England.
"Washington Crime" and "The Case of Congressman
Coyd" took place in the nation's capitol. "The Mardi Gras
Mystery" reflected a New Orleans experience. In "Gangdom's
Doom" The Shadow cleaned up Chicago; and once, in a
story titled "Quetzal," he found himself on the wrong end
of a Mexican firing squad.

In a conversation I once had with Walter Gibson, he
revealed that the 1936 Shadow yarn, "The Northwoods
Mystery," had been based on a trip into the Ontario
Northland. "You know, I was criticized for including a
French Canadian guide named Pierre," he confided.
"Some people thought the character and his name were too
much of a pulp magazine cliche or something. But, darn
it, I really did have a guide who was just like that
character-- and his name really *was* Pierre!"

As the series progressed, important changes took
place. Early Shadow novels had been written in the
discreet non-violent manner of 1920s detective thrillers.
All too often The Shadow's foes were small-time hoods
bearing such cheap names as Squint Preston, Nogger
Tellif and Konk Zitz. (If Mr. and Mrs. Tellif had given it
any thought, they might have known that a name like
Nogger would get their kid into hot water sooner or later).

In those early stories, The Shadow's guns "blasted,"
"roared" and "boomed," sending demoralized punks "howling" and "cowering" back to their miserable rat holes; but

he seldom if ever really *killed* anyone. Fortunately, things improved.

The vaporous night creature of the early stories gradually solidified into an awesome figure of lethal jurisprudence. By 1933, he began cutting a bloody swath through the underworld, judging, condemning and executing bulge-eyed crooks and killers--not neatly, but with an oversize .45 in both hands--and all the while: that low laugh! Atmosphere became charged with action. The newer, sterner Shadow didn't believe in justice--he *was* justice--implacable and inevitable.

> *There were no echoes to his sardonic laugh. The reverbrations of The Shadow's mirth were drowned in the roar of his .45s as the controlling fingers loosed a stream of lead into the midst of the startled mobsters.*
>
> *Bodies thudded to the floor. Gasping oaths spattered from snarling lips that closed to speak no more. Shattered flashlights fell useless. With one fierce volley from his recoiling automatics, The Shadow cleared the way. Upon the floor lay the piled up bodies Gats Hackett's new band of killers--men who would never slay for their black-hearted chief.*
>
> *The automatics disappeared beneath The Shadow's cloak. He had used every cartridge. The hands emerged, bringing forth another pair of pistols. With a forward spring, the black-clad figure swept over the mass of bodies that cluttered the doorway to the hall.*

Readers loved it. They bought magazines. They mailed off dimes for Shadow pins and rubber stamps. They wrote idolatrous letters to his magazine.

By 1937 many of The Shadow's fan letters requested membership in his 'Century Club'--an honor list of readers who claimed to have read one hundred or more of his adventures. One Shadowholic went so far as to express his dedication with the threat of applied torture: "If Maxwell Grant ever quits writing The Shadow stories or runs out of ideas, he should be made to feel the soothing embrace of the Iron Maiden. No offense meant, Mr. Grant."

Numerous correspondents stressed fascination with The Shadow's criminous foes, who necessarily grew more monstrous as he disposed of their wimpy predecessors. Reacting to public enthusiasm, a roll call of master fiends arose in novels bearing their grotesque names: "The Black Master," "Charg, Monster," "Gray Fist," "The Murder Master," "The Creeper," and "The Cobra." One Shadow novel titled "The Hydra" dealt not with a single super foe but with a criminal organization which put forth two new hoodlums whenever one was killed, much as the Hydra of legend sprouted two new heads each time one was severed.

Occasionally a villain would escape The Shadow's wrath long enough to make a return appearance. The first of these was Rodil Mocquino, the evil Haitian voodoo doctor, who led his zombie slaves in "The Voodoo Master" (March 1, 1936), "City of Doom" (May 15, 1936), and "Voodoo Trail" (June 1, 1938). Other recurring villains included The Hand, The Wasp and The Prince of Evil.

From his beginning, The Shadow's favorite crime haunts were the so-called Chinatowns on both coasts, reflecting Gibson's admiration for Sax Rohmer's popular Fu Manchu novels. Known as Ying Ko to the Chinese, The Master of Darkness skulked through New York's Chinatown in "The Living Shadow," "The Fate Joss," "The Chinese Disks," "The Living Joss," and "The Jade Dragon." San Francisco's Chinatown encountered him in "Green Eyes," "The Chinese Tapestry," "Six Men of Evil," "Teeth of the Dragon," "The Chinese Primrose," and finally in "Jade Dragon," the latter not to be confused with "The Jade Dragon" of 1942, which was set in Manhattan's Chinatown.

❖ Theodore Tinsley ❖

MAXWELL GRANT'S SHADOW

©1978 FRANK HAMILTON

After numerous Chinatown combats it was perhaps inevitable that The Shadow would eventually encounter an Oriental super villain whose abilities and resources were the equal of his own.

As Walter Gibson explained it, "That was left for Shiwan Khan in 'The Golden Master' of September 15, 1939. Since The Shadow in his early years had visited Tibet, there to acquire hypnotic powers that helped him to triumph over fiends of crime, it stood to reason that his nemesis--if he should ever have one--would have to come from that mystic land in order to challenge The Shadow on his home ground. Shiwan Khan not only came from Tibet, he claimed that he owned it, along with outlying territories, which made him formidable, indeed."

Shiwan Khan, The Shadow's own Yellow Peril, stalked through four novels, along with his colorful retinue of Mongols, Chinese, Afghans, Tibetan wizards and (shades of Sax Rohmer) Dacoit stranglers.

Ironically, it wasn't superfiends who gave The Shadow sleepless nights, but some of the Master Avenger's own

imitators. By the mid thirties flamboyant rivals like Popular Publications' *The Spider* began cutting into sales. Suspecting that Gibson's intricate, atmospheric style might need boosting, Street & Smith decided to hire another 'Maxwell Grant' in order to inject fresh input into the series. The idea wasn't to replace Gibson but simply to introduce the odd pulp-style action story to give the magazine variety. They found such a thrill doctor in a writer named Theodore Tinsley.

A frequent contributor to the prestigious *Black Mask* magazine, Tinsley was a skilled craftsman who matched the familiar Gibson style while introducing his own brand of hardboiled, cliff-hanging suspense. His most significant contribution, however, was the introduction of scenes featuring females disrobing or having their clothing ripped strategically. This allowed cover artists to introduce mildly titillating situations--at least by Street & Smith's sedate standards. Sales bounced back, probably due to the liberated covers rather than the new author's excellent but unacknowledged contributions. (It was during the Tinsley era that George Rozen's powerful, symbolic covers gave way to Graves Gladney's more illustrative paintings).

Over seven years -- from "Partners in Peril" (November 1, 1936) to "Golden Peril" (June 1943)--Tinsley contributed 27 novels to the series, roughly four a year. While Gibson's Shadow reflected the author's interest in magic, Tinsley's Shadow was never far removed from trains. One of his finest contributions was "The Pooltex Tangle" (October 1, 1937), a lightning-paced ode to steam-puffing chariots and the glimmering sweep of metal rails.

With his Shadow workload reduced to a mere twenty novels a year, Walter Gibson occupied his "spare time" with numerous other assignments. One of these was The Shadow comic book which Street & Smith originated to cash in on the juvenile market that had sprung up as an offshoot of the hero pulps. He wrote the comic book Shadow from the first issue on for six years, condensing highlights from specific novels into the required number of pages.

Small wonder that The Shadow's fame soon spread like wildfire into other mediums, the foremost of which were the classic radio melodramas that outlasted the magazine by five years. While the pulp novels were basically mystery stories enriched with atmosphere and

incident, the radio programs were outright melodramas, often luridly so. Episodes like "Isle of the Dead," "Tomb of Terror," "When the Grave is Open," and "The Gibbering Things" were commonplace, as were yarns about werewolves, ghouls, haunted houses and other trappings of the Gothic spook story. The idea was to chill you a little so that the sponsor, Blue Coal, could warm you up with hearty messages about winter heating.

In addition to the comic book, there were Big Little Books, a syndicated daily comic strip, and a host of commercial tie-ins such as Shadow disguise kits, The Shadow pencil lite, Shadow masks, Shadow capes, games, stationery, ad infinitum. A 1940 issue of the magazine (carrying an illustrated ad for a plethora of Shadow-oriented games and gimmicks) admonished young readers to "Make it a Shadow Christmas!"

The Shadow was also the subject of one movie serial and seven feature films. Silent movie retread Rod LaRocque donned cape and black hat unenthusiastically in Grand National's 1937 turkey, "The Shadow Strikes." He returned again in "International Crime" as a radio crime reporter known as The Shadow, sans cape and hat. In 1946 Monogram starred athletic Kane Richmond in three disappointingly facetious Shadows titled "Behind the Mask," "The Shadow Returns," and "The Missing Lady."

A later Shadow feature, "Bourbon Street Shadows" (aka "Invisible Avenger") was produced by Republic in 1958. Until the 1994 special-effects laden Universal film starring Alec Baldwin, it was notable mainly as the only movie version in which Cranston/Shadow became invisible by "clouding men's minds."

The serial, released by Columbia in 1940, was titled simply "The Shadow." To its credit, it drew inspiration from its pulp magazine source, even if The Shadow did use .38 revolvers instead of his trusty .45 automatics, and even if he did seem to miss every time. In the 15-chapter serial play, the burning eyes and hawk-nosed visage of actor Victor Jory bore a startling likeness to the magazine covers, giving credence to his portrayal. Fans knew he wan't the real Shadow, though, because he spent too much time getting knocked about by low-grade comic hoodlums.

It is ironic that during the war years the radio Shadow maintained and even increased his popularity while his magazine counterpart began falling on leaner times--as did virtually all the pulp hero titles. Loyal readers knew they were in trouble when Margo Lane, the Shadow's radio "friend and companion," joined the pulps and soon became his primary, and sometimes only, assistant. It was an entrance that would herald the beginning of a disheartening slide into mediocrity.

Walter Gibson continued turning out two Shadow novels a month until March, 1943, when declining popularity combined with wartime paper shortages forced the magazine to go to one issue a month. By the end of the year the Street & Smith pulp chain was the first of its kind to adapt to the more "respectable" digest size. For The Shadow it was a reduction in spirit as well as content. In April of 1945 ("Death Has Gray Eyes") Shadowphiles were dismayed to discover that their hero had been pre-empted to the back of his own book, with a routine detective novel shoved up front.

In 1946--following a chain of editorial upheavals--Walter Gibson abandoned the series over a contractual dispute. A new 'Maxwell Grant' was quickly hired. In the "new look" stories, ghosted by Bruce Elliott, The Shadow's cloak and hat were eventually left at home and the uncostumed Lamont Cranston became little more than a glorified private eye in a series of modern detective settings. By this time the Shadow "novels" had been trimmed to little more than the length of short stories, bearing prosaic titles like "Death On Ice" and "Room 1313." Quite a come down from the glory days of The Masked Headsman, The Gray Ghost, and The Creeping Death. Besides, who wants to read a Shadow Magazine without The Shadow? In 1947 the magazine was reduced to a bi-monthly and in 1948 a quarterly.

Then in 1949, in a belated attempt to revive the pulp tradition (and circulation figures) the magazine was again published full size, sporting dynamic Rozen covers. Gibson wrote three final Shadow novels in the grand old style, including one in which he himself made a brief appearance. Alas, the attempted rejuvenation came too late. It was but a last hurrah before the world turned rotten and there wasn't room for pulp heroes anymore.

When The Shadow magazine folded in the summer of 1949 with its 325th issue, it appeared that time (or Time as the pulps would have it) had accomplished what a score of master fiends could not. The Shadow's sinister laughter seemed permanently stilled.

Or was it?

Fortunately, many of the old Shadow radio programs were saved on transcription disks and later on tapes. They are still being played on many stations. Of course, the comic book Shadow never did disappear for long. Various comic book companies, including DC, Dark Horse, and even Archie Comics have had a fling at interpreting the Master Avenger following the demise of Street & Smith's own long-running comic. Even the pulp stories have been recycled by various paperback companies, notably Bantam Books during the late '60s and early '70s. In 1963 Belmont Books even commissioned a string of original

Shadow novels, the first one written by Walter Gibson himself--just for old time's sake.

When the magazine folded, old pro Walter Gibson simply turned to other writing. His career encompassed 149 other books of all types, thousands of newspaper and magazine pieces, comics, radio shows, puzzles, magic tricks and other material under various pen names. Author J. Randolph Cox's monumental guide to the work of Walter Gibson (*Man of Magic and Mystery*, Scarecrow Press, 1988) is in itself a staggering 328 pages long. Ironically, that which Gibson will be remembered for--his 283 Shadow novels--represents but a fraction of his total output.

Walter Gibson died in 1985 at the age of 88. He lived to see his Depression-era phantom attain folk hero immortality. Endless revivals of The Shadow in paperback, hardcover, and comic book form had enabled him to climb out from behind the Maxwell Grant pen name. In his later years he enjoyed increasing public recognition in newspaper and magazine articles, radio and television appearances, and as a guest at various conventions. He even made peace with his famous pseudonym, and designed a signature in which the two names were intertwined.

In 1979 Walter Gibson was awarded a Master's Fellowship by the Academy of Magical Arts and Sciences, an award never before given to a non-performing magician. Another honor--the Lamont Award--was named after his creation and is bestowed at the annual Pulpcon for outstanding contributions to the field of pulp research.

In the final analysis, the greatest monument to Walter Gibson's memory is his own legacy. He accomplished that which only a few people in history have been fortunate enough to do.

He created a legend.

DOC!

There was death afoot in the darkness.
It crept furtively along a steel girder.
Hundreds of feet below yawned glass-
and-brick walled cracks--New York streets.
Down there, late workers scurried home-
ward. Most of them carried umbrellas,
and did not glance upward.
Even had they looked, they probably
would have noticed nothing. The night
was black as a cave bat. Rain threshed
down monotonously. The clammy sky was
like an oppressive shroud wrapped around
the tops of the tall buildings. The naked
beams were a sinister forest.
It was in this forest that Death prowled.
Death was a man.

The foregoing prose is what is known in writers'
parlance as a narrative hook. It was the manner in which
pulp fictioneers began almost every story back in the
golden age of the pulp magazines, and was in fact the bait

used to snag newsstand perusers of the March 1933 issue of *Doc Savage Magazine.*

The magazine's 60,000 word novel "The Man of Bronze" was the opening salvo in a series of monthly adventures that would chronicle the hair-raising exploits of Clark Savage Jr., known to the world as Doc Savage. The circulation of the *Doc Savage Magazine* reached 200,000 soon after publication of that historic first issue.

Doc was a vivid splash of color in the emptiness of the Great Depression. During the 1930s and 1940s generations of youth grew up under the spell of his far-ranging exploits. For years they poured millions of grubby dimes across newsstand counters to follow the monthly adventures of their modern Galahad.

"A man of superhuman strength and protean genius, whose life is dedicated to the destruction of evildoers," Doc Savage was the original inspiration for literally hundreds of superhuman freaks who, in 1933, were yet to be imagined. There is much to indicate, for instance, that when teenagers Jerry Siegel and Joe Shuster created the comic book adventures of Superman, their model was Doc Savage, The Man of Bronze, who antedated The Man of Steel and *his* host of imitators by several years.

Doc could run faster than a horse, bite through nails, untie knots with his tongue, hold his breath longer than a South Seas pearl diver, scale any building that wasn't smoother than a sheet of glass, speak any language known to man and a few others besides. A master surgeon, chemist, pilot, engineer, archaeologist--Doc was a walking compendium of mankind's total knowledge.

Like most of the great pulp heroes, The Man of Bronze supplied escapist entertainment for the Depression-era dispossessed. More important, he was a personification of American ideals at a time when those virtues were being questioned. For Doc Savage, the system had not failed. A self- made phenomenon, his power, wealth, and humanitarian exploits demonstrated to youthful readers that success or failure depended on the individual, that a man could still better himself with effort. Doc was not Superman. He was SuperAmerican. His physical and mental powers were not the result of being born on some alien planet; they were the culmination of extreme dedication combined with two hours of intensive mental and physical exercise each day, a regimen which had been instituted by his father when Doc was barely old enough to walk.

Young Clark was born on the schooner Orion off the island of Andros. His mother died some fourteen months later and he was raised by his wealthy adventurer father to be a perfect human specimen. The boy's unconventional education was handled by experts ranging from Indian fakirs to Yale physicists, from circus acrobats to jungle trackers. He even had a specialty, that of surgery; he was the world's best, of course, and hence earned the sobriquet "Doc."

In order to bone up on newest developments in all fields of science and world affairs the Man of Bronze retired periodically to his mysterious Fortress of Solitude (later appropriated by Superman), a rendezvous built on a rocky island deep in the Arctic regions. This was one of the secrets of his universal knowledge, for his periods of concentration there were long and intense. Whether even a mental giant like Doc could handle today's information explosion is a matter of conjecture but back in the 1930s he more than held his own.

From the beginning, Doc Savage was hand crafted for success. The folks at Street & Smith Publications had a runaway hit with pulpdom's first superhero, The Shadow. It was only natural that sooner or later they would attempt a sibling money earner.

For a while the publishers toyed with the idea of a character called The Phantom but in 1933 Ned Pine's Standard Publications beat them to the punch when they published *The Phantom Detective* magazine. Street & Smith abandoned the idea of a direct Shadow imitation and instead decided to fashion a different type of hero altogether: a strapping adventurer who would use scientific gadgets as weapons.

The Shadow's godparents, Henry W. Ralston, editorial executive at S & S, and Shadow editor John Nanovic developed the character and many of the basic concepts in a series of editorial sessions. They decided that the new superhero would be named Doc Savage and that he should combine "the clue-following ability of Sherlock Holmes, the muscular tree-swinging ability of Tarzan, and the scientific sleuthing of Craig Kennedy." They did not add, but could have, that he should have the morals of a saint. Doc was designed to be a hard act to follow.

According to Nanovic, Doc and his aides were all reflections of real people whom Ralston knew personally. Pulp researcher (and later-day Doc writer) Will Murray has revealed that Doc was based on the character of Major Richard Henry Savage, an American engineer, author, lawyer and soldier who fought in the Spanish-American War and served in the Egyptian Army. To the attributes of this authentic real-life character, Ralston added the superhuman moral, mental and physical abilities of Nick Carter--Street & Smith's original paper hero.

Editor Nanovic handed a 30-page "outline" for Doc Savage, Supreme Adventurer to a dynamic 28-year-old freelance writer named Lester Dent. He had come to their attention through his work on their own *Top Notch* and *Popular* magazines, and on request had pounded out an unpublished Shadow story as proof of his hero writer abilities.

Dent was six feet two and weighed in at around two hundred pounds; if his black hair had been changed to bronze he might have served as a model for Doc himself. Like Doc he was a tinkerer and a gadgeteer as well as being a world traveller with an explosive love of fun and adventure.

Street & Smith gave Dent the unprecedented offer of exclusive production rights to the Doc Savage novels. He was to write them under a house name, Kenneth Robeson,

Lester Dent

but he could if he so wished hire another writer to help out, then pay the other man out of his own salary. Furthermore he was not restricted to work on Doc Savage alone.

Dent was enthusiastic. What he did with the editors' outline was something even they could not have anticipated fully. In a vibrant style that blended globe-trotting adventure and science-fiction concepts with hardboiled prose and quirky humor, he made Doc Savage and his friends spring to life.

In "The Man of Bronze," a unique pledge is sworn by a group of six men meeting on the 86th floor of one of New York's tallest buildings: while a would-be assassin peers down at them from his steel eyrie, Doc Savage and his five aides--"the greatest brains ever assembled in one group"--meet to mourn the death of Doc's father, a man known throughout the world for his work in righting wrongs. The six unique men dedicate themselves to uphold the elder Savage's ideals, "to go here and there, from one end of the world to the other, looking for excitement and adventure, striving to help those who need help, and punishing those who deserve it."

Unlike most superheroes, Doc was no loner. He was aided in his worldwide crusades by his rough-and-tumble aides, the Amazing Five, and, on occasion, by his lovely bronze-haired cousin, Patricia Savage.

Doc and his confederacy of globe-trotting do-gooders were described in the opening scenes of "The Man of Bronze." It was a description that would not vary greatly throughout the 17 years to follow. Surprisingly, it was the portrayal of Doc himself that proved flexible. In the opening novel Doc was six feet tall but it seems that he continued growing until in 1935 he stood nearly six-six. Other than that, Doc remained agelessly constant. If not actually immortal, he was wondrously durable, possibly because of the medicinal properties of an age-retarding plant, silphium, involved in his adventures on the Caribbean island of Fear Cay.

Doc's skin was of a permanent bronze color, a characteristic peculiar to the entire Savage clan. His features were so regular that they might be that of a man sculptured in hard bronze. "The lines of the features, the unusually high forehead, the mobile muscular, but not too-full mouth, the lean cheeks, denoted a power of character seldom seen." His hair was of a bronze a trifle darker than his skin, laying straight on his scalp like a metal skullcap. We are told that Doc's bronze hue has been kilned by the heat of tropic suns. This reference to the tropics may explain the exotic trilling sound which he utters in those rare moments of unconscious stress: possibly the imitation of a jungle bird.

Above all else, Doc's eyes caught and held attention. "They were weird, commanding eyes, like nothing so much as pools of flake gold. They radiated a hypnotic quality, an ability to inspire fear or repect--to convey threat, domination or command. Even in repose, they glowed with the heat of an indomitable will."

Not exactly a description of your modern anti-hero! If Doc himself remained an impossible ideal for youthful readers, his five boisterous aides presented more human fronts as well as a variety of physical types for vicarious identification. Chief among his pals was "Monk" Mayfair, the amiable, apelike being who was described as being one of the world's leading chemists, a millionaire with a penthouse laboratory near Wall Street, a setting in many of the Doc Savage novels.

The most common (as well as the most tiresome) running gag in the Doc Savage yarns was Monk's constant feud with Ham Brooks. Ham was the ying to Monk's yang. Slender, waspish, quick moving, Ham looked like what he was--possibly the most astute lawyer Harvard ever turned out. A dapper dresser, he carried a black walking stick which was, among other things, a sword cane. Those baddies fortunate enough to escape Monk's bristle-covered fists usually wound up on the wrong end of Ham's sticker.

Doc's other aides included: John "Renny" Renwick, civil engineer, who was a big, somewhat gaunt man with a severe puritanical face; Major Thomas J. Roberts, an ectomorphic electrical wizard, also called "Long Tom"; and William Harper Littlejohn, called "Johnny," an archaeologist who had formerly been the head of the natural science research department of a famous university, an environment which perhaps had given him his penchant for big words. "Superamalgamated" was Johnny's favorite expletive, a word which could also be used to describe Lester Dent, the writer of the Savage opus.

In the world of the pulps there existed a curious relationship between the fictitious characters and their creators. Bob Hogan, author of the high-flying G-8 adventures (chapter four) was himself a World War I pilot--even if he did extrapolate some bizarre variations on his own experiences; The Shadow reflected many of the interests of his writer, Walter Gibson, an expert in magic and the supernatural; and Norvell Page, who for a decade chronicled the macabre exploits of the Spider (chapter five) came to identify so completely with his own creation that he took to wearing a black cape and black slouch hat in public.

As for Lester Dent--who wrote 165 of the 181 Doc Savage novels under the publisher-owned name of Kenneth Robeson--he was the kind of man who might have joined Doc's merry band of adventurers. As a boy Dent travelled across Wyoming in a covered wagon. In his adult years he made forays prospecting for gold in Mexico, Death Valley and elsewhere, sailed his small schooner, *The Albatross*, on treasure-hunting expeditions, explored Mayan ruins and prehistoric Indian dwellings, toured Nazi-overrun Europe, invented electrical gadgets, and flew his own plane. As recognition of his travels, he was made a member of The Explorers' Club of New York.

But, according to Dent, it was the lonely life of a rancher's son that prepared him for later success as a storyteller. "I had no playmates," he explained. "I lived a completely distorted youth. My only playmate was my imagination, and that period of intense imaginative creation which kids generally get over at the age of five or six, I carried till I was twelve or thirteen. My imaginary voyages and accomplishments were extremely real. I almost think I learned at the time a form of self-hypnosis."

As a young adult, happily married and working at a night telegraph job for the *Tulsa World*, Lester got deterred when he turned his hand to setting down some of his imaginative daydreams in the form of written adventure stories. His first thirteen stories gathered rejection slips from various pulp editors but his fourteenth sold for $250. The story was titled "Pirate Cay," and it appeared in Street & Smith's prestigious *Top Notch* magazine in September 1929.

Following a number of other sales, the young writer was stunned to received a telegram from Dell Publishing Company of New York. The editor at Dell suggested that if Lester was earning less than a hundred dollars a week at his present job he should quit immediately and be taken under their wing. In return for writing exclusively for Dell, he would be given a five-hundred-dollar-a-month drawing account.

After checking on the editor's sanity, Dent and his wife Norma soon left for the Big Apple. While working at Dell he learned the discipline required to turn out immense volumes of well-crafted fiction. Eventually, the magazines he wrote for folded, but by that time he was skilled enough to tackle the precarious life of the freelance writer.

Dent sold western romances, air-war thrillers, detective yarns and straight adventure pieces to a variety of magazines. One series, the adventures of scientific detective Lynn Lash presaged Doc Savage, right down to crime-fighting gadgets and the inclusion of an apish character named Monk. The

THE CODE OF DOC SAVAGE

Let me strive, every moment of my life, to make myself better and better, to the best of my ability, that all may profit by it. Let me think of the right, and lend all my assistance to those who need it, with no regard for anything but justice. Let me take what comes with a smile, without loss of courage. Let me be considerate of my country, of my fellow citizens and my associates in everything I say and do. Let me do right to all, and wrong to no man.

young author's skill at characterization and plotting combined with his scientific knowledge and technical virtuosity soon brought him to the attention of the editors at Street & Smith, the fabled "fiction factory." They were looking for a writer who could handle Doc Savage. Lester Dent was born for the job.

For the next 15 years Dent was reponsible for one Doc Savage novel a month, at $500 a story to begin with, and later at $750 a crack. In his spare time he knocked out the Click Rush series for *Crimebusters* as well as a variety of tales for such top pulp markets as *Black Mask* and *Argosy*.

A native of La Plata, Missouri (pop. 1400), Dent moved back to his hometown to continue churning out the monthly Savage adventures.

Because of Dent's own adventures, the Doc Savage thrillers were characterized by an authenticity of background. As for Dent's writing style, an anonymous *Newsweek* writer suggested that it read "as if he had a stopwatch in one hand and a thesaurus in the other." Certainly the yarns were written in a bravura, hell-for-leather manner which carried youthful readers along in a phantasmagorical series of fights, chases and escapes all tied together with remarkably fluid transitions.

A successful pulp hero writer--and few were more successful than Dent--had to work fast and never look back. Dent's typewriter keys flew like machine-gun bullets. Sometimes he got carried away.

Long-time Doc Savage editor, John Nanovic related how his own son would humiliate him by reading aloud a sentence from one of the stories: "Doc's arm drifted outward with lightning speed."

As Nanovic explained, "You had to be a Doc Savage fan to know that there was nothing wrong with that. If anybody could drift his arm outward with lightning speed, Doc could do it. And the way Dent wrote it, you believed it. It was just right."

Lester Dent's work was not rich in allegory or poetic symbolism. It was not intended to be. His stories were jolting, exotic, antic, throbbing with narrative drive and cliff-hanging suspense. They usually started with a stinger:

> *The man carried a .30-.30 rifle in one hand and two boxes of cartridges, both open, in the other hand. He acted as if ready to drop the cartridges and use the rifle any instant.*

or

> *Five men were running across the golf links of the Widebrook Country Club.*

> *They kept in a compact group, and their manner was determined and sinister. Each carried a hooded golf bag. The hour was near midnight.*
>
> or
>
> *It was too bad that nobody actually saw what happened to the new army X-ship on its test flight. It happened that there were clouds that night, and anyway, the impossible thing occurred twenty thousand feet in the air.*

Pulp writers knew how to set the scene quickly and get on with the mayhem.

Like most single-character series, the Doc Savage stories were written to a strict formula. Author Dent's own personal recipe for plotting high-powered adventure fiction appeared under his by-line in a 1939 issue of *Writer's Digest*. The article was as unpretentious as Dent himself. Suspense, he opined, is the sugar that draws the flies. Among other things he admonished the would-be writer to introduce the hero as quickly as possible and immediately swat him with a fistful of troubles; introduce a menace strong enough to hang like a cloud over the hero; have at least one minor surprise to a printed page; keep shovelling grief onto the hero. "The idea," Dent wrote, "is to avoid monotony."

Dent did his best to avoid monotony. Turning out 200,000 words a month and selling every word, he often earned two to four thousand dollars a month--and this in the days of breadlines and hobo jungles.

The Savage novels flooded from his pen, each one bearing an evocative title: "The Land of Terror," "The Lost Oasis," "The Phantom City," "The Thousand-Headed Man," "The Squeaking Goblin," "Poison Island," "The Sargasso Ogre," "The Man Who Fell Up."

Doc and his boys went everywhere and did everything. Adventurers all, they discovered lost cities and forgotten races in the world's secret recesses. From The Valley of the Vanished to the oceans' depths, to a prehistoric world in the arctic, they pitted brain, brawn and super-science against such foes as The Sargasso Ogre, The Mind-Changing Monster, The Living Fire Menace, The Stone Man, The Vanisher, The Annihilist, The Mystic Mullah and The Roar Devil. They stopped wars, prevented a new Ice Age, battled dinosaurs and ancient mummies, and saved humanity from one world-wrecker after another. Throughout it all raced the beguiling Savage mystique: Eyes of flake gold. Muscles bunched like cordwood. That eerie trilling whistle.

Even the covers contributed to Doc's image. One of the greatest of pulp artists, Walter Baumhoffer, was the initial Doc portrayer and he set the standard for all to follow. Many of his paintings were really portraits of Doc frozen in the middle of some adventurous situation. One such cover ("Quest of Qui," July 1935) was *only* a close-up study of Doc, refuting the pulp belief that action and action alone sold copies.

To millions of young readers, Doc Savage assumed the proportions of a real life hero. Street & Smith did nothing to shatter the illusion. The magazine carried a Doc Savage credo, a Doc Savage Club, Doc Savage portraits, Doc Savage lapel pins and a gold Doc Savage award which went to deserving nominees.

Doc's daily calisthenics were such an important part of his adventures that Street & Smith began to publish a series of articles on the various exercises. These instructions for self development were touted as the open sesame to Doc's physical prowess, but keener fans may have noticed their similarity to the brand of isometrics taught by Charles Atlas, another superhuman figure often represented in the pages of the pulps.

Street & Smith was the contractual owner of all of Dent's Doc Savage novels but, surprisingly, they allowed the author ancillory rights to film, radio, and even newspaper comic strip versions. (The reason Dent did not bargain for comic book rights was because such magazines did not exist when Doc was first created.)

Unfortunately, while the Doc Savage magazine equalled and even surpassed the success of The Shadow, Doc did not fare as well in other mediums. The Shadow starred in his own Street & Smith comic book for nine years (Doc was sometimes a back-up feature) but Doc's own comic premierred in May of 1940 and ended twenty issues later in 1943.

The Shadow was at least a moderate success in movie serials and grade B features but poor Doc never hit the flicks at all--at least not at the time.

And of course The Shadow was one of the most popuar radio characters of all; even today children who cannot possibly have heard the program are able to recite its opening lines like a litany. The radio Doc, on the other hand, appeared briefly in a 1934 syndicated series produced by the West Coast Don Lee Network. Although the scripts were written by Dent himself, the program suffered from a format that restricted each story to a mere 15-minute time slot. Although the *Doc Savage Magazine* carried advertisements for the show, listing scores of stations throughout the United States and Canada which carried it, no surviving transcriptions exist today and few, if any, old time radio fans remember even hearing it.

Doc Savage hit the airwaves again in a 26 week run over station WMCA in New York in 1943. The new version bore little resemblance to the bronze hero of the pulps, even though some of the melodramas bore titles similar to the kind of thing Lester Dent might have written: "The Pharoah's Wisdom," "Monster of the Sea," "The Screeching Ghost," "The Miracle Maniac," etc. The first two broadcasts featured Doc's "two-fisted assistants Monk and Ham," but by episode three Ham was dropped in favor of a Brooklyn-born secretary named Myrtle. When the radio Doc was in trouble he donned a hood from which glowed a sacred red ruby, blinding the eyes of his enemies and protecting him from harm. This juvenile schtick was never

DOC SAVAGE
On Your Radio

You can now hear the adventures of DOC SAVAGE and his pals on the Air—More than 75 stations carry the DOC SAVAGE programs.

THROUGH THE COURTESY OF CYSTEX YOU CAN HEAR THE DOC SAVAGE EXPLOITS OVER THESE STATIONS

City	State	Station	City	State	Station	City	State	Station
Birmingham	Ala.	WAPI	Omaha	Neb.	WOW	Nashville	Tenn.	WLAC
Mobile	Ala.	WALA	Atlantic City	N. J.	WPG	Amarillo	Texas	KGRS
Phoenix	Ariz.	KTAR	Albany	N. Y.	WOKO	Dallas	Texas	KRLD
Little Rock	Ark.	KLRA	Buffalo	N. Y.	WGR	El Paso	Texas	KTSM
Denver	Colo.	KLZ	Newark	N. J.	WNEW	Houston	Texas	KPRC
Hartford	Conn.	WDRC	New York	N. Y.	WMCA	San Antonio	Texas	KTSA
Miami	Fla.	WQAM	Rochester	N. Y.	WHEC	Waco	Texas	WACO
Tampa	Fla.	WSUN	Syracuse	N. Y.	WSYR	Salt Lake City	Utah	KDYL
Atlanta	Ga.	WGST	Asheville	N. C.	WWNC	Richmond	Va.	WRVA
Savannah	Ga.	WTOC	Charlotte	N. C.	WBT	Roanoke	Va.	WDBJ
Peoria	Ill.	WMBD	Raleigh	N. C.	WPTF	Seattle	Wash.	KOMO
Chicago	Ill.	WIND	Akron	Ohio	WADC	Spokane	Wash.	KHQ
Indianapolis	Ind.	WKBF	Cincinnati	Ohio	WKRC	Milwaukee	Wis.	WISN
Des Moines	Iowa	WHO	Cleveland	Ohio	WGAR	Honolulu	T. H.	KGU
Sioux City	Iowa	KSCJ	Columbus	Ohio	WBNS	St. Joseph	Mo.	KFEQ
Kansas City	Mo.	WREN	Toledo	Ohio	WSPD	**CANADIAN STATIONS**		
Wichita	Kans.	KFH	Oklahoma City	Okla.	KOMA	Calgary	Alb.	CFCN
Louisville	Ky.	WAVE	Tulsa	Okla.	KTUL	Vancouver	B. C.	CJOR
New Orleans	La.	WDSU	Portland	Ore.	KGW	Winnipeg	Man.	CKY
Baltimore	Md.	WBAL	Harrisburg	Pa.	WHP	St. John	N. B.	CSHJ
Boston	Mass.	WAAB	Philadelphia	Pa.	WIP	Halifax	N. S.	CHNS
Detroit	Mich.	WJR	Pittsburgh	Pa.	WCAE	Sydney	N. S.	CJCB
Duluth	Minn.	WEBC	Providence	R. I.	WJAR	Toronto	Ont.	CFRB
Minneapolis	Minn.	KSTP	Charleston	S. C.	WCSC	Windsor	Ont.	CKLW
St. Louis	Mo.	KWK	Chattanooga	Tenn.	WDOD	Montreal	Quebec	CKAC
Butte	Mont.	KGIR	Memphis	Tenn.	WMC	Regina	Sask.	CKCK

FIND YOUR NEAREST STATION IN THE ABOVE LIST. CHECK THE TIME FROM YOUR DAILY BROADCAST SCHEDULE AND LISTEN TO THE EXCITING ADVENTURES OF THE BRONZE MAN.

DOC SAVAGE IS A STREET & SMITH MAGAZINE··

used in the pulp yarns but it was integrated into the Street & Smith comic books, where it seemed perfectly at home.

If Doc Savage's gold-plated success was limited to the pulp magazines and subsequent paperback reprints, it was probably for a very good reason. The name of the reason was Lester Dent.

As fast as he required them, author Dent's facile mind invented hundreds of gimmicks and bits of business for the Savage saga. In "The Man of Bronze" he introduced Doc's rapid-firing supermachine pistols; they bore resemblance to oversize automatics but featured curled magazines which held sixty rounds of either 'mercy bullets, incendiaries, tracers, magnesiums or even armor-piercing slugs.'

In the line of hand weapons Doc's group had everything from recoiless rapid-firing elephant guns to pocket knives which fired single bullets from their hilts. Doc himself did not favor the wearing of guns because of his theory that they made the bearer dependent on them. Instead, what Doc did become hooked on was an incredible array of gadgets and gimmicks hidden on his person.

In "The Red Skull," he first wore his armor-scaled vest. Its contents included delicate mechanical devices, strange scientific weapons, and glass vials containing "chemical concoctions calculated to accomplish the unusual." In short, almost anything Doc (or Lester Dent) needed to pull him out of a particularly rough spot.

Stripped of his vest, Doc was still a walking arsenal. The hollow heels in his shoes contained everything from tiny radio transmitters to explosives and miniature drills. His belt housed a silken cord with a collapsible grapnel hook at one end. The buttons of his suit were a thermite compound. The suit itself was impregnated with chemical weapons, his undershirt loaded with tear gas.

In addition to fireproof and radiation proof suits to fit the occasion, he also developed a spray-on overskin that acted as a perfect insulation against heat or cold.

Even denuded he still had his metal skull cap that

simulated his bronze hair. A false scar on his back contained still more explosives, as did a pair of hollow capped teeth. Another hollow tooth contained a tiny coiled saw!

In order to attempt to get the best of him, wily captors sometimes stripped Doc down to the buff. Once, in "The Submarine Mystery," assailants shampooed his hair to wash out chemicals; they even checked out his teeth with instruments. But even bound and gagged Doc remained a holy terror. He could still hypnotize a man with his flake-gold eyes or anaesthetize him with the tiny needles hidden beneath his fake fingernails.

Out of the bronze man's lonely Fortress of Solitude poured a harvest of scientific miracles. In "The Golden Peril" and again in "The Motion Menace" Doc treated thugs to the spectacular effects of the world's first atomic disintegrator.

In "Mystery Under the Sea" he first tried out the special oxygen pills which, when ingested, rendered it unnecessary to breathe for periods up to half an hour.

In his precious spare moments he invented the world's first wire recorder. The first telephone answering service. High speed elevators. Advanced brain surgery techniques. A cure for the common cold. A radar device that could differentiate between metals. An early version of the aqualung. Futuristic airplanes (he even toyed with jet travel). Sophisticated electronic bugging devices. Disposable parachutes. The list could go on and on.

Doc and his aides were communicating via two-way wristwatch television while Dick Tracy was still pounding a beat. Then too, they often employed an ultra-violet projector and "blacklight" goggles in order to work by night or in Stygian quarters. It was a common plot gimmick to leave messages which could only be revealed through the use of this method. In "The South Pole Terror" Doc's rocket-powered dirigible is even equipped with an ultra-violet searchlight.

Doc was a great believer in lighter-than-air transportation (a faith which is only now being substantiated by aeronautical experts), but his adventurous life created a high mortality rate for his prototype dirigibles. In "The Land of Long Ju Ju" he unveiled a wing-shaped lighter-than-air craft which was capable of speeds up to and surpassing 500 miles an hour. Unfortunately the wing met the fate of so many of Doc's advanced gas bags: it didn't survive its maiden launching.

He had better luck with his Cousteau-style yacht, The Seven Seas, which saw action in "Fantastic Island," "Land of Fear" and "The Red Terrors." Beneath the seas his streamlined submarine vehicle Helldiver (complete with collapsible seaplane and infra-red TV scanners) was the scourge of aquatic supervillains. The Helldiver was especially designed to work beneath polar ice but in "The Phantom City" it travelled beneath the Arabian desert to reach a mysterious city of white-haired inhabitants. In "Haunted Ocean" the Helldiver's baby sister, a pocket-sized glass sub, was used to zip Doc from peril.

Although Doc scrupulously avoided publicity, everybody appeared to know about him and his 86th floor headquarters in a certain New York skycraper. The most exotic of Doc's adventures often began in this tri-suite fortress perched high above the Empire City. From his admirable vantage point, Doc looked down on a sunny, Art Deco version of New York of the 1930s--a locale as colorful and as nostalgic as any of the Oriental ports or tropic islands in which his adventures placed him. The Savage manse was guarded by a veritable armory of scientific gadgets, alarms and traps. In "The Flying Goblin" even a radio-controlled missile attack on HQ is thwarted by a force-field projector which emerges on call from Doc's futuristic lab.

The Hidalgo Trading Company, Doc's Hudson River warehouse, was in reality no trading company at all. It was the gateway to lost valleys and far sunsets. Within its windowless walls were housed all the mechanical magic carpets Doc needed to whisk him to the world's inaccessible places. It contained his turbine-powered sub as well as various armored motor boats and launches. There were a variety of helicopters, autogyros and super-speed amphibious airplanes, and even the latest thing in dirigibles. Doc could flit from his skyscraper eyrie to the warehouse via a pneumatic capsule--a route he nick-named the 'flea-run.'

The vast sums of money required for these expensive appurtenances came from a hidden valley in Central America, a lost retreat presided over by the descendants of the ancient Mayan race, and was supplied to Doc solely for the purpose of furthering his cause of right. At noon on a prescribed day of the week, Doc had but to broadcast, over powerful radio stations, a few words in a mysterious tongue. Some days later a supply of pure gold would arrive for his use.

It need hardly be mentioned that pulp writers were in the business of supplying dreams that money could buy. For a mere ten cents a month they gave pretty good value.

Lester Dent's own penchant for adventuring sometimes caused him to miss deadlines. While he was off treasure hunting in The Albatross, fellow pulpsters Harold Davis, Ryerson Johnson, William Bogart, Laurence Donovan, and Alan Hathway occasionally filled in. Often the ghostwriters' work was a bare-bones narrative which Dent reworked in his own zippy prose style. To speed things up Dent also experimented with dictation, using a dictaphone to record some of Doc's high-speed adventures.

During the 1940s a gradual attrition took place in *Doc Savage*. The hero pulp magazines had been hurt by the coming of the comic books with their colorful compacted stories and their modest demands on young readers' time.

The pulps retrenched. Street & Smith decided to aim at a more mature, more sophisticated audience. As Lester Dent put it, "After the flood of super people and phantoms and bat men and such people that Doc started coming out of the cartoonists' and writers' inkwells, my stomach kind of turned. I've toned Doc down now to where he is not the

slambang fire-eater he was. He still discovers strange
tribes of people in the heart of the world's deserts, but he
doesn't come across nations in the interior of the earth
anymore."

The coming of World War II produced even greater
changes. In "The Fiery Menace" (Sept. '42) Doc travelled
to Washington to confer with President Roosevelt and
other government officials. He begged to be accepted for
military duty and was politely but firmly refused. During
the war most folks looked askance at a healthy male who
claimed deferment from armed service. To a patriotic
superman like Doc it must have been a crushing humili-
ation.

Fortunately, the U.S. government (and Doc's publishers) eventually gave in, allowing him to fight against
the Axis as a civilian agent. "The Black, Black Witch"
(March '43) saw Doc preventing the Nazis from acquiring
a gas that would enable them to foretell the future. In "The
Three Devils" Doc confounded an Axis plan to shut down
Canada's wartime pulp paper industry (thus saving his
own magazine, one presumes), and in "Time Terror" he
kept a super-evolution element from the Japanese. Just to
prove he could still hack it, Doc rescued Winston Churchill
from the Nazis in 1944, and in 1945 captured Adolph
Hitler himself. But something was clearly missing. Some
of the heart had gone out of Doc. He was a Bronze Man in
a world turning colorless.

The far-out fantasy of the 1930s stories had became
muted. It was replaced by a hard brittle quality: the cold
light of reality. The Man of Bronze was caught in the
middle of a world-shaking battle which was to test the very
concept of a superhuman elite. Like a character in a
nightmare he felt his powers slipping away. He became
cautious, testy, less idealistic. He began to question his
own invulnerability. Poor Doc. It was a wonder he made
it through the war at all.

In the postwar period there was little mention of his
five aides and Doc himself became little more than a

scientific detective assisting the FBI. In January of 1944 the magazine came out in the more "respectable" digest size. Under the aegis of a new editor, young Babette Rosmand, the magazine was retitled *Doc Savage, Science Detective* and became a semi-slick publication, far removed from its rough-hewn pulp glory. Adding insult to injury, the Doc Savage novels were shoved to the rear of the magazine and a conventional detective novel placed at the front.

The last issue of Doc's magazine was number 181, published summer 1949. With an inspired effort, Dent turned out a final novel, "Up From Earth's Center," which proved to be one of the best and most well-written of all the Doc Savage stories. In that final adventure Dent strongly suggested--and never retracted--that Doc and his cronies (reunited at last) had met and battled the minions of Satan right up from hell.

After that, what else was left? It was the Gotterdammerung of the pulps.

Following the wholesale demise of the once ubiquitous pulp magazines Lester Dent continued to write fiction. The style of his later stories (mostly full-length mystery novels) was assured, mature, polished, realistic. He had always wanted to be regarded as a fine writer but early in the game had found himself trapped on a gold-plated treadmill.

In February of 1959 Dent was stricken by a massive heart attack. He was rushed to the Grim-Smith Hospital in Kirksville, Missouri, where he died March 11 at the too-young age of 54. Shortly before, he had confided that in his opinion the Doc Savage stories would be of little interest any more. "They would be so out-dated today," he said, "that they would undoubtedly be funny. Hell, when I wrote them, an airplane that could fly 200 miles an hour was science fiction."

For once, Dent had misjudged Doc's appeal. Unfortunately, he died too soon to witness the emergence of a new generation of fans who would snap up the monthly

Savage thrillers with as much dispatch as did their fathers nearly thirty years before.

Doc's reincarnation occurred in 1964 when Bantam Books under the leadership of Marc Jaffe, a Doc Savage fan in his youth, put out three Doc Savage novels in a brand new softcover format. Wisely, Jaffe prevented Bantam from updating Dent's original plots.

In addition, Jaffe commissioned a top illustrator, James Bama, to paint new covers for the series in a uniform format similar to the old pulp covers. While differing greatly from the interpretations of Walter Baumhoffer, the original Savage cover artist, Bama's paintings were magnificent pieces of commercial illustration which contributed immensely to Doc's second coming.

Even so, long-time pulp fans were shocked by Bama's radical interpretation. They maintained that while the artist had lifted Doc's skull-cap hairline from the pulp descriptions, his portrayal of their hero as a seamed and constantly tattered giant is at odds not only with Dent's descriptions but with the original pulp covers and interior illustrations. (Philip Jose Farmer wrote that Bama's Doc looked to him like a 55-year-old ex-Mr. Universe down on his luck; author and pulp historian Robert Weinberg saw him as a cross between the Jolly Green Giant and a Nazi stormtrooper!)

It should be noted that there has always been controversy over the manner in which Doc has been depicted. Back in 1933, the original Doc Savage cover artist was given specific instructions to mold Doc in the image of Clark Gable. Walter Baumhoffer, who had little time to read the pulp stories he delineated, ignored the dictate and cast his superb Doc portraits in the handsome image of a model he was then employing. It was left to Paul Orban, a Street & Smith staffer who did the interior illustrations for many years, to bring Doc's image closer to the Gable ideal.

In any case, despite Jim Bama's revisionist interpretation--and more likely because of it--the new books were

instant successes. They sold in the millions. It was 1933 all over again.

Other mediums began looking at the superannuated hero as grist for their mills. In 1966 Gold Key Comics timidly assayed a Doc Savage comic book. They brought out their four-color version of "The Thousand Headed Man," complete with a Jim Bama cover painting. The interior art by Jack Sparling was less than dynamic, however, and the book lasted but one issue.

There was even talk of a movie series in 1966, and once again "The Thousand Headed Man" was chosen as a pilot project. It is possible that the Gold Key comic was meant to be a tie-in with the movie, but the project never got off the ground and Doc's filmic and comic book possiblities lay dormant for several more years.

In 1973 Stan Lee's Marvel Comics purchased the rights to produce still another graphic picture version. This time the possibilities were more encouraging. Back in the early sixties Lee had reintroduced the comic book superhero, making household names of such creations as Spiderman and The Fantastic Four. It was intriguing to conjecture what he might accomplish with Doc and his Fantastic Five.

Unfortunately, Marvel's Doc turned out to be a modified costumed hero with a Bama-inspired widow's peak. He limped through a handful of lacklustre adaptations that failed to capture either the mood of the original stories or the mystique of the character. DC Comics, the home of Doc-inspired Superman, attempted a more recent Doc Savage comic, but also failed to generate much excitment, possibly because of a mistaken editorial decision to update Doc's adventures.

The Doc Savage revival of the seventies did produce a couple of interesting spin-offs, however. Top science fiction writer Philip Jose Farmer turned out two book-length Savage pastiches, *A Feast Unknown*, published by (zounds) a porno book company called Essex House, and *The Mad Goblin*, issued by Ace Books. Both novels featured Doc Caliban and his sidekicks Jocko and Porky, and both were interesting examinations of the hero psyche.

Apparently this was still not enough to purge Doc from his system, so in 1973 Farmer wrote a monumental "biography" of his hero: *Doc Savage: His Apocalyptic Life*. The book was conceived in the manner of William Baring-Gould's famous *Sherlock Holmes of Baker Street*; that is, Farmer postulates that Doc was a flesh-and-blood individual and that Lester Dent served as a mere chronicler-- and sometimes exaggerator--of real events. Farmer's engaging literary conceit was a monument to Doc's mesmeric hold on his once youthful readers.

It was probably coincidental that at almost the same time movie producer George Pal announced plans to do a series of Doc Savage feature films. The first film was to be produced by Warner Brothers and it was to be shot on a multi-million dollar budget. George Pal was the Hungarian-born puppeteer who parlayed a knack for single-frame animation into a career as one of Hollywood's most successful producers of imaginative cinema. His credits include such science fictional extravaganzas as *War of the Worlds*, *The Time Machine* and *Destination Moon*. His participation in a Doc Savage series of films was enough to set any fan's heart to flutter.

In February of 1974 I interviewed Pal by telephone for a newspaper article I had been commissioned to write. He was on the set of *Doc Savage...the Man of Bronze*, overseeing a spate of night shooting. Pal told me that he had become interested in Doc's movie possibilities when he learned of the phenomenal success of the paperback reprints.

"I bought a few of the books and found them great fun to read," he said. "Almost everybody was buying them-- from nostalgic old-timers to a whole new generation of youngsters who still find them exciting. Right from the beginning we knew they'd make a fabulous movie series. They have almost everything, including that marvellous 1930s background. It took us over a year to clear the rights--we had to buy all 181 books--but it was worth it."

Alas, Pal's initial Doc Savage film was neither a critical or financial success. No further movies were produced, even though Philip Farmer had written an excellent screenplay for a follow-up effort.

In the meantime, Doc continues his literary blitz-krieg. All 181 of the original pulp stories have been unearthed, plus another that was editorially supressed in 1949. In fact, the reprints have proven so popular that Bantam Books commissioned Philip Farmer and Will Murray to write new Doc Savage novels in the Lester Dent style. The Murray Docs were all based on Lester Dent plot outlines and bear such arresting Dent titles as "Python Isle" and "The Frightened Fish."

As of this writing the Doc Savage novels have sold tens of millions of copies, making ex-telegrapher Lester Dent one of the most popular--although largely unrecog-nized--authors of our time. Where it will all end no one knows. Whether Clark Savage Jr. will take a place in history beside such fictional immortals as Sherlock Holmes and Tarzan only time will tell.

Doc and his boys were products of the pulp magazines, those gaudy but ephemeral records of a more
innocent time. Like most of the pulp heroes, they emerged
during the Great Depression in a time of fear and
deprivation--a time of international crisis when ordinary
people required a simple escape from the complexities of
life. Pulp fictioneers like Lester Dent supplied that
escape--in spades. They wrote of a simpler world of
dastardly villains and unblemished heroes, a world in
which you could tell one from the other; you *knew* whose
side you were on.

In today's age of ecological horrors and global human
overpopulation, who can fault readers for once again
plunging into that simpler, more innocent age when the
worst the fates could muster was The Sargasso Ogre, or the
Living-Fire Menace or perhaps the red-fingered survivors
of an ancient, lost civilization.

With a gent like Doc Savage on your side, that was
but the best of all possible worlds.

G-8's WEIRD WAR

To the very young, war, from a distance, can appear to be an exciting adventure. When this writer was a kid growing up in the peculiar milieu of World War II, not learning anything in school was generally considered a badge of manhood, but God help the male youngster who couldn't spot a P-40 from a Zero, or who failed to recognize the square-tipped wing outline of a Messerschmitt 110.

We constructed model planes from balsa wood, used our hands to simulate choreographed aerial dogfights, and pursed our lips in snarling imitations of diving Stukas and chattering Vickers guns. Wise kids collected bubble gum cards with enemy aircraft spotter identification--just in case!--and many of us whiled away countless Saturday afternoons devouring the air-war pulp magazines. Even now, some five decades and a state of mind away, who can forget their titles...or fail to thrill to the images they evoked? *Air Trails! Wings! Dare-Devil Aces!*

Who was the greatest aerial hero of them all? If you ask an old-time pulp reader, the chances are he'll give you a name you can't research in any history book. One of the earliest and unquestionably the greatest of all the high-flying pulp heroes was a man who had no name at all. He was known to friends, foes and readers alike as 'G-8'.

G-8, to the initiate, was also known as The Master Spy. His enemies--they included some of the choicest fiends in the Valhalla of scoundrels--frequently referred to him as "the verdammt one," an accolade of frustration which described his effectiveness as both spy and fighter.

"Gott in Himmell," his foes would rage, "Germany would have won the war months ago if it had not been for the verdammt one."

Debuting in October of 1933, the verdammt one's magazine, *G-8 And His Battle Aces,* ran for an incredible 110 issues, each number featuring a collision-course adventure in the career of the World War I master spy. For over a decade, while one air pulp after another went spiraling down, G-8 winged on, carrying his fight with the Kaiser's minions into the heart of World War II.

G-8 was but one of the many pulp heroes born in the fertile mind of publisher Henry Steeger. By 1933 his Popular Publications' once-popular *Battle Aces* magazine was nose-diving and the dynamic young businessman realized that it needed some fast thinking to bail it out. Over at Street & Smith, The Shadow and Doc Savage had proved to be instant successes. Popular would counter with their own larger-than-life hero, the Spider. Why not, Steeger reasoned, add a super hero of the air. The publisher discussed the idea with top air writer Robert J. Hogan and they quickly restyled the mundane *Battle Aces* into *G-8 and His Battle Aces.* The rest, as they say, is history.

While constructing the first G-8 novel, "The Bat Staffel," Steeger and author Hogan decided that a full-length aerial adventure series might bog down without stronger, more bizarre plots. In pulp magazine terms, they conceived the G-8 publication as a hybrid of *Dare-Devil Aces, Amazing Stories* and *Weird Tales.* To this outre stew Hogan added a hero who, with the aid of disguise, could mask himself in any role. Jaded pulp readers--those hardy

souls who enjoyed their yarns considerably larger than life--found the blend irresistible.

It was in the area of the weird and frankly preposterous that Hogan really excelled. Surely no protagonist since the days of the Greek heroes ever faced such an horrendous array of foes both natural and supernatural. Even his titles suggest the horrors he ladled out: "Squadron of Corpses," "The Headless Staffel," "Scourge of the Sky Beast," "Flight From the Grave," "Staffel of Invisible Men," "Claws of the Sky Monster"...well, you get the idea.

Flying Dragons. Legions of defrosted Vikings. Death Rays. Robot soldiers. Invisible Monsters. Tiger-men. Zombies. Hordes of giant, man-carrying bats from the Matto Grosso. Nothing, simply nothing was too fiendish or too gruesome for the Kaiser's mad scientists. And nothing was so horrific that it daunted the unswerving courage and youthful good natures of G-8 and his two loyal Battle Aces.

One of the oft-voiced criticisms of the G-8 series is that the Battle Aces were little more than Rover Boys at the Front--perennial boy scouts who supplied a bulwark of cheerful normalcy against the horrors of the charnel house and man's ultimate madness. Pulpwood paragons all, it's true that they seemed to face each supernatural challenge with wisecracks and apple-pie aphorisms. Even so, the criticism is probably unfair. A writer for the pulps could not afford to make abstract projections of human motives. His job was to supply vicarious adventure for a largely youthful audience; to do so he was required to invent protagonists with simple and easily identifiable characteristics.

Nippy Weston, the terrier ace, was tow-headed, pint-sized and quick as lightning. He practiced magic for a hobby, could laugh in the face of death and superstition, and did so by flying Spad number 13.

Nippy's buddy, Big Bull Martin, was twice the terrier ace's size, with a face like a thundercloud and a jaw that appeared to be built out of solid rock. A former All-American half-back, Bull always figured, in spite of his power and strength, that he could use all the luck he could get. For that reason, his Spad was adorned with a lucky number 7 on the side.

The third Battle Ace, G-8 himself, is given even less description and nary a name at all. We learn that he is of medium height, athletic build, and has steel gray eyes and sandy hair. We discover his tastes in food and learn that his favorite phonograph record is "Raggin' the Scale," a jazzy tune he uses to stimulate his thoughts. Like many of the great pulp heroes, his outstanding characteristics relate to such traits as courage, devotion to duty, and plain dumb luck.

Battle Aces headquarters was at the airdrome near Le Bourget, just north of Paris. Here, attached to the end hangar which housed their three Spads and an anonymous "long powerful roadster," was the private apartment in which the indomitable trio lived. It was (the magazine informs us) as though these young men at the end hangar had deliberately chosen the point nearest the enemy as their headquarters.

It has been said that disguise was virtually a way of life for the great pulp heroes. The Master Spy was unique among pulp mummers in that he employed his own English manservant, a gent know only as Battle, to apply his numerous disguises. A master of malapropisms and

SQUADRON OF THE DAMNED

Diving out of shell-shredded skies, G-8 flies uncharted avenues of Death to keep a rendezvous with the Red Raider who holds the fate of civilization in his hands. Here, from the pen of Robert J. Hogan, comes another action-packed novel of thrills and matchless courage in the bomb-seared skies of yesterday! Don't miss SQUADRON OF THE DAMNED IN THE BIG DECEMBER issue of

G-8 *and His* BATTLE ACES

muddled Yankee slang, Battle's uncanny ability with a make-up kit was equalled by his prowess as a cook, although the Battle Aces' tastes placed few demands on culinary imagination. Their sallies against the night and its secret shadows often wound up back at Le Bourget airdrome with one of Battle's breakfasts of buckwheat cakes, sausages and real maple syrup.

This contrast between the horrors of the dark and the sanguine comforts of home was a recurring image in the G-8 yarns. It is an empathic theme that lies at the root of much vicarious adventure, from Sherlock Holmes to *The Lord of the Rings*, from *Homer's Odyssey* right up to and including the pulp hero pantheon. Hogan understood it well and made the most of it. In order to make the comforts of home even homier, he found it necessary to make the perils of the unknown even ghastlier.

The author of a thousand-and-one horrific, action-packed encounters, Robert Jasper Hogan was one of the few men to write pulp hero novels under his own name rather than that of a "house name" supplied by the publisher. The son of a Dutch Reformed minister, Hogan was born in 1897 and raised in Buskirk, New York. A graduate of St. Lawrence University, he served his apprenticeship as a cow-puncher, amateur boxer, piano player, pilot, and airplane salesman, before settling down to a career of writing.

Like many fiction writers, Hogan drew upon his own experiences to fabricate the wild plots and outrageous inventions of his pulp yarns. Hogan's friendship with a fellow flyer named Harold "Bull" Nevins, who had done

Intelligence work in France during the war, served as inspiration for both G-8 and for G-8's fictional sidekick, Bull Martin. The third Battle Ace, and Bull's friendly rival, was named Nippy Weston in honor of one of Nevin's wartime buddies, Nippy Westover, whom Hogan never met.

One of the fabrications that earned reader loyalty was Hogan's idea of basing the G-8 novels on a supposed secret wartime diary maintained by the Master Spy himself. G-8's well-worn notebook is featured a number of times throughout the series. In "Wings of the Hawks of Death," it is even captured by the enemy. In addition, there was the use of historic characters and real events as background for many of the extravagant plots. Fans were convinced that G-8 (and his secret diary) really existed when they spotted each month's contents page. There it was...."Bombs From The Murder Wolves," as told by G-8 to Robert J. Hogan.

NEXT MONTH—

G-8 flies again to answer a challenge in the skies—with Nippy and Bull beside him in a final showdown with Death! Who were the Monsters of Destruction that rode roughshod over the earth and ruled the sky with a murderous hand?

You will learn all this and live through the high adventure of the airways when you have read

The Flames of Hell

By Robert J. Hogan

May Issue Out April 1

The truth is that every word in the G-8 magazine came from the head of Bob Hogan. In addition to the monthly "book-length" novel, Hogan also managed to write the short stories that filled up the balance of each issue. Posing as the Master Spy himself, he wrote the editorial badinage in a column titled "G-8 Speaks," in which readers were introduced to the G-8 Club and coerced to purchase their own copies of each issue. (In his column, G-8 routinely refers to Hogan as "old horse-face.")

Under his own name, Hogan was also responsible for two other major pulp character magazines: *The Secret Six* and *The Mysterious Wu Fang*. Although it failed to catch on, The Secret Six was one of the most imaginative of pulp series, while Wu Fang was an entertaining derivative of Sax Rohmer's famous Fu Manchu novels. For a brief time this amazing wordsmith was producing lead novels for all three of these books as well as numerous short stories each month. A *Reader's Digest* article of the time claimed that he sold more words than any other living author.

Hogan was churning out a minimum 200,000 words a month in this period, dictating to two secretaries in his New Jersey home, or typing under a palm tree in a Florida retreat. He worked six days a week from early morning until lunch time, and in the afternoon again if deadlines demanded. In the evenings he planned the next day's scenes out loud with his wife.

In a letter written to me in 1988, publisher Steeger recalled his writer friend with the following description: "Bob was never complicated or burdened with any of the restrictions of the academic world. He invented everything from his own fertile imagination. To look at him you would say this is the last perons on earth who could be an author. He had a long, thin face and he was a very thin gangling type of person put together with steel wire rather than glue. He had sort of pale washed-out eyes and thinning hair but was most active physically and, of course, his fertile mind never stopped for a moment dreaming up dramatic situations. He loved nothing better than telling me about new evil doings of his villains and also of the great heroics of his heroes."

G-8's author was under orders never to rewrite or edit copy, but simply get the material in on time. Edythe Seims was the first of his hard-working editors, succeeded by Bill Fay, with Alden Norton taking over in the late '30s. In the magazine's final years diverse hands took turns smoothing out Hogan's increasingly frenzied prose.

MURDER threw its loathsome cloak across the Front again! Murder that walked the night on padded feet and ripped the throats of sleeping men whose souls cried out for justice! These were the words that rode the midnight skies and filled men's souls with horror—"The greatest fighters among you shall die—unless this war is ended!" It was no empty threat, no idle boast, for spotted killers stalked their prey and murder was their work! G-8 and His Battle Aces were themselves attacked, and The Master Spy staked his wits and courage against the greatest menace the civilized world had ever known.

Popular Publications is pleased to announce "The Patrol of the Sky Leopards," which we consider to be the best of the long series of G-8's adventures from the pen of Robert J. Hogan.

In the March issue

G-8 and His BATTLE ACES

On Sale Jan. 29!

The Secret Six magazine lasted but four issues and *Wu Fang* a mere seven, which must have been a relief to Bob Hogan, who had enough work on his hands just inventing super villains to harass his Three Musketeers of the air.

Of all of G-8's master antagonists, the ultimate bad guy was Herr Doktor Kreuger. Kreuger was the Kaiser's prize fruitcake--the maddest mad doctor of them all. Compared to him, other mad doctors appeared to be general practitioners. He was called "the little fiend," and battled G-8 some twenty-seven times across the years, usually producing quite a bloodbath.

As conceived by Hogan, the little fiend is a study in pure evil--a man absolutely dedicated to his pursuit of high standards of viciousness. Introduced in the first chapter of the very first G-8 adventure, he immediately disclosed his modest plan to murder every man, woman and child from the Rhone to Paris by means of giant poison-breathing bats. Foiled in that initial endeavour, he returned the following month with a scheme to enlist captured Yank airmen, their faces turned to a ghastly purple, in leading savage suicide attacks against their own men.

And so it went over the years, with the hell-spawned runt of Hunland continually frustrated in his simple plans for world destruction. In June of 1943, a full decade after his initial introduction, in a story titled "Scourge of the Sky Monster," he appeared to finally meet his maker. Whether or not the devil accepted him went unrecorded.

Another popular baddie, Stahlmaske, or Steelmask, spilled blood in almost a dozen G-8 novels. An enigmatic genius with Messianic delusions, he created awe and fear even among the German High Command--the Kaiser himself sent informants to check up on what he was doing. A victim of G-8's marksmanship, Stahlmaske hid what was left of his face within a conical, midnight-black steel mask; slits in the heavy metal allowed his eyes to burn through like crimson brands. The twisted but fertile mind of the man in the steel mask invented such devices as exploding pellets, monstrous land carriers, catapults for launching planes, and even one ingenious tank device which solved Germany's incipient food shortage by scooping up Allied soldiers and processing them into canned meat.

Such inventiveness was not limited to the minds of Aryans alone. G-8's adversaries ran the gamut of racial stereotypes, including at least two Orientals. Chu Lung, a Chinese, was known as the Oriental Master of Death. He threatened the flying spy eight times in such adventures as "Wings of the Dragon Lord," "Skies of Yellow Death," and "The Sky Serpent Flies Again." Described as a gaunt man with glowing jade-green eyes, Chu Lung boasted an arsenal undreamed of even by Sax Rohmer's infamous doctor. (Would you believe poisonous clouds, mechanical banshee wails, and a gas-powered fire-breathing dragon plane?)

Author Hogan even introduced a Japanese villain to the series--Herr Matzu. While history records that the Japanese entered World War I on the side of the Allies, Herr Matzu preferred the life of a freelancer. Diminuitive of body, possessing a soft and diffident voice, he seems at first to be the antithesis of Rohmer's yellow peril and Hogan's own Chu Lung. In the midst of carnage he is polite and eager to please--like a small boy playing a deadly game. "I don't hate anyone," he explained. "I like being friendly with everyone, even though I must kill them."

At the climax of his initial encounter with the Master Spy, Herr Matzu is shot and left for dead. Later, however, in an adventure titled "Red Fangs of the Sky Emperor," he returns in an alliance with Doctor Chu Lung. "I was shot in the head," Matzu explains to his unholy chum, "and that delayed my operations."

While the introduction of werewolves and vampires to the Western Front appeared to offend few readers' ecological sensibilities, at least one disgusted fan took umbrage with the idea of a Chinese warlord fighting in the service of the Kaiser.

"It must have been pure accident," the reader wrote, "that I struck a good story when I read my first G-8 yarn. I thought to myself, 'Here's a swell mag' and I looked forward to the next issue. Well, the next issue came out. So what? It was a lousy story about guys who rose up from the dead and went on fighting and all that silly stuff that everyone knows is impossible. So I bought the next copy after that. So help me, it was worse. That was a story about that crazy Chinaman you call Chu Lung who was supposed to be helping the Germans. Of all the goofy things I ever read."

Well, you can't please everyone. But Bob Hogan certainly tried. The long-term success of the G-8 pulp magazine was due in no small part to the numerous fiends

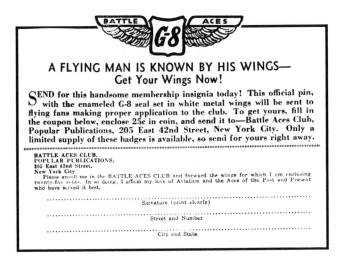

who stalked its pages. The bestiary was so large that one can only suggest the diversity. There was the giant Man in Armor, who commanded an army of bloated corpses; the Raven, a beak-faced avian travesty; the Vampire Hag, queen of the winged dead; Herr Doktor Wormer, the Death Master, who planned to blow up the world--quite literally; Herr Feuer, the asbestos-garbed super pyromaniac; and last but not least, there was Grun, the American-born ape man who hated everything lovely and beautiful on earth. The high incidence of stigmata-bearing villains would indicate that either the Kaiser's surgeons were criminally inept or that frantic pulp writers often regurgitated their own ideas.

The writer suspects that a number of Hogan's villains and their devices were the inventions of cover artist Fred Blakeslee, working in collaboration with publisher Henry Steeger. One of Popular Publications' greatest strengths was that Steeger made a near scientific study of readers' tastes and personally supervised the execution of each cover with a master chef's understanding of ingredients. There are numerous occasions in which a cover scene is described graphically in the final pages of a story but sometimes with little conviction. Details are brought painfully into the scene, then disposed of summarily, as if Hogan had achieved his goal of justifying some preposterous cover concept. This theory would explain such macabre villains as Baron von Todschmecker--a walking skeleton with the hilt of a dagger protruding from his gun-blue skull--as well as scores of insane aerial confrontations.

Another unsung hero was interior illustrator John Fleming Gould. Gould's planes were less convincing than Blakeslee's, but his dark-toned sketches excelled in the vivid imagery of awesome aerial combat, shadowy Black Forest castles, and ghastly moonlit monsters. It was these disparate elements that gave the magazine much of its surrealistic appeal.

Author Hogan knew this of course. He took delight in spinning tall tales of fantabulous invention. His only concern-- expressed occasionally in the stories and sometimes in the editorial comments--was a fear that readers would think he meant that war was fun. The magazine had sprung up when there was no holocaust in Europe. People thought that the greatest war of all was past, and dead history is always fair game for stories of simple thrills and heroism.

Clearly the yarns were not meant to be taken seriously, for Bob Hogan was a man who wrote with a twinkle in his typewriter.

In one of the Chu Lung adventures, Nippy taxis up to the 128th drome, having dropped the flying spy somewhere over Germany. A concerned Bull Martin challenges him:

> "Well, come on. Tell me what happened on the flight will you?"
>
> The terrier ace shrugged.
>
> "Oh, I just flew G-8 over," he said. "He hopped out when he got ready and I came back."
>
> "There's something you'll never be, Nip," he said, "if you do come out of this war alive."

> "What's that?" the terrier ace asked.
> "You'll never be a writer," Bull told him. "As far as you're concerned, nothing happens unless about fourteen million people get killed."

If you listen carefully, you can hear the ghost of Robert J. Hogan--laughing at himself. For the man who wrote the G-8 stories just had to have a sense of humor.

With a story set in mysterious Burma, "Wings of the Death Tiger," (June 1944), the saga of G-8 and his Battle Aces finally came to a close. Hogan put the pulps behind him forever, making an effortless transition into the slick magazines as well as producing a series of hardcover Westerns. One of his books, *Stand at Apache River*, was produced as a movie in 1953. Many of his stories were adapted for television, and several of his books have been translated into foreign languages. Robert J. Hogan died in 1963, with the last G-8 story written nearly twenty years before. Like Conan Doyle, he had once hoped to gain recognition as a writer of serious historical novels, but had been trapped by the runaway success of his bread-and-butter hero.

Today, Hogan's chief claim to immortality is as sole author of the G-8 stories. While attempts to revive his famous flying spy have had little effect (notably a series of Berkley paperbacks and a 1966 one-shot comic), pulp collectors and readers with long memories remain forever loyal.

If the G-8 yarns were trash--and millions of parents must have regarded them as such--then they were the best of all kinds of trash. They were trash for connoisseurs of trash. Trash for people who understood just how good trash could really be.

Even so, it is not easy for an adult to read G-8 today and still rekindle that precious sense-of-wonder which the stories once engendered. You have to suspend critical faculties. More than that, but better still, you have to rediscover that part of you which is forever young and naive--the lost boy who stirs within the consciousness of any man who has ever known a boy's dreams.

Perhaps, on nights when the wind howls fitfully in the chimney, you remember other such nights. Nights when the boy who dreamed dreams curled up with an apple in one hand and a copy of G-8 in the other. For a glorious hour or two, the sound of Hisso engines fills his mind. Once again, he is with G-8 in the midnight sky, some 10,000 feet over Germany. He is on the wing of Nippy's Spad, his eyes on the luminous dial of his German watch, his body curled to keep from freezing.

The little plane drones over the Vosges mountains. Somewhere down there, in the midst of the Stygian darkness, looms the secret laboratory of Herr Doktor Kreuger. The boy's heart pounds for he knows that within moments he will dive with G-8 into the blackness of the night. End over end he will spin in a series of somersaults until he feels the tug of the shroud cords, hears the parachute making a sound like a bursting paper bag as it snaps open.

Before him are all the exciting, horrifying, suspenseful adventures that a boy could possibly dream.

Bob Hogan understood those dreams.

He wrote directly to them.

THE SPIDER'S WEB

He scurries out of the night's black vortex, a stooped horror seemingly spawned from the pits of hell:

> *The skin was sallow, shining where it drew tightly over cheek bones, his mouth a lipless gash, the nose a predatory beak. He wore a wig of lanky black hair. About his twisted, deformed shoulders, a billowing black cape, and beneath the wide brim of a black hat long fangs gleamed in a horrid, sharp-toothed mouth.*

He is the *Spider*, pulp fiction's most ferocious masked vigilante. Half saint and half headsman, the Spider employed his never-cool .45s to scythe the city's streets of some of the most bizarre criminal vermin to erupt from a pulp writer's overheated imagination.

For a solid decade, from May of 1933 to December 1943, the Spider--cryptically billed as "the Master of Men"--entranced loyal readers who may have found The Shadow too tame for jaded tastes. Even compared to his chief rival in the phantom hero game, the Spider was one creepy character. When The Shadow laughed it seemed reasonable that he did so to scare the hell out of criminals. But the Spider's weird howl, his shivering peel of maniacal cackles, spoke another language.

Beneath the fright rags and vampiric make-up lurked Richard Wentworth, millionaire philanthropist. He gave thousands of dollars to the poor, and relaxed by playing his Stradivarius like a virtuoso; but as the Spider he killed without mercy and used his cigarette lighter to brand the foreheads of murdered thugs and their gloating masters with a vermillion seal of tensed hairy legs and poison fangs--his weird symbol of swift and ruthless justice.

As pulp historian Will Murray once put it, "No stranger hero ever existed in popular literature. The Spider was so weird that his publishers refused to showcase him on their covers as he *really* was. Instead, he was depicted with cloak and hat, set off by a black domino mask. For a four-issue stretch in 1940, the editors bowed to reader pressure and the Spider swooped across his own covers, long hair flowing, white fangs gleaming. Then, abruptly, their better sense reasserted itself. Some sights are just too strong for the light of day."

Like G-8, the Spider was the brainchild of Popular Publications' resourceful young publisher Henry ("Harry") Steeger, a gradudate of Princeton University and the University of Berlin. Admittedly an attempt to cash in on the success of Street & Smith's Shadow character, *The Spider* shared the spotlight with G-8 as the first of Steeger's pulp magazines to bear the name of a character rather than a genre.

In late 1929, when Steeger was in his mid-twenties, he borrowed some money from his stepfather and, with a partner named Harold Goldsmith, started the Popular Publications pulp chain. At first the partners had only four titles, a western, two detectives, and an air war, but by the 1940s they were running the biggest pulp publishing house in the world.

The youthful partners at the upstart company ran a happy ship, their offices described as a constant madhouse of larks and bantering. The entire staff was under thirty and they and played as hard as they worked. Shirley Steeger, Henry's wife, read the "slush pile" to pick out stories and ideas, and was reponsible for naming the company. It must have been fun--even the story titles mixed sensationalism with wry wit-- "You're the Crime in my Coffee," "The Corpse Belongs to Daddy," "This is the way we Bake our Dead." A chance remark, a joke, anything would suggest a new title which was immediately rushed into print.

As new fads replaced old, new magazines sprang up or disappeared like flamboyant weeds. Steeger instituted a sassy, extravagant style for his popular fiction and developed an instinct for cover art that bordered on genius. Eventually, the Popular Publications colophon identified some of the most exciting fiction magazines ever published: *Black Mask, Adventure, Dime Detective, Famous Fantastic Mysteries, Dare-Devil Aces, Argosy.* The list could go on and on. Over one hundred titles in all. It was Harry Steeger who dreamed up *The Spider.* He said he got the idea one day when he was playing tennis and noticed a huge spider at the edge of the court. In the earliest pulps and silent movies the spider had been employed as a frequent symbol for all that was creepy. Harry figured that it would work as the title for a new character magazine designed to compete with The Shadow. As usual, his instincts were spot on.

Touted as "a new magazine with a dynamite punch," the initial issue featured a novel titled "The Spider Strikes." The story was supposedly written by the popular Canadian writer R.T.M. Scott, who the publisher billed as "one of the finest mystery-action writers of the present day." I say supposedly because it appears that Scott's son, R.T.M. Scott II, may have written the first two Spider sagas, based on his dad's series of short stories and novels featuring a Secret Service agent named Aurelius Smith.

What is known is that young Scott was an associate editor at Popular and that he did write a number of stories for the mystery pulps. Unfortunately, whatever writing career he may have developed was cut short by service with the 48th Highlanders of Toronto during World War II. He was killed in action in Holland in 1945.

Scott's two Spider novels were, by pulp hero standards, fairly routine stuff. They are slickly written but nowhere in them is there a hint of the dreadful night demon who will soon debut as the authentic star of the title. They did serve to introduce wealthy Richard Wentworth, his society paramour Nita van Sloan, and the redoubtable Ram Singh--his fiercely loyal Hindu (later Sikh) manservant. But bigger and better, not to mention wilder, events were in store for Dick Wentworth. Beginning with the December issue a new writer took over, lurking behind the publisher's distinguished-sounding house name, Grant Stockbridge.

The new writer on the block was actually Norvell W. Page, an ex-newspaperman turned pulp paper pounder. Over the next ten years Page would blow up a storm in the magazine, producing some ninety-one Spider novels pulsing with anguish, fury, and blood sacrifice. Under his deft hand Richard Wentworth, uncostumed playboy detective, suffered a mutation into the *real* Spider, a "ruthless and terrible" cloaked apparition bound by his hero's oath to protect society from the forces of anarchy at whatever personal cost. Other pulp heroes did the same thing, of course. But the Spider did it better.

Norvell Page was one of the pulp field's most reliable professionals, a dynamic purple proser whose work invariably sported a flair for the dramatic upheld by powerful imagery and content. He worked hard at it, as suggested by his article in the 1935 *Writer's Yearbook*, in which he confessed: "I never turned out a story in my life that wasn't plain, hard work. Not that the writing itself isn't enjoyable. I don't have to sweat out words, or worry about action when my characters 'come to life.' But somewhere in that

story, the work was hard. Getting the idea, working out the outline, revising the copy, trying to get a fast opening that still would carry all the information it should; straining to tell a scene just as I see it in my mind's eye. On my Spider stories I have written as many as six different opening chapters, and spent a full day getting the first two thousand words on paper. I may have written eight, ten, twelve thousand in getting those two, and even then, I don't always like them."

But pulpmaster Page did get it right, and almost every time. Under his firm hand, the Spider tread boldly in The Shadow's footprints but wielded an even bigger schtick. Page quickly dispensed with Scott's mild plotlines and plunged deliriously into a mad netherworld threatened by masterfiends as bent as boomerangs. To state that he brought a level of emotional intensity to the Spider's world of death, torture, and apocalyptic terror is raw understatement. Potboilers those wild old yarns may be but, thanks to Page's scalding prose, the pots bubbled like corked volcanoes.

In Page's premier outing, the Spider waged all-out war with a pulp-style criminal monster, The Black Death, amidst the befouled air of a Manhattan swept by bubonic plague. This approach to the pulp hero formula--the sheer *magnitude* of the villain's crimes and his utter disregard for human life--was an element that typified the Spider epics of the 1930s. Manhattan itself was usually under siege, its major landmarks destroyed by flames, bombs or death rays, tens of thousands--perhaps millions--of innocent citizens destroyed by disease, drugs, or the ruthless incursions of subhuman hordes. One story alone ("The City Destroyer," January 1935) began with the destruction of the Empire State building and Grand Central Station, then went on to polish off Brooklyn Bridge and the New York subway system along with miscellaneous real estate and the usual cast of hundreds of thousands of screaming extras.

As Page's plots sped recklessly past the borders of reality, his horrors moved beyond the Big Apple into state-wide and even nation-wide settings. Snarling Neanderthals pillage the countryside. People burst spontaneously into flame. Hordes of poison vampire bats swarm. Giant robots with fire-squirting fingers stalk. And tigers and hyenas roam the ravaged streets as tens of thousands die from a green gas that strips flesh from bone. In a 1937 epic, "Machine Guns Over the White House," the government of the U.S.A. is captured by storm trooper minions of an Eastern occult order. The President himself is impeached on a trumped up charge of looting the Treasury and, in a cataclysmic finale, fights at the side of the Spider against armed troops and Eastern killers. (FDR was practically an ongoing character in the series, appearing as more than an incidental figure in several of the novels).

It should all seem ludicrous--if only the author gave you time to think or catch your breath. But his stories race along as if there is a warrant out for their arrest. Perhaps their tail pages are on fire. You can almost smell the cordite as pistols bark, machine-guns stutter, victims topple, blood splashes. The body count is relentless. Events careen from one unimaginably hideous predicament to something even worse. The prose is taut, vivid, muscular, throbbing with blood and resounding with the thunder of overwhelming tragedy. Even the titles leap out furiously: *Prince of the Red Looters. Death's Crimson Juggernaut. The Red Death Reign. The City Destroyer. Legions of Madness.*

It is the Spider's purgatorium.

Dreadful Night shrouds the world's greatest city. *Wings of the Black Death* descend. *The Flame Master* strikes.

The Grey Horde Creeps.

The Mayor of Hell reigns.

Oh, Spider! They're burning the city! Those people...Oh, Spider!

So little time until dawn! Alone, injured, perhaps near death, his beloved city in flames or ruins around him, the law, the public, and even his loved ones turned against him, the Spider must fight on. For he is The Master of Men. And for the Master of Men there is no surcease, no rest.

Like most things that excite disapproval, the Spider stories proved to be addictive. He was easily the most popular character produced by Popular Publications, rivalled only by The Shadow and Doc Savage over at Street & Smith. Even his author took to the character with the enthusiasm of his fans. Henry Steeger once confided: "Norvell Page was a very colorful character who enjoyed identifying himself as the Spider. I remember frequently that he would appear in the office in a black cape and a big floppy hat, and on his finger he wore a Spider ring."

The wearing of Spider garb was not the only connection between author Page and his unusual protagonist. In many ways Richard Wentworth, the Spider, was the most outlandish of the great pulp heroes. And yet, in some ways, he was the most human. Chalk it up to author identification.

When Norvell Page assumed the role of Spider scribe, he inherited a cast of characters invented by another author. The roll call, fairly complete, included not only Richard Wentworth and his fiance Nita, but also featured Wentworth's chauffeur Ronald Jackson, who served under him in the Great War, Wentworth's aged butler Jenkyns, the aforementioned Ram Singh, and Professor Brownlee who puttered about in his private lab to supply the Spider with such crime-fighting gimcracks as "the web," a long silken cord with a break strength of seven hundred pounds. Another major character was long-suffering Police Commissioner Stanley Kirkpatrick who was at once Wentworth's best friend and the Spider's sworn enemy. Under Page's skilled manipulation each of these stock characters began to take on flesh...or at least the fictional illusion of real flesh and human warmth.

But it was Richard Wentworth that Page identified with most, not just because he shared his hero's passion for costumery, but because the author found in Wentworth a perfect conduit to express his own deeply held beliefs regarding idealism, faith, and duty...even if those concepts were shrouded in blood-soaked science fiction nightmares. Under Page, Richard Wentworth emerged as humanity's paladin, a man of patrician tastes whose heart was kind but whose actions were ruthless because of his stern sense of justice and the measureless malignance of his enemies. He was, in a sense, pulpdom's tragic hero. The Spider's monthly triumphs came only through Herculean efforts against impossible odds. And the price he paid was awesome. Readers had met his kind before but never with such heart and feeling. Compared to The Shadow, who seemed to possess no overt emotional life, the Spider was *all* emotion, often to the detriment of common sense and logic.

As pulp historian Robert Sampson explained it, "The best Spider stories carry an emotional field strong enough to attract nails. They sweep you along, the paragraphs radiating emotion with almost physical intensity, numbing the critical sense. it is basic, simple stuff, overpowering in context. It works wonderfully well. You care for the people. As in other wish- fulfillment worlds, the hero is young, wealthy, adored. Unlike many other heroes, Wentworth is regularly abased, rejected, and scorned. He is alone--staggering, exhausted, gripped by agonies, bleeding from assorted wounds. Forward he reels in solitary struggle--leaving behind a trail of corpses, each neatly shot in the forehead."

The red badge of the Spider's justice was expressed by those nasty little seals he dispensed so generously. Hundreds of dead bodies, hundreds of burning symbols stamped indelibly on pallid foreheads...human detritus abandoned in the wake of the Spider's Old Testament war against vast conspiracies. Occasionally, even Wentworth had pause to consider. In "Green Globes of Death" we read: "He turned the lighter over curiously in his hand, looking at it with eyes that saw through and beyond it. How many times had that gleaming metal touched the dead foreheads of his victims? A strong shudder shook him."

But it didn't shake him for long. Only a month later, in "The Cholera King," the Spider's guns produced yet another red harvest, each dead thug tatooed with the familiar vermillion trademark. It was the Spider's version of the Puritan's scarlet letter: payment meted out as punishment for sin. So much to do, so many criminals to be punished.

In the Spider's mad universe, freakish enemies with names like The Red Mandarin, The Blind Man, The City Destroyer, and The Death Fiddler are not paranoid nightmares--they are a day-to-day reality. As repetition and the sheer virtuosity of break-neck prose made suspension of disbelief progressively easier, Norvell Page's imagination spawned armies of even more improbable megalomaniacs to add to his hero's overburdened work schedule: The Flame King, The Sandman, The Skull, The Conqueror, and The Emperor of Vermin, among others. In "Prince of the Red Looters" (August 1934) the Spider even met The Fly. Guess who won?

You had to admire the Spider, though. (How could you *not* admire a guy who figured that dressing up like a fanged hunchback would terrify hardened criminals)? Through years of rage, sacrifice and injury, with friends and the forces of law turned against him, madmen forever on the loose, and so little time to practice his violin, he underwent a purgatory of injury and defeat. The dreadful things that befell poor Dick Wentworth and his loyal group are almost too awesome--and certainly too numerous--to describe. Other pulp heroes operated under a bell jar of author security--you just knew they were going to come out of scrapes relatively unharmed. But the Spider suffered...*really* suffered. And most of the time his author convinced you that Wentworth wasn't going to make it through to next month's issue.

Drugged, paralyzed, disgraced, punctured by bullets through the chest, stomach, brain and other allegedly vital organs, the Spider fought on to illustrate to loyal readers the benefits of excellence under stress. But the bad guys never got his message. They returned time and time again to make his life a living hell. In "Legion of the Accursed Light," that eccentric fellow, The Eye of Flame, spread his lethal influence over New York, burning to charred cinders thousands of citizens and innocent commuters who crossed his path. As usual, the fate of America hung in the balance. And the Spider, the only man capable of penetrating to the heart of the enemy's stronghold, was captured and hung by his feet like a trussed chicken from a beam. How to escape? Being the Master of Men, he figured cooly that if he could remove just one of his feet, the anklet holding him would come loose and the chain could be pulled over the beam. It was just the Spider's way.

A Norvell Page capper, though, was the scene illustrated on the cover of "The Spider and the Slaves of Hell" (July 1939). The story featured a mad extortionist who specializes in blowing up landmark buildings. With his Sutton Place headquarters obliterated, his body torn by police bullets and chained to great balls of iron, the Master of Men rescues his beloved Nita by climbing up the sheer face of a building, dragging his metal balls behind him. It's all a matter of will.

Despite Wentworth's vigilance, lovely Nita was herself the subject of uncounted injuries, tortures, and emotional upheavals. In her efforts to aid the Spider in his battle against the ungodly, she was turned into a gibbering drug addict in "Slaves of the Crime Master," threatened with rape by an orangutan in "The Red Death Rain," had some of her brain cells suctioned out by "The Scarlet Doctor," and in "Rule of the Monster Men" was transformed into a surgically-altered cripple by that crazed practitioner, The Wreck. She was a spunky gal, though, and occasionally, when the Spider was either wounded, crippled, infected with rabies, blinded, dying, or sentenced

to Death Row in Sing Sing, she'd don his old cape and fright mask and off a few bad guys on her own.

One of the things that distinguished the Spider series was that it was a kind of ongoing serial with interrelated events in which the fate of characters changed dramatically. Wentworth's friend Stanley Kirkpatrick was Commissioner of Police throughout most of the stories but he ran for Governor of New York State in "Reign of the Death Fiddler," was elected and served until "The Mayor of Hell," eight issues later. He suffered a nervous breakdown in the late 1930s, and was felled by a major heart attack. But he was back to his old self in 1941 when he met and fell in love with Lona Deeping, whom he later married. But not all of Wentworth's pals got off so lightly. Like the Spider himself, they all suffered numerous wounds and near-death experiences. In "Laboratory of the Damned," his beloved Great Dane, Apollo, died of eating poisoned chocolate. His chief aide, Jackson, was bumped off in another story, as was clever old Professor Brownlee. Miraculously, Jackson was later restored to life, explaining that it had only been a bad wound. Perhaps because of his age, Professor Brownlee found it more difficult to shrug off three bullets through his skull; he tended to remain dead.

Not even Wentworth's residences were safe. He had three, perhaps four "permanent" bases in the stories. Despite secret passages, concealed steel doors, and yards of armor plating, most were either routinely invaded by criminal hordes or occasionally blown to slag. (Everybody seemed to know where the Spider lived, except possibly the police). Crime fighting took a similar toll on his high-powered automobiles, including his beloved armoured Daimler, his Hispano-Suiza convertible, and several Lancias, which he had hidden away in various places around New York City. In "Hordes of the Red Butcher," Wentworth comments: "I'll have to get a less expensive car. I've destroyed at

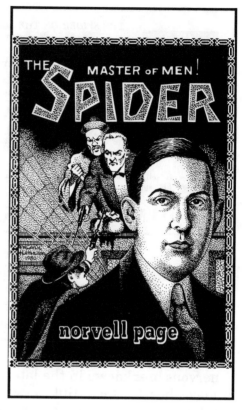

least a half-dozen of these and they run into money after a while."

It will appear to gentle readers that homicidal hero Wentworth may have been wound at least one turn too tight. Frankly, it's difficult to synopsize the Spider stories without presenting them as targets for satire. But clearly they weren't meant to be taken too seriously. They were disposable entertainments improvised at white-hot heat by a master pro who no doubt entertained himself by stretching nearly everything to near snapping point. Readers back in the "dirty thirties," however, not only found the stories great fun to read (they still are today) but responded enthusiastically to the author's subliminal messages concerning love and trust, loyalty and duty.

Other pulp heroes went about fighting petty crooks and chisellers, but the Spider specialized. He struggled against the things that Depression-era readers *really* feared--the death of friends and loved ones, the breakdown of social order, and the destruction of ideals in the face of chaos. The Spider of the pulps had begun life as yet another playboy detective. Under Norvell Page's influence he gradually metamorphized into something quite different. He became unofficial king of the tenement dwellers. For the disposessed he was God's messenger with a gun, a self-sacrificing saviour who fought evil that the law did not address. Faced with criminal conspiracies as vast and as frightening as the Great Depression itself, all the police could do was stumble about, banging away at the Spider's departing figure as if he were the cause and not the solution. But only the Spider could triumph, because his heart was pure and his moral judgment unyielding.

The new, improved Spider's colorful mix of action, sensationalism, and quasi-religious moralizing proved to be a formula for success. A Spider club was soon formed, grandiloquently titled "The Spider League of Crime Prevention." Thousands of metal Spider rings were sold to enthusiastic readers pledged "to aid the Spider in his ceaseless battle against crime." Members were urged to uphold the law on all occasions, even though that was a lot more than their hero ever did. There was even a Spider radio show (on KMOX St. Louis) and two Columbia Pictures serials, *The Spider's Web* (1938) and *The Spider Returns* (1941), the former earning its gun-blazing reputation as the most cadaverous kiddies' movie ever lensed.

But the Spider's glory was due to more than Norvell Page's scorching typewriter. Thanks to publisher Steeger and editor Rogers Terrill, the magazine was a total environment, from its curiously misshapen title logo to its scarlet spine inset with dripping dagger. Even inside, there were unique editorial touches like creepy little spider sketches and the manner in which the *Spider's* name was always italicized.

Beneath the crooked yellow logos lurked exquisite cover paintings detailing marvels of maniac action involving underdraped females and slobbering wingnuts waving blow-torches and whips, or pouring molten metal from bubbling cauldrons. Even the story titles demanded youthful attention: *Master Of The Night Demons. Scourge Of The Yellow Fangs. The City That Dared Not Eat.*

In the world of the pulp hero, such icons as Doc Savage and The Shadow were defined by the cover portraits of Walter Baumhoffer and George Rozen. As for the Spider, few would argue that John Howitt's masterfully lurid tableaus of pandemonium and carnage helped sell copies like ballpark hot dogs. Even so, it seems to me that the Spider's definitive artist was John Fleming Gould, the magazine's pen-and-ink man. Even the publisher must have thought so: cover artists Howitt and the great Rafael De Soto never received a byline, but Gould often did--and right on the contents page.

Gould was a favorite at Popular Publications. His work not only graced such other hero pulps as G-8 and Operator #5, but was used to launch a staggering number of first issues of other titles. He usually did *all* the pen-and-inks for any magazine he worked on, from column headings and character portraits down to spot sketches and those tiny hairy spiders. For the Spider he slashed out kinetic mini-murals full of the red-hot mayhem described so breathlessly in Norvell Page's apocalyptic melodramas. It seemed at the time--and still does--a perfect fusion of writer and artist. If Page could draw, I am sure he would have done so with Gould's harsh energy.

In "The Citadel of Hell" (March 1934) Page had introduced the real Spider--that sallow, stooped hunchback with the fake canines. A month later, in "Serpent of Destruction," artist Gould pictured Richard Wentworth in his new fear form: a scuttling apparition in black ankle-length cape, grotesquely out of place on a night club dance floor. And look! He's stapling some gink's forehead with the point of a venom-tipped cane. What a man, the Spider.

In the years that followed, Richard Wentworth's guns never cooled; and artist Gould was there to illustrate author Page's horrific visions of a world gone mad. "The City Destroyer" (January 1935) kicked off with a spectacular view of the Empire State building crumbling into pedestrian-jammed streets. "Reign of the Vampire King" (November 1935) featured hordes of vampire bats nipping Broadway theatre goers, bats attacking a night- flying airplane, and a giant bat racing a bi-plane over a vampire-infested carnival. Wonderful. "Master of the Flaming Horde" (November 1937) began with a panoramic street scene gutted by fire, an eerie horrorscape defined in flames. Explosions and flames were a Gould specialty; some of his best double-pagers nearly leap off the page with pyrotechnic fury--just like Norvell Page's scorching stories.

But even Page's fury had to wane. From the start his technique had been to escalate all the elements: bigger threats, more calamitous horrors, more action, wilder plots and villains, and more searing emotional tension. It all built up a glorious head of steam. Unfortunately, once you go over the top, it becomes increasingly difficult to climb higher. Inevitably, old ideas began to be recycled. And then, in the middle of the Living Pharoah series in late 1937, Page wasn't there at all. A new writer took over. The new man's name was Emile C. Tepperman.

Beginning in 1934, Tepperman had contributed a series of short stories to the magazine, all featuring his character Ed Race, the Masked Marksman. Late in 1935, he took over the publisher's *Operator #5* series from Frederick C. Davis. He would write some twelve Spider novels in all between 1936 and 1940.

In July of 1937 Norvell Page re-emerged with a Spider story titled "The Man Who Ruled in Hell." But the next issue saw yet another writer, Wayne Rogers, begin writing Spiders, more or less alternating with Page, who must have been suffering from author fatigue. Rogers was a conscript from the publisher's so-called "weird menace

pulps"--magazines that featured tales of grue and horror
based on the tradition of the legendary Grand Guignol
theatre of Paris. His Spider novels usually reflected those
sensational elements, culminating in his notorious "The
City That Dared Not Eat."

The new Spider scribes tried hard--their stories were
shrill and furious--but neither would or could reach the
emotional heights climbed by author Page. They tried to
copy the Page mystique without understanding it. In their
skilled but uninspired hands, Richard Wentworth slipped
in and out of character. Sometimes he seemed more like
The Shadow and sometimes even the Phantom Detective.
The real Spider waited in the wings for the second coming
of his creator.

Norvell Page, presumably rested and recharged,
returned to glory in 1939. He would continue to write most
of the Spiders until the magazine's demise four years later.
In the August 1941 issue, it was announced that a fire at
the author's hunting lodge had destroyed his entire
collection of *Spider* magazines. This was a genuine loss to
Page, who often spoke of Wentworth and his loyal circle
as if they were his own close friends. Perhaps inspired by
his loss, subsequent novels contain increasing flickers of
the author's philosophy and faith, woven like silken
threads through crude tapestries of destruction.

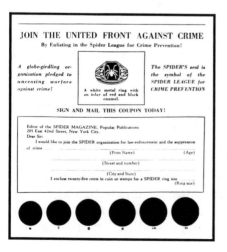

It is in this period
that Page engages his
readers with overt dis-
cussion of Wentworth's
extraordinary inner
strength and nobility of
purpose. In a footnote in
"Slaves of the Ring," he
states unequivocally,
"Self-less strength is what
men attribute to gods."

January of 1942 saw publication of the one hundredth Spider novel, "Death and the Spider." It was an event of some celebration in the magazine's editorial pages. For this special issue, Page concocted a stew of mysticism and menace that was strange even by his own iconoclastic standards. In it, an ancient Tibetan Lama prophecies that when Death walks the earth in the form of a man, the Spider will die. And Death does walk the earth in the classic form of a cowled skeleton with a bloody scythe. Death is, of course, impervious to the Spider's bullets, and Wentworth is only able to save himself by reciting the Twenty-third Psalm like an incantation. (Meanwhile, in Tibet, ten thousand holy man pray from him). And the Spider, in order to save the President of the U.S.A. from Death, endures a mortal chest wound. He dies. Dies dead. Or seems to die. Or perhaps only his physical being dies. With the Master of Men, such things were always tricky judgment calls. But then:

He drove his lagging body upward from the snow. He seemed to be detached from his body. He was up there in the air above his head somewhere, looking down. He felt sorry for his body, but it had to obey him. It had to live.

The dead man got up and walked. He pushed himself up with arms like broken sticks. He got up on legs that were limp and bent. His body sagged and his chin rested on his chest.

A man turned and saw him, and his white set face. He stepped aside. Wentworth's body sagged, but his head was up. His jaw line was carved from granite, and his eyes were chips of fire. He walked, and paid no heed to the mob, and it opened before him like the Red Sea.

Inside, Death has hypnotized the President into heart failure. In lurches the Master of Men, his body a bloody mess, but his mighty will strong enough to defeat even Death himself. When the President recovers, the church bells of Christmas ring out, and the great man is able to deliver his scheduled speech in that familiar, resounding voice: *"People of America, we have nothing to fear save fear itself."*

It is all very exciting. But strange. It is pure Spider. And pure Norvell Page.

There would be nineteen more Spiders--all but one written by Page--but never again would they reach the delirious heights of that one-hundredth issue.

And then, abruptly, it was over.

The Spider magazine was terminated during the Christmas season of 1943, a year that was to take a heavy toll on familiar heroes. In fact the war years were boom years for the pulps. But paper was limited, so less popular titles had to make way to supply increased print runs for better selling books. The fact that such "character" magazines as *The Spider* and *G-8 and His Battles Aces* were axed within the same period would indicate that infallible heroes were finding less favor with increasingly sophisticated readers. Many of the Spider's youthful fans were now in uniform, and they were embroiled in battling real-life villains on foreign shores. The new bad guys dressed in neither hoods or masks and didn't bother to pose behind secret identities.

The last Spider novel, "When Satan Came to Town," was ghosted by Prentice Winchell, a writer also known as Stewart Stirling. It was a poor story, and must have been a letdown for those who remembered the great days of the Spider's former glory. Suitably, the final lines belonged to Nita. "I could do with a night's sleep," she said.

As for that typewriter titan, Norvell Page, he had already deserted the sinking pulp ship for government work in Washington, where he wrote for the Office of War Information and, later, for the Atomic Energy Commis-

sion's Information Division. His death of a heart attack in 1961 at the age of 57 was recorded in the *New York Times*. He was credited with "writing more than 100 detective novels". No mention was made of the real nature of those novels.

So the question remains, what kind of a man was responsible for churning out those totally outrageous Spider stories? Acquaintances remember him as a nice guy who took delight in dressing in the fright garb of his famous hero, and who probably took equal delight in scaring the hell out of impressionable readers.

But the other Norvell Page, the amateur philosopher who dared inject unmistakable messages regarding the meaning of love and duty, trust, honor, and the consequences of responsibility, into bleeding pulp hero melodrama, seems to have emerged, like his character, on paper.

In a series of sensitive, revealing letters addressed to a young fan, the author of the Spider sagas once wrote, "Consult your conscience and you will know what is good. Consult your God and you will conquer. I make no forecast of bliss undisturbed, or of ease or luxury. If you have developed strength, it is because you will need it. God wastes nothing, not the smallest tear. If you love battle, you will win. If you are good, you will triumph."

It was the Spider's code. And the Spider was Norvell Page.

PULP PARANOIA: THE OPERATOR #5 SAGA

On the twenty-second day of the invasion of the United States by the Purple Emperor, a crowd of stunned, hopeless men and women gathered in Union Square in New York City to hear a proclamation of the conqueror.

The gray-shirted, steel-helmeted, stony-faced guards of the Central Empire used their sabers indiscriminately to keep the crowd in order. In the center of the square, a wide platform had been erected and upon it was a gruesome block, with a groove in the top, upon which a man might rest his head before it was chopped from his body by the executioner.

Suddenly, a stir ran through the sullen thousands in the square as a squat, broadshouldered man stepped up on the platform in the center. He was naked from the waist up, and his chest was entirely

> *covered with hair. His trousers were*
> *spattered with blood, and there were*
> *flecks of blood on his shoes. Black hair,*
> *matted and uncombed fell over a low*
> *forehead to his eyes. He carried a huge*
> *broadsword on his shoulder, and when he*
> *stopped beside the block, it took both*
> *hands to rest the cumbersome weapon on*
> *the floor.*
> *A low growl arose from the throng at*
> *the sight of him. Voices murmured: "The*
> *Executioner! God, when will they stop?"*

The above scene, which began the June 1936 issue of *Operator #5* magazine was but the beginning of a group of thirteen apocalyptic novels known as the Purple Invasion series. By pulp magazine standards the Purple Invasion was daringly inovative. In the past other paper heroes had grappled with avaricious dictators but never before with such horrendous consequences.

In a series of catclysmic cliffhangers, the Purple Invasion chronicled an assault upon America by the hordes of dictator Rudolph I of "Bulkaria," the Purple Emperor. The complete saga ran well over three-quarter-of-a-million-words. Each novel detailed immense battles in America's second War of Independence. Numerous major characters were introduced, fought for several issues, then were disposed of summarily. At the end, America was left in ruins, Canada and Mexico under the subjugation of vandal rule. Small wonder that the Purple Invasion has been called the War and Peace of the pulp magazines.

While Operator #5 is best remembered for the Purple saga, in fact the magazine ran for some 48 issues from April 1934, with a novel called "The Masked Invasion," until December of 1939 with "The Army From Under-ground." It treated an isolationist United States to not one but scores of paranoid daymares without parallel in the history of literature.

Unlike his contemporaries, Doc Savage and The Shadow, Operator 5 is long forgotten, replaced in the hearts of readers by hordes of pallid, latter-day imitators. But back in the thrill-hungry thirties his adventures were devoured by hundreds of thousands of youths and adults. To his fans he was a combination of James Bond, Tarzan, John Wayne and Superman all rolled into one. Furthermore, in the early thirties the secret service agent was almost a fresh concept in genre fiction. There were a few well-known undercover sleuths, notably George Bronson-Howard's Norroy in *Norroy, Diplomatic Agent* (1907), *Slaves of the Lamp* (1917), and *The Black Book* (1920), Melville D. Post's *Walker of the Secret Service* (1924), and R.T.M. Scott's Aurelius Smith in *Secret Service Smith* (1923). But there was nothing like the deluge of secret agent novels engendered by today's political machinations.

Secret Service Operator #5 was in reality James Christopher, a young man of incredible attributes. One is tempted to call Operator #5 the James Bond of the thirties

but, compared to Jimmy Christopher, Bond is a piker, a
johnny-come-lately whose adventures pall into bland
obsequies.

To be frank, Jimmy Christopher was a Superman.

Like most of the pulpwood heroes, Jimmy was a
larger-than- life figure absolutely dedicated to the eradi-
cation of America's enemies. He bested Bond in almost
every field save one, that of sexual gymnastics. While
Jimmy Christopher had a girl friend--Diane Elliot by
name--there was little or no hanky panky between them.
If there was some dalliance it happened not between the
sheets but simply between issues. The probability of
Operator 5 even finding time for such shenanigans seems
statistically unlikely. Instead, Jimmy's days (and nights)
were taken up with the most incredible series of adventures ever to pour from the high-speed typewriter of a pulp
thriller writer. The titles alone were enough to prickle
hairs on a reader's scalp: "Invasion of the Crimson Death-
Cult," "The Coming of the Mongol Hordes," "Corpse
Cavalry of the Yellow Vulture."

Savage hordes from mythical lands like Balkaria,
actual enemy powers like Germany and Japan, aliens from
other worlds and even creatures burrowing up from under
the earth plunged America's Secret Service Ace into one
overheated paranoid fantasy after another. As a surreal
social mirror of the collective phobias of its time, the
magazine remains unparallelled in the history of popular
culture.

Even so, Operator #5's position in the pulp pantheon
seems open to controversy. Some fans place him on the
very top of the heap, up there with the Spider and Doc
Savage. Others find his adventures to be naive and
jingoistic, particularly when compared to the fashionably
modern cynicism of today's post-Watergate spy thrillers.
Clearly the stories belong to an earlier age when such
words as patriotism and sacrifice were not regarded as
tools in the vocabulary of political fanatics. They were
addressed to the youth of the 1930s, young men as
wholesome as apple pie and as American as Gary Cooper.

In an early novel, "Master of Broken Men," the Vice-President of the United States is introduced to Operator #5. The description of Jimmy is typical:

He was in his early twenties; his face was clean-cut and strong. His bright blue eyes flashed with the alertness of youth; his forehead was high, his chin firmly determined. He possessed a poise that added stature to his years and obviously he was American through and through.

The young man removed from his pocket a flat silver case. His thumbnail pressed upon a corner of it, and a shining leaf of metal sprung up. The Vice-President gazed curiously at the right hand of the young man as the case was proffered toward him.

On the back of that hand shone a peculiar scar--a black and white marking shaped strangely like a spread-winged American eagle. Its wings seemed to flex, as though straining to take flight, as the young man's fingers moved.

Inside the silver case reposed a credential. The Vice-President's faded eyes brightened as he read:

THE WHITE HOUSE
Washington

To Whom It May Concern
The identity of the bearer of this letter mustbe kept absolutely confidential. He is Operator#5 of the United States Intelligence Service.

The signature affixed to the document was that of the President of the United States.

*Quickly Operator #5, otherwise known
as James Christopher snapped the case
shut and returned it to his pocket. "I am
at your service, sir," he said.*

If the scene appears corny now, not to worry.
Operator #5 was written in the grand manner of pulp
tradition. The invention was unflagging, the action fre-
netic. Even today the stories hold up remarkably well from
the standpoint of pure, hell-raising thud and blunder.

The scene in which Jimmy is introduced to the Vice-
President occurs at the very beginning of "Master of
Broken Men." It takes place in Washington at the annual
ball of the Daughters of the American Revolution, a scene
of pomp and splendor as the General Staff and the highest
heads of State regale themselves with music and laughter.
Yet, within paragraphs of Jimmy's meeting with the Vice-
President, incredible horror explodes.

As if at a signal, the doors of the ballroom entrance
swing open. Ten, twenty fearful apparitions appear.

They stride inside, naked bodies glistening, faces
turning slowly right and left, their arms raised, hands
gripping broad-bladed knives--a score of savage tribes-
men--in the midst of the most fashionable event of the
social season.

*Behind them the doors stood open.
Startled hundreds saw a path marked by
violent death. Still bodies lay in the
corridor. Others sprawled on the steps
rising from the street. Each bore the
fearful marks of blows struck by the
bright-bladed knives in the hands of the
intruders.*

*They had literally slashed their way
into the hall and now, weapons held
poised to hack again, they began a slow
advance.*

Operator #5 stood in a cleared space, alone. Darkness clouded his blue eyes as he watched the living menace spreading. Moving with queer, dancing steps, they formed a ragged circle, their grotesque faces outward. Two of them peered straight at Jimmy Christopher, brandishing their knives, their black eyes glinting like beads.

Operator 5's hand clicked loose the buckle of his belt. He whipped it away, and it sprang out straight. It was a narrow sheath of leather; he flicked it off the thin, bright blade of a rapier. It flexed in the light, slender, supple, a needle-pointed line of steel.

This scene was typical of openers in the hero pulps. The writer usually set up a bizarre, arresting situation, embroiled the hero in immediate action and then kept the poor devil riding a roller-coaster plot for some 80 or 90 relentless pages. There was no time out for commercials and little time for the reader to catch his breath. It was story-telling in the grand manner--large than life, chock full of audacious, delicious hokum.

In order to cope with assorted fiends and monsters, Jimmy's belt-rapier was but one of the weapons he carried in his wardrobe arsenal. Others included his famous death's head ring which bore the numeral 5 and contained a powerful explosion in the hollow top. There was a small gold ornament, a reproduction of a skull with ruby eyes, which Jimmy usually had clipped to his watch chain; inside the skull there was a silver ball containing Diphenolchlorasine, a death-dealing liquid which would change into gas upon contact with air. Jimmy was strong on belts. In addition to the belt rapier, he sometimes wore a three-strand leather job, the strands of which could be unloosed and opened into one continuous length of leather rope some nine feet long.

The Secret Service Ace needed these and all the other weapons he could muster to combat such scourges as "The Melting Death," "The Red Invaders," and "The War Dogs of the Green Destroyer." As in all the hero pulp magazines, the contents page for each issue gave a fair sampling of what the hero had in store for him. In "Attack of the Blizzard Men" the synopsis read:

> *It was a sultry day in August when the ghastly cold first came. Snow began to fall; ice formed, and in a brief hour, New York City was paralyzed. A new and deadly weapon had been directed at America by a ruthless, international syndicate, for, under the cover of the sub-zero weather, barbarous, armored warriors swarmed into the United Staes, turning our country into a helpless colony to be exploited savagely. In quick succession, other cities--Washington, Los Angeles, Chicago, New Orleans--fell before the assault of the astute enemy and the marrow-chilling cold. Could Operator 5 of the disabled Secret Service--Jimmy Christopher to his friends--save our land from shameful slavery?*

Well, you had to pay your ten cents to find out. Certainly with monthly problems like that a fellow needed all the friends he could get. Jimmy was blessed with a number of close aides; foremost among them was Diane Elliot (spelled Elliott in later stories). Diane was a special writer for the Amalgamated Press news service but became a full fledged Intelligence agent during the Purple invasion crisis.

As Jimmy's girl, Diane led a life of harrowing adventures. Many of the Operator 5 cover paintings bear likenesses of Diane: strapped to the muzzle of a cannon;

about to be hurled from a giant catapult; facing firing squads; tied to dynamite kegs; and once--shades of Pearl White--bound to railroad tracks, the thundering locomotive mere yards away.

Young Tim Donovan was Operator 5's unofficial assistant. They had met one drenching night on the lower East Side when Tim, a bootblack huddling in a dark doorway, had saved Operator 5 from death by a bullet from a criminal's gun. Jimmy had virtually adopted the plucky youngster, accepting him into his family circle and into his numerous adventures. Young Tim appeared in each of the Operator 5 novels, the only sustaining character to do so. He was even allowed to mature in the course of the series and eventually entered the Intelligence Service himself.

A leading character in the series was the man who was Commander-in-chief of the United States Intelligence Service, a man known even to his most trusted agents only as Z-7. Dressed entirely in gray with black hair and black, glittering eyes, he is described as an older man of stocky build and grim visage. There is a bond of affection between Z-7 and Operator 5, a bond which is sorely tested in the course of the novels. Later in the series, Jimmy replaces Z-7 as head of Intelligence.

Another character who figured in many of the stories was the President of the United States. Although never mentioned by name, there are reasons to assume that he was intended to be Franklin D. Roosevelt. The identification with FDR becomes strange indeed when, in the August 1936 issue, the Chief Executive places a gun to his temple and pulls the trigger rather than agree to an ultimatum from the Purple Emperor. This was just one of the reasons why the Operator #5 novels have to be regarded as science fiction. They were sf set in a curious parallel world--a world sharing a common history with our own yet diverging at right angles somewhere in the 1930s.

Jimmy's twin sister, Nan, was an important figure in the novels as was his father, ex-Secret Service Operator Q-6. In spite of a bullet lodged near his heart which constantly threatened his life, John Christopher managed to assist his son on a number of cases.

The elder Christopher was, in fact, one of the most durable invalids in fiction. In the first Purple Empire story, "Death's Ragged Army," he is one of the initial victims of the Emperor's deadly green gas. Later, in "The Suicide Battalion," Jimmy discovers his father alive, dressed as an old bearded peasant in an alpine inn. After being discovered by his son, Q-6 explains that he had been captured and kept as a slave behind enemy lines, and finally brought to Europe. It is one of the most miraculous recoveries in the history of the pulps, particularly for a man who has been "dead" for some fifteen novels.

Later, in the penultimate Operator 5 adventure, the old man is again laid low--along with the new president, the cabinet and the congress--when the Japanese drop an atom bomb on Washington. But in the very next issue he is alive and hale enough to lead a mass counter-migration from west to east through hordes of Oriental forces. Obviously Jimmy's own invulnerability was hereditary in nature.

As "America's Secret Service Ace," Jimmy himself played many parts. Among the aliases he often assumed were: Huntley Walsh, Morton Clagg, George Wakley, Anthony Andrews, and, in particular, Carleton Victor, noted portrait photographer.

It was in his guise as Carleton Victor that Operator 5 employed a manservant by the name of Crowe. The estimable Crowe, gentleman's gentleman extraordinary, did not dream that Carleton Victor, photo-portraitist of world-wide reputation, was a convenient cover for Jimmy Christopher. Like the

tion, was a convenient cover for Jimmy Christopher. Like the famous personages who considered it a privilege to sit before Victor's camera, the manservant considered his master a great artist.

The sharp-nosed, stiff-shouldered Crowe was, in fact, one of the few "in" jokes in pulp hero history; his colossal cool was a running gag that consciously or unconsciously satirized the sensational nature of the pulp series. Though Crowe was sometimes baffled by his master's eccentricities he permitted himself no curiosity whatsoever. The four walls of Victor's penthouse were the boundaries of Crowe's entire world. Outside, the nation reeled; havoc and ruin stalked the streets; dead men marched; Mongol hordes raided; America's proudest cities were reduced to ashes or frozen with giant neutron projectors. But Crowe was oblivious to it all. He was the one "normal" person in a universe overtaken by madness.

Crowe was dropped from later issues, as were other characters and schticks from the early numbers. In fact, unlike most other hero pulp novels, the Operator 5 books can be divided into two distinct series. The first, running for some twenty issues, was in the mold of prevailing bizzare fantasy pulps. The second, beginning in early 1936, concentrated more heavily on militaristic exploits. Even the style of writing changed at this point, leaving even a casual reader to conclude that there were at least two writers--perhaps more--who worked under the resounding pen name of "Curtis Steele."

The first of these men was the late Frederick C. Davis, author of the famous Moon Man series in *Ten Detective Aces*. In order to help pay his way through college in the 1920s Davis wrote and sold a story a week to the then burgeoning pulps. By the 1930s he had developed a daily regimen of writing from nine o'clock in the morning to four in the afternoon, six days a week. His daily output-- thirty completed double-spaced pages, or 125,000 words a month. He wrote over a million words a year for nearly a decade before World War II.

It was Davis who originated the Operator #5 series and developed most of the characters and situations. I asked Mr. Davis (in a letter dated December 1972) why he abandoned his famous character after some twenty novels. He replied:

"There were several reasons. One, suitable ideas were becoming increasingly hard to dream up. Two, I was sadly underpaid--$500 per story, about half my word rate with other pulp publishers and with other magazines of the same publisher. Three, I was feeling the strain of my heavy work load. While writing Operator #5 I was also turning out more than an equal number of words for other markets--among those, the long-runnig Moon Man series, a novelette every month.

"I never read any of the Operator #5 stories after I stopped writing them, which accounts for my ignorance of the Purple Invasion. (I never read any of the Doc Savage or Shadow stories either.) I had had a surfeit of him and I was busily putting my nonworking time into the pleasure of dating a lovely girl whom I later married and who still later presented me with a son whose name is neither Jimmy nor Christopher."

Following Davis' exit, the series was taken over by Emile C. Tepperman, that prolific pulpster who was to perform similar duties for the Spider and the Avenger, in addition to continuing work on numerous series characters of his own invention.

Tepperman was the sole author of the epic Purple Invasion stories. It would take an article in itself to synopsize the events of that momentous conflict. Even the highlights can only be skimmed: the conquests of the Purple Emperor over Europe and most of Asia; his invasion of America and the establishment of his head-quarters amid the ruins of New York City; the deadly green gas; Diane's rescue as she is about to be hung from the Liberty Bell on the fourth of July; the attack on the gold train; the battle against the Purple Naval Fleet; Operator 5's destruction of the Panama Canal; the cholera march into Phoenix; the bombardment of San Francisco; the suicide charge of the Canadian Lancers (sic); the destruction of the Maximilian Dam and the Pittsburgh steel mills; Jimmy's destruction of the giant blimp; the capture of Chicago by Mongol troops; the Emperor's pact with the Yellow Warlord; Operator 5's battle to the death with Urslup; the second battle of Valley Forge; the siege that brought the Black Plague; and, finally, the fall of the Purple Empire and the rebuilding of America.

A common ruse used throughout the Operator 5 stories was the attempt to lend verisimilitude with the use of footnotes. Some of these footnotes make for fascinating reading, particularly in the early stories of Fred Davis, when they consist of actual news items from journals of the era--the footnotes alone constitute a popular history of the political machinations of the 1930s. Later, in Tepperman's Purple Invasion series the footnotes become part of the fiction; references are made to such pseudo-historical documents as "Harrison Stiever's monumental History of the Purple Wars."

The editorial opinions in the magazine were no less fascinating, both in the unsigned editorial columns and in a monthly feature titled The Secret Sentinel. In the June 1936 issue, The Secret Sentinel column ruminated:

"In spite of the fact that Italy is the only great nation today with an army of veterans, Mussolini did not, and does not want, and cannot afford war.

"Another dictator also attempted a bluff. Nazi Germany is today developed along military lines to a point where some observers claim she is far more powerful than the empire of the Kaisers. Yet, ringed around as she is by hostile neighbors she cannot risk war. But the successful bluff of Benito Mussolini encouraged the unimaginative mind of the Nazi leader to try the same thing. He moved his troops into the Rhineland and barked at his neighbors.

"But Hitler has not the personality of Mussolini. And he has done nothing to stimulate love or admiration. And he has no imagination. He did not understand that by his unconsidered move he was only playing into the hands of Mussolini."

So much for political acuity.

The *Operator #5* magazine was another offspring of Henry Steeger's Popular Publications, a giant of the pulp adventure field. The editor was Rogers Terrill, who served on the equally crazed *Spider* magazine. Jerome Rozen (of Shadow fame) painted the cover for the first issue but most other covers--and there were some beauties--were executed by John Howitt. Amos Sewell and Rudolph Belarski were responsible for interior illustrations in the first issue. John Fleming Gould, the "inside man" responsible for vivid delineations of the Spider and G-8, carried on beginning with issue two and running through until December of 1936. Ralph Carson illustrated the remaining issues excepting that of January 1938 when Harry Fisk helped out. The magazine ran monthly from April 1934 through April 1936, when it became bi-monthly. At the end of 1936 it resumed monthly publication but quickly dropped back to bi-monthly, reflecting an obvious weakness in sales.

By the time Jimmy mopped up the remnants of the Purple Invaders the year was 1938. Earlier villains had masqueraded under Graustarkian labels, but in the battles still to be waged there was little need for euphemistic nationalities. The enemies were clearly named: Germany, Japan, Italy.

It was at this point that a third and final writer--Wayne Rogers--took over the series, still writing under the familiar Curtis Steele by-line. In Rogers' "The Suicide Battalion," the three bandit nations stage an assault from "friendly but helpless Canada," a country now prostrate under tyrant rule. Only the Ferrara Line--a long string of entrenchments which stretch from the Great Lakes to Vancouver--stand between the U.S. and total annihilation.

Jimmy organizes a band of 200 suicidally loyal volunteers. Together they wage an underground war that takes them to the German dictator's own headquarters.

"Now it is our day" the dictator gloats to a captured Operator 5. "The day of the deprived nations who were forgotten when their greedy neighbors carved out colonial empires for themselves. Now it is our turn to take colonies--west of the Mississipi has been allotted to Japan, east of the Mississippi and below the Great Lakes to Italy, and Canada will be the German portion. Colonies worth having, those will be."

As usual Jimmy faces a number of personal crises, but in the final minutes he turns the enemies against one another, makes peace with the Italians and pursues the fleeing Germans into Canada.

Just one month later, though, in "The Day of the Damned," Mexico proves an adequate base for invasion by heavily-armored Japanese forces. "In the hot hills of Old Mexico," the synopsis reads, "Operator 5 launched his great counter-espionage campaign against a plotting Asiatic horde which threatened to loose the entire barbarous Mexican guerilla Southwest upon America, in an attack that also combined modern Japanese mechanized warfare and dread tropical disease. Then, in the final, decisive minutes, America seemed to turn back the very pages of history as she made her last stand for freedom at the Alamo!"

And so it went. Month after month a nervous nation was subjected to one bizarre onslaught after another. In one episode, "Invasion from the Sky," the enemy appeared

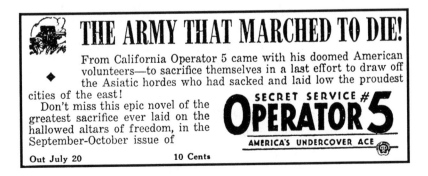

to be chimeras from some other world, landing in the midst of cities in immense space ships--a yarn undoubtedly inspired by Orson Welles' Martian panic broadcast.

Fantastic weaponry abounded in the stories, some of it pre-dating actual World War II devices. The most advanced terror tools were employed by a foe known as The Yellow Vulture--Japanese warlord Moto Taronago.

The Yellow Vulture stories were among the most imaginative of Jimmy's adventures. The series might have eclipsed the Purple Invasion saga had it not ended abruptly after only four episodes due to the demise of the magazine itself.

The final story, "The Army From Underground" (November 1939) contained an especially prophetic scene-- a description of the effects of the first atom bomb dropped on a civilian population--with victors and victims eerily transposed:

> *Soon they reached the edge of the recognizable ruins and were picking their way through a desolation that resembled the debris-littered trail of a devastating tornado. Wreckage encompassed them on every side. Tall buildings had been flattened, stout steel girders twisted and snapped, concrete shattered and crumbled. Streets had ceased to exist, except as barely distinguishable canyons through the mounds of litter. And nowhere was there a living human being...only mangled, half-burned corpses to indicate that this stricken wilderness had once been a great city.*
>
> *For more than a mile they trudged through that ghastly shambles, into a district where the leveled buildings were not so completely obliterated, where the streets were less choked with wreckage--*

*and where the tortured moans of impris-
oned sufferers came to them from out of
the darkness. Here they encountered the
first survivors--a hastily organized patrol
seeking trapped victims.*

*"Everything is destroyed," one dazed
worker told them as he tore away tumbled
wreckage in an attempt to reach a screaming woman pinned beneath the debris.
"Philadelphia is wiped out...everything
but the suburbs. It's all gone--disap-
peared. Houses, cellars, bomb-proof shel-
ters--all blown to nothing."*

*His incredible words were all too true.
Operator 5 found them corroborated even
before the grey light of dawn revealed the
tremendous crater that was the huge
empty grave of the Quaker City. Philadelphia had been utterly obliterated, wiped
from the face of the earth--with a loss of
life that probably would reach a million!*

*"They never had a chance," he said
bitterly as he stared out over that terrible
waste. "This is the most ghastly mass
murder the world has ever seen--the most
heinous crime ever committed against an
innocent and defenseless people!"*

In almost every story Jimmy's beloved nation suffered a purgatory of conflict and defeat. Victory came only
when all seemed darkest. But even victory was often
Pyrrhic. At the end of "The Army From Underground,"
with Philadelphia, Washington, Knoxville and Baltimore
completely demolished, with giant slaughter machines
burrowing out of the ground and carving bloody furrows
through the countryside, Jimmy receives further news:

> *"There is no more Canada,"* Quillen's
> *whisper cut like a cold wind. "The Japa-*
> *nese have wiped it out...destroyed the*
> *remaining cities...annihilated the popula-*
> *tion. The Dominion is a great*
> *wilderness...and the Japanese are using it*
> *at this very minute as a base from which*
> *to sweep down into New England...coming*
> *down to destroy arms...ammuntions..."*
> *His dying voice faded, was gone.*
>
> *In that moment Operator 5's triumph*
> *turned to bitterness. He had won back*
> *territory and snatched a great population*
> *out of the hands of the Japanese, yet*
> *certain destruction and merciless annihi-*
> *lation now faced them all... Instead of*
> *into safety, he had led the millions of*
> *Pacific coast emigrees into a death trap*
> *worse than the one from which they had*
> *fled...A death trap out of which he*
> *somehow must deliver them and build*
> *again a new and great America!*

That November 1939 issue was destined to become
the biggest cliffhanger of them all. Another novel, "Hell's
Last Battalion", was announced but never saw publication. Jimmy Christopher's battles were over.

America's real war was soon to begin.

TWENTY YEARS
OF MURDER

1933.

It was a dynamic year not only for Depression-weary America, but for America's favorite form of lowbrow entertainment, the pulp fiction magazine.

In March Franklin Delano Roosevelt became the 32nd President of the U.S.A. and soon instituted his famous fireside chats. As if to celebrate the New Deal new pulps sprang up like public works programs: *Magic Carpet, Nick Carter, Black Book Detective, Ten Detective Aces, The Lone Eagle* and dozens more.

Nor was FDR alone among superheroes that propitious year. Four of the most durable of all pulp characters were introduced: The Spider, G-8, Doc Savage, and the Phantom Detective.

Of all the major pulp heroes the Phantom best reflected the 1130's passion for yet another form of escapist literature: the classic detective story.

In hardcovers such sophisticated sleuths as Lord Peter Wimsey, Ellery Queen, Hercule Poirot and Philo Vance sold books by the millions. It was this type of detective novel--the story of ratiocination--which attracted the attention of most critics and literary pundits of the era. But, in America in the 1930s, for every reader of S. S. Van Dine there were dozens of readers of *Dime Detective* and *Black Mask* magazines. The pulps alone had introduced a new kind of detective who was in some ways a city version of the wild west hero. Unlike the police, the hard- boiled detective was bound by no rules other than his own. He was armed and dangerous, and he walked down mean streets simmering with the potential for ready violence.

If the Phantom (he was not called the Phantom Detective in the novels--that was the magazine title) deserves any place in the history of mystery fiction it is because he was a calculated attempt to blend the inde-structible action detective of the pulps with the cerebral problem solver of the Sherlock Holmes school. It was not always a comfortable amalgam but the attempt paid off handsomely in two decades of successful publication.

In all of those twenty years the Phantom had but one policy from which he never deviated. He would not take on a case unless he felt that it had elements unusual enough or sinister enough to warrant his efforts. But when such a case did present itself (usually about once a month) he struck like a hawk in the dark underworld of crime.

According to the magazine's own carefully concocted legend, the Phantom was Richard Curtis Van Loan, one of the wealthiest playboys in the country, a man who was believed to live only for the pleasure he could get from life. As the Phantom Van Loan was called into action by a crimson light blinking on the apex of the towering *Clarion* building.

The Phantom was the only pulp hero to be sponsored by a newspaper--or to be more precise, by a newspaper publisher, kindly old Frank Havens of the *Clarion*. An early issue of the magazine explained their relationship:

> *Young Van Loan's father had been a*
> *lifelong friend of Havens, and it was*
> *after the elder Van Loan's death that*

Frank Havens had been responsible for the existence of the Phantom. The idea had first been born when Havens had suggested that Dick Van Loan, bored with life and restless, try his hand at solving a mysterious crime which had stumped the police of the nation. And so successful had he been that the young heir to the tremendous Van Loan fortune had gone on and on perfecting himself in that which had become his lifework. The name of the Phantom led all the rest in the annals of crime detection, a name known and admired by the police of every nation.

One of the unusual aspects of the playboy's secret war on crime is that it was conducted in a dispassionate style. Van Loan did not fight crime out of some personal rage. He fought it because it was wrong, and because crime fighting was an anodyne to boredom.

The Phantom had no supernormal powers but, like most of the great pulp heroes, possessed an awesome range of abilities. Wide-shouldered, powerful, Van Loan could stay on his feet for ninety-six hours at a stretch. He was adept at nearly all sports, an expert with the fencing foils, at ju-jitsu, la savate, and his markmanship with guns of all kind was uncanny. In addition he was a skilled pilot, a master of ventriloquism and hypnotism, and could speak a dozen languages fluently.

If there was one thing Dick excelled at, however, it was the art of disguise. Van was the finest make-up man outside of the Actor's Union. He had to be because death was the certain penalty for a single botched job.

While the sleuth of a thousand faces often wore a small black cloth mask (as depicted in Rudolph Belarski's cover paintings), mostly he preferred to adopt the guise of another living being. Like a shadow passing the sun, a layer of skin cream would blot out his own familiar features and then, with the aid of crayons and shadow pencils, he could assume any other identity. He carried a compact portable make-up kit on him at all times, another more elaborate one in his special souped-up car.

Headquarters for the Phantom was Van Loan's own Park Avenue penthouse apartment. It was serviced by a private elevator and was curiously devoid of servants or valets out of respect for the Phantom's lone wolf life style.

Within the hushed luxury of his apartment, Van needed only to press a button concealed on the back of his Louis Quinze bed and a section of the wall would unfold to reveal his inner workroom. Here the Phantom kept a small but complete scientific laboratory, a wardrobe containing some of his various disguises, a make-up table, and a staggering arsenal that included small pistols tiny enough to fit into the palm of the hand, large-bore Lugers, Colt Peacemakers, derringers, nickel-plated S & W's, and blue-steel automatics with easy-action triggers made to the Phantom's order.

An even more impressive lab and armory was set up in an old warehouse along the waterfront. All that the people in the neighborhood knew about the building was that it belonged to a Dr. Paul Bendix, a bearded, querulous old scientist who had the reputation of being a recluse. Only Frank Havens was aware that Dr. Bendix was but one more version of his friend the Phantom.

The Phantom Detective magazine was the property of a publisher named Ned L. Pines. Fresh out of college, Pines entered the pulp publishing field in 1931. Throughout the

FRANK
HAVENS

MURIEL
HAVENS

CLARION

The Phantom
Detective

RICHARD CURTIS
VAN LOAN

FRANK HAMILTON ©1974

years his firm remained one of the big three of the pulp world (trailing only Popular Publications and Street & Smith). For some reason Pines' company was variously identified as Standard Magazines, Beacon Magazines, and Better Publications, although they were known in the trade as "the Thrilling group," partly because of a logo running on the covers and partly because of editor Leo Margulies' penchant for magazine titles with the world "thrilling" prominently displayed: *Thrilling Mystery, Thrilling Adventure, Thrilling Wonder Stories, Thrilling Ranch Stories*, etc.

One reason the Thrilling magazines have often been underrated by pulp fans and collectors is that they were less flamboyant than many of their rivals. But if the Phantom lacked the pure sensationalism of Operator #5 or the bizarre melodrama of the Spider, you couldn't tell it by titles dreamed up for his stories: "The Corpse Parade," Master of the World," "Cities For Ransom," "The Talking Dead," "The Criminal Caesar" and so on.

The covers portray casual homicide, either real or threatened; above it, the masked face of the Phantom looms symbolically like--well, like a phantom.

Inside, the slaughter continues. A man is turned into a human torch by a booby-trapped cigar. Wealthy men are found chained to moving vehicles...each with one arm missing. Kidnapped victims cry out from buried coffins. Bodies plummet from an empty sky. Rampaging lions turn Manhattan into a concrete jungle.

They called them "the bloody pulps," and not without reason. There were 170 issues of the Phantom Detective magazine, thousands of pages. And throughout them all the action is violent, unremitting. The need for pace dictates the narrative; whenever the plot flags, another body bites the dust--or plummets from a seemingly innocent sky.

It is all hackwork, of course, but hackwork developed to an art by old pros who constantly demonstrate their instinctive timing and their well-developed flair for the preposterous and the melodramatic. For the world of the Phantom is that heightened universe of the pulp hero where violent physical action is the dominating law of man and nature.

Despite the Phantom's claim to be "The World's Greatest Detective," his is a milieu alien to such cerebral detectives as Sherlock Holmes or Philo Vance. Holmes proved that thought is action; he did not need to leave his flat to solve a case. Indeed, Holmes' closest American counterpart, Nero Wolfe, makes a point of seldom venturing forth from his old Brownstone on West Thirty-fifth Street.

The Phantom Detective stories were written for a hero-oriented audience. Phantom readers did not demand that they be given a chance to solve a detective riddle on their own; instead, they were content to enjoy the Phantom overcoming an intellectual problem--just as they were content to watch their indestructible hero overcome such physical obstacles as getting knifed or being tossed off a cliff.

To be sure, there was always the obligatory denouement scene in which the Phantom strutted his mental stuff before a room full of red herrings--at least one of whom would be unmasked as the villain of the piece. These scenes were in the tradition of the classic mystery and sometimes ran for three or more pages. Perhaps this is why the Phantom's publishers saw fit to call him "The World's Greatest Detective," and who was there to argue?

But, for a mental marvel, Van spent a lot of his time getting out of physical scrapes. In fact, if anything distinguished the Phantom plots it was the number of capture and escape scenes featured. Many of the escapes were reminiscent of cliffhanger endings in the then-popular Saturday afternoon movie serials. Even the chapter headings, "Tommy-Gun Rampage," "Pawn of Death," "The Well of Murder," suggested greater fealty to chapter plays than to the intellectual puzzler.

EVERY STORY BRAND NEW

The PHANTOM DETECTIVE

Vol. XXXIX, No. 1	JUNE, 1942	Price 10c

Featuring the World's Greatest Sleuth
in
A Full Book-Length Novel

MURDER MAKES A MOVIE

By ROBERT WALLACE

Taken from the Case-book of Richard Curtis Van Loan
(Profusely Illustrated)

The Phantom would have made a good movie serial character, but no one seems to have thought of it. Curiously, he elicited very little interest outside of the pulps. His publishing company did have its own chain of comic books and for a number of years his adventures appeared in strip form in *Thrilling Comics*. But in the comics he was a mere back-of-the-book figure--a masked dandy in tophat and tux--who held limited appeal for young fans of Captain America and Superman.

Until recently no one seemed certain just how the Phantom came to be created or who dreamed him up. Years earlier a writer named Herman Landon had written some books featuring a character called the Gray Phantom, also a disguise whiz. It's unlikely that the Gray Phantom was the Phantom Detective's literary ancestor, though, because the character was rather uninspiring except to lovers of oddball names (his civilian sobriquet was Cuthbert Vanardy).

The real inspiration for the Phantom was undoubtedly the same as that of the Spider. They were both calculated to cash in on the great success of Street & Smith's *Shadow* magazine. Not only did the Phantom cognomen sound as mysterious as that of The Shadow, but even the author's name rang bells. "Robert Wallace" was a fictitious byline chosen by editor Leo Margulies because he felt unsophisticated readers might link it to Edgar Wallace, a popular writer of the day whose name symbolized mystery and detection.

The truth was that "G. Wayman Jones" (author of the first eleven titles) and "Robert Wallace" (credited with the balance) were not the exclusive pseudonyms of any one indivdual. They were house names which cloaked the work of a stable of writers operating under first the Jones and then the Wallace identity.

Editorial Director Leo Margulies claimed that he and a writer named D'Arcy Lyndon Champion created the Phantom Detective in 1932. Certainly many of the early Phantoms appear to have been the work of Champion, who also wrote under the name Jack D'Arcy. (As D. L. Champion he was one of the mainstays of *Black Mask* in the 1940s).

The problem with Champion was that while he was a fine writer and a witty fellow, he had a reputation for giving editors angina attacks concerning deadlines--a cardinal sin in the hero pulp game. Other writers were called in to keep the Phantom on course. Chief among these was the dependable, awesomely prolific Norman A. Daniels.

According to his own records, Daniels began writing the Phantom with novel #20, "Merchant of Murder" (October 1934). For another two years he wrote better than half of the monthly novels, contributing some 36 Phantoms in all, including the final one, "Murder's Agent," published in Summer of 1953.

Of his part in guiding the Phantom, Daniels confided to this writer: "It might be interesting to you if I tell you that the publisher Frank Havens really had a live counterpart. His name was Marcus Goldsmith. He had some kind of financial interest in Ned Pines' outfit, though I believe that it was only in regard to the Phantom. I also believe that he thought of himself as Frank Havens. In his opinion, the Phantom was the best crime magazine in existence. Mr. Goldsmith was extremely wealthy and one of the finest gentlemen I ever had the privilege of knowing.

"He discussed each synopsis with me in detail, sometimes in his Manhattan apartment, a luxury residence if I ever saw one. We got along fine. Other writers who worked with him, hated him. He would nit-pick and was not easy to please. However, he certainy enjoyed his role in the Phantom and he could dream up some mighty hard revisions which I learned how to simplify.

"He would invariably pick a section in the middle of the book which he didn't like and give me his idea of how it should be done. So I used to write the book in its entirety, just as I felt it should be, give him the manuscript with an inserted middle part weak and absurd. He would pick that

part to pieces and instruct me how to improve it. I'd simply remove the inserted part, replace the pages already written. He was always completely satisfied. How the other writers handled him, I don't now, but I assume they met with the same reception I did."

Unlike such rivals as the Spider, and Operator #5--whose adventures were controlled by one or two writers with a little help from their friends--the Phantom was a wide open market for freelancers. "Ghosting" the Phantom was practically a cottage industry. The roll call of ghosts included Laurence Donovan, W.T. Ballard, George A. MacDonald, Edwin Burkholder, C.S. Montayne, Stewart Sterling, Whit Ellsworth, Charles Green, G.T. Fleming-Roberts, Ryerson Johnson, and even science fiction specialists Henry Kuttner and Ray Cummings. It became a standing joke that *every* writer had polished off at least one Phantom.

Pulp hero books like the Phantom Detective were frankly mass production goods written to formulas as rigid as gun metal. To the average reader there was little to separate one author's contribution from another, although a single writer would occasionally recycle identifying phrases and descriptions. Thus, in a 1938 adventure,

"Yellow Shadows of Death," one writer wrote "The little Chinese, a crimson devil's stitch across his chest, was hurled a dozen feet by the terrific impact of that spray of lead." A full five years later in "Murder Money" he wrote "He had practically been decapitated by bullets, and there was also a crimson devil's stitch of machine-gun lead across his chest."

Despite multiple authorship, the Phantom Detective format was reasonably consistent over the years. Such recurring characters as Frank Havens, Muriel Havens, Steve Huston, Inspector Gregg and others remained inflexible personalities because each writer drew them from the same template.

Frank Havens' petite daughter, Muriel, supplied romantic interest in the stories. Unfortunately for her, the Phantom's true mistress was Adventure.

Pity poor Muriel on a date with her amorphous boyfriend. As recorded in a scene from "City of Dreadful Night," she had to keep her eyes open just to recognize him--and, once spotted, her lover was less than solicitous.

> *Muriel leaned back and watched the entrance to this smart restaurant. Through that door would come a man who was an utter stranger to her. She had no idea what he would look like. He might be stocky and give the illusion that he wasn't very tall, or he might be lanky and rangy. He might look like a prosperous professional man, a down-in-the-mouth failure, an indolent cafe-hopping playboy, or a shifty-eyed gangster. She wouldn't know it was the Phantom until he sat down beside her and smiled, and she looked into his eyes.*
>
> *She hardly noticed an ordinary-looking man who did enter unobtrusively. It would have been difficult for anyone to tell whether or not he belonged to this*

place, though he had a certain assurance about him. He stopped for a moment on the low balcony at the entrance, and his eyes quickly scanned the room and everyone in it.

Then he made his way down the steps to the main floor, between tables, and came straight to Muriel's booth. His right hand slowly moved up as if to massage his jaw. Instead he gently tugged at his left ear lobe, and that was the signal by which Muriel knew him.

"Phantom!" she said softly. "It's so nice to work with you again."

He grinned at her as he sat down. "You might not think it's so nice by the time this is finished, Muriel. We're bucking a tough proposition. Let's order first, then I'll brief you on all the details!"

So much for Romance.

Not even Muriel was cognizant of the Phantom's true identity, at least not until one of the last adventures, "The Silent Killer," Winter 1952.

Another of the regulars in the Phantom saga was Steve Huston, one of the *Clarion's* star reporters. Steve was a brisk, red-haired freckled-faced young fellow for whom Frank Havens had an almost parental affection. Steve was of inestimable help to Van on any number of cases and, in the adventure "Stones of Satan" revealed his intense admiration for the Phantom when he blurted to a disguised Van, "As often as I've worked with you I can't get over the thrill I always feel when meeting you. I'd rather be on a case with you than own the *Clarion!*"

In that same adventure the Man of a Thousand Faces repaid the compliment by disguising himself as Steve. It was a scene typical of the way in which pulp writers tried to suggest the Phantom's magical way with make-up:

> *His first step was to remove his current disguise--the swarthy complexion, the pellets which flattened his nose, the hard-rubber gadget over his lower gum which lent a pugnacious cast to his underjaw, the thick shading of the eyebrows. Richard Van Loan's handsome face was now reflected in the mirror.*
>
> *And then, magically, that face again began to change. Something which looked like powdered rust, diluted with a table-spoon of water and rubbed into his hair, in a matter of seconds made a redhead out of Van. He used some of it on his eyebrows, too, and combed his hair the way Huston did. An orange paste from a tiny jar gave his face Huston's pinkish complexion. And a fine-pointed brush, dipped into a vial containing some fluid, dotted heavy, brownish freckles over his nose and cheek bone.*
>
> *Next out of the make-up kit came a pair of what looked like tiny clamps. They were rubber-tipped and cleverly made to lock at any angle. He adjusted them to a certain width and thrust them into his nostrils. They were invisible, and what a moment ago had been a straight nose now was the exact replica of Huston's. The final move was to wedge a little rubber gadget under his upper lip to give it a protruding effect.*

There were other recurring minor characters. A streetwise boy named Chip Dorlan was allowed to mature in the series, eventually entering military service. Most of the other characters remained more or less static. There was a Police Inspector Iverness in the early stories, replaced by Captain Brady by 1936, and eventually by

DEATH BELLS RING OUT
ON NEW
YEAR'S EVE

in

THE BROADWAY
MURDERS

*A Long Complete Novel of
Manhattan Mystery*

By ROBERT WALLACE

Featuring THE PHANTOM *in Rapid-Fire Action*
In Next Month's Issue of THE PHANTOM DETECTIVE

Inspector Gregg, who remained a fixture until the end. Inspector Gregg was typically Headquarters from the brim of his felt hat down to his square- toed brogans. When it came to the Phantom, however, Gregg displayed open cooperation.

The World's Greatest Detective was unique among masked avengers in that he operated with the full sanction of the law. The Spider, the Whisperer and dozens of other pulp vigilantes were condemned murderers wanted as much by the police as by the Underworld; in their pragmatic and possibly psychotic minds what worked was not Law but Justice.

The Phantom was a teacher's pet by contrast. He had only to display his secret emblem--a tiny, jewel-studded platinum domino mask--and the minions of the law fell over themselves in open relief. They knew, as did every one else, that the publisher of the *Clarion* was the Phantom's only contact, and when things got really tough they hoped that Havens would send along a call for their mysterious ally.

Like The Shadow, the Spider and even Doc Savage, the Phantom's home base was Manhattan. The Big Four

of the Big Apple may actually have met at some time--
perhaps in Lamont Cranston's elegant Cobalt Club--but if
they did there was no record taken. Most of them worked
for rival publishers who probably weren't too eager to
publicize the event.

Also, each hero's Manhattan was a uniquely different
city. The Doc Savage novels record it as a bustling, sun-
washed Art Deco Shangri-La, home of the world's tallest
building where Doc moors his dirigible and maintains his
fabulous scientific headquarters.

The Spider's turf is a city under siege; a nightmarish
metropolis of yawning chasms filled with the crackle of
flames and the screams of dying citizens. It is a vibrant,
bleeding setpiece for unlimited science-fictional terrors.

The Shadow's urban world is a surrealistic nighttown
reminiscent of the Expressionist German cinema of Fritz
Lang.

The Phantom, fittingly, operated in a rather charac-
terless Manhattan--a city interchangeable with most
others, in the manner in which the Phantom himself was
the compleat interchangeable avenger-hero: a black mask,
a top hat, a disguise kit for all emergencies.

Sometimes his writers rose to the occasion, as in "The
Broadway Murders," in which the opening paragraphs
shrilled:

> *A million lights! Broadway! The heart
> of Manhattan!*
>
> *New Year's Eve! Ear-splitting sound
> and fury! The old year marching out to a
> cacophany of blaring horns, racketing
> noise-makers, and the screeching, roaring
> joyousness of thousands of throats.*
>
> *Throats of thousands given to unfet-
> tered merriment and mirth as they voiced
> humanity's ever reborn hope for the new
> year, due to arrive in four short hours.
> Thousands who surged and swirled in the
> aimless, purposeless tide of packed bodies*

*flooding the width of Broadway in the
space above the gray, old wedge of the
Times Building, with its flashing, brilliant band of ceaselessly moving words in
new parade.*

*Words conveying the news of the world
to those who paused long enough in the
mad carnival to lift their eyes. Ever-
moving words of silver light that could
exhilarate or play upon the fear-chilled
sense of throngs avid for sensation, or
quick to sense through the glittering
words the pulse of a moving world.*

Well, with all those exclamation points and hyped-
up description, you might know that something unusual
was going to happen.

Within moments the sensation-seeking crowd is
treated to spectacle beyond expectation: the burning of two
living men before their eyes...two fiery bodies hanging
from a Broadway sign. A pretty girl cries out and falls to
her knees. The body of one of the burning figures strikes
her in its plunge. Minutes later three charred corpses are
ghastly heaps under the still moving, still brilliant sign of
the Sunny Seas Cruise Line.

Welcome to the Phantom's New York. There isn't a
mugger in sight.

Many of the magazine's openings were real grabbers.
Pulp scribes called it the narrative hook--that first scene,
paragraph or even sentence which hooked the newsstand
browser into a commitment involving his hard-earned
dime:

*Hundreds saw the death plane before it
dived.*
(The Curio Murders)

*Nothing about the quiet residential
street on the outskirts of Fairmount indi-
cated that death lingered there. Yet murder waited on that summer day.*
                (Murder Under the Big Top)

*Night, black and rain-swept, shrouded
the Kirty Institute for the insane. Gusts of
howling wind attacked the ugly gray
buildings like seas pounding some bleak,
rocky coast. There was the same impres-
sion of desolation, of a savagely forbid-
ding place that humans shunned.*

*A small car lurched to a stop in front
of the guard-house at the gate. Two men
got out, collars upturned, hats pulled low.
They dodged toward the booth--and paused
involuntarily, lingering despite the drenching rain. There was a brief lull in the
wind, and from within the buildings
somewhere, they heard a voice lift in song.*
                    (The Melody Murders)

*It was a huge house; a venerable house.
And it was articulate with the eerie
creaking voice that comes with architectual
age. It spoke now, and the single man who
heard was pale with terror. Ghosts trod
the carpeted stairway. The weird, crack-
ling sounds peculiar to old wood, old
brick, old mortar sighed audibly through
the emptiness.*

*Roger Arkwright paced the study and
listened. He was alone. He was the only
living thing in all these scores of high-
ceilinged rooms. His heart thudded against
his breast, and his nerves were darting
quicksilver...*

A bell tolled in the empty house.
(Death Glow)

The editorials in the *Phantom Detective* magazine were usually written by the Phantom himself in a chummy hero-to-reader fashion. Usually they touted the following month's Phantom novel in much the same manner as a movie trailer.

The Phantom would write: "Bob Wallace has taken the story of the menace to the Mattling shipping interests and its relationship to the American overseas export trade and has woven it into an intriguing and challenging detective story in 'Masterpiece of Murder,' the Phantom Detective novel appearing in the next issue of THE PHANTOM DETECTIVE MAGAZINE.

"I, personally, got a great kick out of working on the case, and I know that when 'Masterpiece of Murder' comes your way that you'll get just as much satisfaction in reading about the incident that led up to the uncovering of the whole nest of criminal vipers in the plot."

Sometimes the Phantom was less modest.

"'Murder Acres' is a story that is as dramatic as human emotions can ever be, as forceful as the evil powers involved can make it, and as superb as the triumph of justice can become for us all! You'll like the story."

For most of the Phantom's career his magazine carried a membership offer in a Phantom Club called FRIENDS OF THE PHANTOM. There were no dues or fees, although a special bronzed replica of the Phantom's badge could be obtained for 15 cents (for the traditional 'postage and handling'). Membership in the club and the special badge came with a dire warning--"It must be clearly understood that membership in THE FRIENDS OF THE PHANTOM gives you no special privileges or police powers whatsoever."

The Phantom often seemed perturbed about this problem.

"A question that comes up frequently in connection
with FRIENDS OF THE PHANTOM," he wrote, "is
whether or not membership confers special police powers.
Naturally joining our group does not give you any special
rights or priviliges with regard to your local or Federal
law-enforcement agencies. There is no connection between
our organization and any of these law-enforcement bodies.
Our chief purpose is to express, tangibly and collectively,
the feelings of the right-thinking, law-abiding readers who
follow THE PHANTOM DETECTIVE."

The right-thinking readers were even invited to mail
in their comments on the magazine. Their letters were
either addressed to "Bob" (for author Robert Wallace) or
simply "Dear Phantom." Nearly all were self revealing.

> *Dear Phantom:*
>
> *I love to read your magazine. It has
> some interesting stories in it. I do a lot of
> reading because I live in a small town and
> there isn't much to do here in the way of
> entertainment. I'm eighteen years of age
> and a junior in high school.*

> *Dear Phantom:*
>
> *I sure get a big kick out of reading your
> story, "The Chinese Puzzle," in the Janu-
> ary 1947 issue. I happened to be serving in
> the Army in the South Pacific, and before
> coming back to the States this year I got
> into China. I found out a good deal about
> some of the intrigue that was going on
> there, and your story sure stirred up some
> colorful memories. More power to you.*

> *Dear Phantom:*
>
> *I am a friend and admirer of the
> Phantom, and have been for some time.
> Richard Curtis Van Loan is a real person
> to me, and I glory in his every triumph.
> Sometimes, however, when the 'enemy'*

*gets him, my heart is in my mouth, but I
should know I can count on him every time
getting out of all kinds of danger...*

*Van Loan never ceases to be a gentle-
man, even if he has to twist the neck of a
gunman at times. He does it so that my
heart swells with pride. I can see him
dusting off the soil accrued from the
crook, probably saying "This hurts you
worse than it does me." It is odd, that it
never makes me feel anything but happy
when he bests a criminal, but when Van
Loan gets hurt, I die.*

(signed) Just a Bad Old Gal, I guess.

*Dear Bob:
Your stories are all good except that I
don't like your main character. Your plots
are interesting, but not the Phantom.*

"Occasionally," (the Phantom replied testily) "letters
that come in are a bit difficult to interpret, but they do
provide food for thought."

The *Phantom Detective* magazine ran from February
1933 to Summer 1953. It was one of the last surviving
pulps.

In the early issues the stories were suitably melodramatic with bizarre murders perpetrated by such spook
villains as The Fang, The Beast-King, The Satan, and
even (gulp) The Green God. These Depression-era issues
betrayed the poor man's fixation with the wealthy; not
only was Van Loan fabulously rich, but most of the victims
were bank presidents, heads of large companies, and
famous politicians. (Pity the poor rich man was a basic
theme).

As the magazine moved into the War Years the
masked villains were phased out and such earlier setpieces
as waterfront warehouses and blood-flecked back rooms

began to be described in the hard, unblinking style of the *Black Mask* school. The atmosphere became sleazier, denser; the criminals diminished in size toward realistic dimensions.

There were some good yarns written in this middle period, but by the end of the 1940s even the new format had calcified. The magazine went quarterly in 1949 (a certain sign of diminished vigor) and it sleep walked through another four years to its final story, "Murder's Agent." Like most fictitious heroes, the Phantom never announced his retirement, he just faded away.

The pulp hero magazines were a short-lived phenomenon; they lasted but twenty-two years in all. The Phantom blasted and slashed his way through twenty of those flamboyant years. It was an honorable record.

Each issue of his magazine would do a wrap-up scene in which the Phantom faded into the shadows, always promising to return. Any one of these farewells would serve as a fitting tribute to the character:

> *But as the Phantom turned from them all, to fade inconspicuously from sight of the excited, chattering group, he was weary--weary of death, and with the realization that there were other men in the world like the Green Mask and his cohorts who fattened on murder. Perhaps, someday, thanks to the efforts of the Phantom and the men who aspired to be like him, the criminal population would be decreased appreciably.*
>
> *Even now the world was cleaner, freer, because one such group no longer breathed the world's air. But it would be a long, hard battle still, and no one realized that more fully than the Phantom, world-famed nemesis of the underworld.*

> *He would keep on, however, always on call when there was need for him and his uncanny powers. But now he was tired-- tired. The life seemed to have sagged in his over-wearied body. As he slipped away from ancient Half Mansion to make his way to the nearest railroad station, he pondered his next step. Should he refresh himself with a plunge into New York Social life, or would a cruise best suit his needs?*
>
> *But whatever it would be, he knew it could not be for long. Some day--perhaps soon--a red light would flash atop the Clarion Building, and the Phantom would come eagerly to answer that call, to do battle again with some dire force of evil.*

It was the detective story version of riding off into the sunset.

The Phantom never failed.

And he never really died.

BLACK BATS AND GREEN GHOSTS

In their roistering heyday, pulp heroes were almost a dime a dozen. Only a handful achieved genuine fame, returning issue after issue for a number of years. The rest fell victim to the ruthless odds of showbiz: for each success, a hundred failures.

In the late thirties and early forties Ned L. Pines, publisher of *The Phantom Detective* magazine, decided to push his luck by introducing a quintet of Phantom-type heroes--the Black Bat, the Ghost, the Purple Scar, the Crimson Mask, and the generically named Masked Detective. Of these, only the Black Bat triumphed. The others are mostly forgotten now but deserve appreciation as one small part of the colorful pulp hero mosaic.

If the Black Bat's position in the pulp hero heirarchy is not of the first magnitude it is perhaps due to the fact that he had to be content with filling the front pages of *Black Book Detective* and lurking as a background figure on the magazine's covers. Despite this handicap and a late start, the masked and cowled Bat was the only mystery man hero to rival the Phantom's admirable run from the thirties into the final dissolution of the pulps in the fifties.

While he is seldom mentioned in the company of such icons as Doc Savage or the Spider, he did offer his fans a long series of well-crafted stories, most of them produced by the estimable Norman Daniels.

Born in Brooklyn, Connecticut in 1905, Daniels was one of the most prolific of all pulp hero writers. He sold his first story in 1931 and remained a highly successful freelance writer until his retirement many decades later. He and his wife Dorothy were a fiction factory; he turned out the stories and Dorothy typed and edited. Later, she became an author on her own. By their own admission, there were months when they turned out a Black Bat novel, a Phantom Detective, a Crimson Mask, and maybe even a Candid Camera Kid as well. They also produced many of the Dan Fowler novels in *G-Men Detective*.

"As I recall," Daniels wrote, "I originated the series characters of the Masked Detective, Candid Camera Kid, the Crimson Mask and, though I can't call them to mind at this writing, many others. But of them all, the Black Bat was my favorite, mainly because the characters seemed so real to me.

"Many years ago Leo Margulies asked me to come up with a series to be in competition with The Shadow. I concocted the set-up which, without change, became The Black Bat. Originally, I called him The Tiger. It seemed a natural since the hero's face was scarred from an opening sequence in the first book. The scars on his face resembled the markings on a tiger's. However, as it was going into *Black Book Detective*, Leo decided to change the title for the character to conform with the magazine and so, to blend with Black Book, he renamed it Black Bat. I suspect that was what they were after anyway."

Daniels' Black Bat was yet another refutation of the trite observation that "bad guys wear black." In fact the good-guy hero outfitted himself in black from head to toe-- black shoes, black gloves, black shirt, black mask and cowl, and a ribbed black cape almost identical to that legendary creation of the comic books, Batman. Interest-

Norman A. Daniels

ingly, the Black Bat and Batman made their initial appearances at almost the same time. Batman was introduced in *Detective Comics* #27 in May 1939 and the first Black Bat novel, "Brand of the Black Bat" appeared in *Black Book Detective* a mere two months later. After a brief flurry of litigious wrangling by the two publishers, cooler heads prevailed when they realized that the synchronous appearance of the nocturnal bat guys was too close to be anything but coincidence. In fact Daniels had actually submitted his first Black Bat novel in December of 1938, several months before Bruce Wayne donned his own trick suit to become a crime-fighting rodent.

In the long pulp tradition dating back to Zorro and beyond, the Black Bat was a wealthy young bachelor who fought criminals while disguised as a masked phantom. He was actually ex-district attorney Tony Quinn, who would have been handsome except for the deep, disfiguring scars burned into the flesh around his eyes, the result of acid thrown at him by criminals. To the world at large Tony Quinn was "as blind as as a bat," but readers of his magazine were informed that a secret, miraculous operation had not only restored his vision but had also given him supersight with the ability to see in the dark. Then too, during his blindness, other senses had developed. His touch was acute, his hearing almost uncanny.

Tony used his new-found powers to bring justice to criminals that the law could not touch. He pretended to be blind so that he could moonlight as the Black Bat--the cowl obscuring his telltale facial scars. As a lawyer Tony Quinn worked patiently within the justice system but, in his persona as the night-prowling Black Bat, he frequently hurried things along.

"We'll use whatever means we think best in our fight against crime," Tony vowed. "We'll fight them with their own weapons--with treachery, intimidation, theft. We'll worry them until they are as jittery as a one legged man on a tightrope. We'll work with the police or against them if need be. We'll make our own laws and we'll enact our own judgments."

Daniels' early Black Bat novels were less vivid reflections of the vigilante themes blazed by Norvell Page in his Spider epics. In titles such as "The Faceless Satan," "The Black Bat's Dragon Trail," "Murder Among the Dying," and "City of Hidden Death," the Bat squared off with super-fiends and Nazi spies intent on wide-spread schemes for conquest. And, like the Spider, his .45-caliber automatics thundered out messages of death to the ungodly, accompanied by his personal signature--a tiny black bat in flight--stuck on rapidly-cooling foreheads. Superstitious criminals believed him unkillable and, because of his membranous cape, actually thought he could fly.

Quinn shared his secret identity with a trio of helpers: ex- con man Silk Kirby, pugilist Butch O'Leary, and Carol Baldwin, the mysterious lady whose generosity had restored Tony's sight. It was Carol's donation of the eyes of her murdered police officer father that had enabled the super-sighted Black Bat to be born. Tony only dropped his pose as a blind man when he operated as the Black Bat or when he was in his laboratory, hidden behind a door in his large home on a spacious estate within the city limits. An underground passageway led from the laboratory to a secret exit from his estate, and a dilapidated, souped-up coupe parked on a nearby side street served as his own personal batmobile.

Like the Spider, the Black Bat was branded a criminal by the authorities and thus faced the threat of capture or death at the hands of the police as well as his numerous criminal foes. His persistent nemesis was a cigar-chomping police lieutenant named McGrath, who not only set out to prove that Quinn was the Black Bat, but constantly set up wily traps to prove that the young lawyer's supposed blindness was a sham. He would slam doors in the "blind" man's face, throw lit cigars at him, or offer his hand in a friendly manner, all to trick Tony into an instant of forgetfulness. For his part, Tony appeared to enjoy the game. I suppose it kept him on his toes.

In a 1944 story titled "Markets of Treason," McGrath's bag of tricks hit a new low--even for him. He presented Tony with the gift of a "seeing eye" dog named Gwendolyn. Secretly, McGrath had trained the normally docile pet to attack any man wearing a cloak. So when Quinn next donned his familiar bat costume, Gwendolyn launched a murderous attack on her new master. The incident so unnerved Tony that he actually discarded the cape that had been his near undoing. The story was probably an editorial dictate emblematic of a "new look" for the Black Bat and of a new, more realistic trend in the single character hero magazines as well. In the 1940s, as war gripped the nation, readers turned indifferently from the wild old plots involving master fiends and costumed heroes. By the end of the war the realistic crime story was firmly entrenched. Soon there would be no more hero pulps at all.

"I wrote all of the Black Bat series over a period of eleven years," Daniels once confided. "I was paid ex-

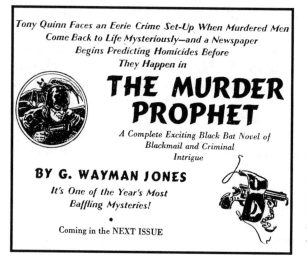

actly what (Walter) Gibson was paid and raised when he was raised. The final Black Bat was taken over by a new group (pulps were rapidly fading then). They wanted to load the story with sex and I wasn't about to comply. They loaded it, I understand, and it was the final book."

Norman Daniels' commitment to the Black Bat resulted in a long-running series for his publisher. Despite a late start, the character lasted more than 13 years, topped only by the Phantom at 20 years, The Shadow at 18 years, and Doc Savage at 16 years. Even the Spider did not last as long, although he saw more adventures. Alas, the publisher's four other "Thrilling" tryouts were to prove less successful.

The titular hero of the *Masked Detective* magazine (written by Daniels as "C. K. M. Scanlon") was something of a dull fellow by comparison to the the author's own Black Bat. Perhaps this was because he had so few characteristics of his own, and not even an interesting name or costume to alleviate the problem.

To be fair, the Masked Detective novels were all fast-paced stories with the same brand of cliff-hanger captures and escapes that helped make the Phantom so successful. A number of his adventures, often violent, reflected the dynamism of his wartime milieu: "The Fifth Column Murders," "The League of the Iron Cross." In "The Canal Zone Murders," the Mask was even sworn in as an offical FBI Agent, although nothing was made of this in future installments.

Like the Phantom, the Masked Detective was a master of disguise and ventriloquism, and was a trained boxer to boot. Despite cover artists' delineations, he seldom resorted to weapons. His one real secret weapon was his proficiency in the ungentlemanly art of *la savate*, the French type of fighting with the feet. His specially built shoes, with square, hard toes, could deliver bone-crushing kicks to crooks and killers. He spent long hours practicing on a life-sized dummy which--unlike the crooks--kept bouncing back for more.

The gumshoe with the killer feet was really Rex Parker, a crime reporter for *The New York Comet*. The public and criminals alike recognized newshawk Parker as the one man who was able to reach the Masked Detective in times of trouble. Why they didn't also suspect him of being the mysterious crime fighter was never explained. Perhaps he just wasn't impressive enough--the stories usually described him as being "lazy" and "easy going."

Unimpressive or not, Parker did have a girl friend-- a fellow reporter named Winnie Bligh, cozily referred to as "Cap'n Bligh" by the occasionally insufferable Rex. Winnie was also lacking in original attributes; her main talent seemed to be that of inviting frequent kidnapping by crooks.

While most of the Mask's adventures were routine detective yarns, he occasionally bumped into villains worthy of more flamboyant rivals. "The Poison Puzzle" introduced a white-hooded master menace, and "Crimes of Stilicho" featured a mysterious art vandal who fancied himself the modern version of a Fifth Century marauding general. One novel described a scene of purest pulp invention--the sight of a corpse apparently standing on its head in the East River. "Whose were the murderous hands which held the doomed man's ankles and dipped him into the dark water as a man might dip a roll into his morning coffee?" the magazine asked. "Whose brain directed those hands?" Fans had to read on to find out.

Unfortunately, it was the Masked Detective himself who failed to capture readers' overburdened attention, probably because his publisher had conceived him as little more than a utility-grade hero in a cheap domino mask. Even the covers reflected this problem; most were previously used paintings retouched by adding a mask to some central figure like an afterthought (sometimes they didn't bother). "Death Island" was a title that referred to the island of Moaxacelo in the Gulf of Mexico, yet the issue's cover inexplicably featured an Oriental menace and a gun-blazing hero sans mask. The cover on the Spring 1942 issue features a masked character, but he's wearing a welder's hood, not the Masked Detective's slash of eye-covering silk. With such half-hearted endorsement it was no surprise that after a mere dozen issues the Masked Detective received his early retirement. Fortunately for him, he still had his dummy to kick around.

Unlike the Masked Detective, who at least commanded his own magazine, the Crimson Mask and Purple Scar appeared as features in the publisher's existing titles.

Like the Masked Detective, the Crimson Mask was yet another proletarian version of the Phantom. In real life, or at least what passed for real life in the detective pulps, he was known as "Doc" Clarke, a young pharmacist who was the son of a cop killed in the line of duty. The flash of a small red bulb beneath the counter of Doc's old-fashioned pharmacy was his signal to stop dispensing pills and start dispensing justice as a masked vigilante. It wasn't a bad premise, but it wasn't original either, and few of the CM adventures (all of them written by the indefatigable Norm Daniels under the penname Frank Johnson) ever attempted to rise above routine status.

Of course the Crimson Mask was not designed to set the pulp world on fire. He was launched in *Detective Novels* in 1939 when the publisher attempted to boost circulation with the addition of series characters. Another character, Jerry Wade, "the Candid Camera Kid" appeared first in a series of snappy novelettes featuring a young red-headed news photographer. When the Crimson Mask was brought in to help out, the two series ran as a double feature in each issue. Later they began to alternate.

Impressively, the Candid Camera Kid series was also written by Norman Daniels, using the penname John L. Benton. This was at the same time as the one-man fiction factory was churning out the Black Bat novels along with much other material. If readers did not respond to the Masked Detective or the Crimson Mask, it was not a reflection of Daniels' proven ability to entertain but simply a rejection of mundane masked detectives at a time when such certified loonies as The Shadow and the Spider were still cutting their ferociously melodramatic swath through crime.

Yet another of the publisher's masked crime fighters suffered the misfortune to appear as an infrequent character in an ongoing magazine. *Exciting Detective* was host to the Purple Scar, a lesser known but intriguing gent who appeared briefly in a series of full-length novels in 1941 and 1942. One might be tempted to say that the Purple Scar was unusual because he was *not* written by Norman Daniels, but that would be unfair to a hero with distinct, although somewhat unrealized possibilities.

Like most of Standard's "also ran" series, the Purple Scar novels barely rise above the level of routine detective thrillers. What makes this aborted series noteworthy is the utterly bizarre nature of the character's masked identity.

In civilian life the Purple Scar is Doctor Miles Murdock, described by author John S. Endicott as "the most brilliant young plastic surgeon of his time." Six feet tall and handsome as a movie star, young Murdoch decided to fight crime as a masked avenger when his brother, a member of the city's police force, was murdered by gangsters. Because most of his publisher's mystery men chose to fight crime while wearing skimpy domino masks of red or black, Murdoch must have decided he had to be different--really different. That was where his skill as a plastic surgeon came in handy.

Miles Murdoch had stood in the morgue and had viewed the acid-destroyed face of his murdered brother, turned a ghastly purple by its days of soaking in river water. From this personal horror he had conceived the nemesis of evil known as the Purple Scar. From police photographs taken of his brother's bloated, scarred face, Murdoch had made a grim mask of purple-dyed gum elastic. It was a perfect reproduction, copied skillfully even down to the smallest detail: A ghastly network of torn, acid-destroyed tissues, features almost totally eaten away, eyes only empty shriveled sockets, mouth a twisted slash. A face so horrible to look at that even the least sensitive recoiled at the sight of it. It was the face of a corpse!

"I'll use the mask when I want it known the Purple Scar is on the trail," Murdoch decides. "It's a name the underworld will find easy to remember. I choose purple because I want to imitate my brother's features. Flesh that's been eaten by acid and submerged in water turns a dark purple. Purple becomes black at night, which will make my face invisible instead of a betraying pale glow in the darkness."

Unfortunately, the Purple Scar novels were less imaginative than their protagonist's wild disguise. Abetted by the usual coterie of helpers, a nurse-fiance, a friendly police Captain, and a reformed second story man, the dreaded Purple Scar confined his cases to such routine problems as stolen gold and poisoned meat shipments-- hardly the stuff of great pulp melodrama. One can only guess what bizarre possibilites a Norvell Page might have wrung from a hero who stalks the night wearing an imitation of his own brother's dead face.

Of The Thrilling group's less successful tryouts the Ghost is perhaps the most noteworthy, partly because he also terrified crooks with a frightful countenance and partly because he belonged to that interesting sub genre known as the magician detective.

From the days of folklore involving witches and warlocks and other practitioners of the Black Arts, a vague sense of the sinister has always permeated the air around magicians. The affinity between magic and mystery proved irresistible to thriller writers of the thirties and forties. Various magician types skulked through pulp paper pages. They ranged from genuine sorcerers and necromancers like Dr. Satan and Dr. Death to such hocus-pocus hawkshaws as Norgil the Magician and Don Diavolo, the Scarlet Wizard. (In fact the creators of Norgil and Diavolo, mystery greats Walter Gibson and Clayton Rawson, were in fact real-life prestidigitators).

It is interesting, although not surprising, that two pulp heroes known as "the Ghost" should have shared a similar magical background. In my book *The Super Feds* (Starmont House, 1988) I wrote of the Ghost series that ran in 14 issues of Popular Publications' *Ace G-Man Stories*. That particular shade was known in civilian life as Brian O'Reilly, a former stage magician who used his tricks of sleight-of-hand and ventriloquism in a freelance vendetta against the FBI's most vicious foes.

The G-Man Ghost first appeared in a yarn titled "The Ghost Wears a Badge" by Wyatt Blassinghame in the September 1939 *Ace G- Man*. A mere four months later Thrilling Publications brought out *The Ghost Super-Detective*. The new magazine also featured the exploits of a mystery man outlaw who, in civilian life, was a former stage magician who used his showbiz background to confound criminals and the police alike.

Such creative synchronicity was not unusual in the copy-cat world of pulp publishing. Once you have a Shadow, and then a Phantom, can a Ghost be far behind? But there are laws governing such things, coincidence or not. And occasionally a phone call from one publisher to a friendly rival would solve copyright problems short of litigation. This may be the reason that *The Ghost* magazine became *The Green Ghost Detective* with its fourth issue.

Unfortunately, the Ghost/Green Ghost was another failed attempt at a major pulp hero by the Thrilling group, even though they gave the character a good sendoff with his own magazine and a series of eye-catching covers. He lasted but seven issues in his own title and then was relegated to a further six novelettes in the publisher's *Thrilling Mystery*, a popular dumping ground for failed heroes. Even so, he deserves a special place in the pulp hero old boy's club, if only for his imaginative entrances:

> *Through the open door of the den*
> *eddied a thin column of grayish mist,*

barely visible in the uncertain light. An unearthly laugh sounded from the darkness just beyond the door.

"Who's there?" Turrin's voice was taut.

The mist expanded until it seemed to clog the darkened doorway with swirling gray. A pinpoint of greenish light seemed to be the nucleus of the misty cloud as it moved slowly into the room. The green light brightened, caught the highlights of a ghastly death's head that seemed floating without bodily support.

"Don't you know, gentlemen?"

The voice came from the skull-teeth of the green-tinted death's head.

"The Ghost," Werges whispered. "The Green Ghost. I've heard of him."

Small wonder. The face of the Ghost is a bloodless white (or a sickening green, depending on which issue you read). Teeth the color of old ivory pop naked from fleshless gums, nostrils gape, dead eyes threaten. When occasion demands, the head comes right off, floats across rooms, or is hurled at suitably impressed thugs. Not an easy thing to forget.

The Ghost's alter-ego was a little less impressive, but only when compared to a head-throwing dead man. The first of the novels is titled "Calling the Ghost" (January 1940) and in it we are introduced to George Chance, magician-detective. Surprisingly, Chance introduces himself. Unlike other hero pulp journals, all transcribed by omnipresent authors from "case books" or secret diaries, the Ghost's adventures are credited as autobiography, recounted in a chummy manner by Our Hero himself. While some of the "hard-boiled" detective hacks had already worked the first-person narrative into near parody by 1940, it was still a novel form in pulp hero terms.

"I was born in the show business," the Ghost confided to his readers. "My father was an animal trainer and my mother a trapeze performer in a circus....I learned much of the secrets of makeup from a clown named Ricki. To the grave-eyed man with the long black burnsides who traveled with the show under the name of Don Avigne, I am indebted for knowledge that has made the knife one of the deadliest of weapons in my hands. Then there was Professor Gabby, who taught me principles of ventriloquism which are today responsible for the hundreds of voices of the Ghost. But most important of all, while I was hanging around the circus, I won the confidence of Marko, the Magician....Magic was the ladder that helped me climb from the circus to vaudeville and from there to my own revues".

What further prompted George Chance, a showbiz success, to dress up as a spook and run around New York risking his life and reputation fighting criminal maniacs is never explained. In the world of the pulp hero it was just the thing to do.

As the Ghost, Chance surrounded himself with loyal assistants, from a lady friend named Merry White to a middle-aged cigar-smoking midget called Tiny Tim. His real ace-in-the-hole was a man named Glen Saunders. Chance and Saunders were identical doubles. By assuming the part of George Chance while the real George Chance, suitably disguised, was out playing cops and robbers with his magic, Saunders supplied the Ghost with a perfect alibi to confound criminals and the police alike.

Like Norgil and Don Diavolo the Ghost uses illusion as a nucleus of misdirection. To make the magic stick he togs himself in fright clothes and a horror face to scare hell out of superstitious criminals. Even the police are impressed.

Chance worked his Jekyll-and-Hyde act with the full knowledge of New York Police Commissioner Edward Standish. Unlike many pulp top cops, Standish not only approved of his friend's nocturnal vigilanteism but even kept in touch with the Ghost via the private wire from his apartment. In addition, Standish allows Chance to haunt police headquarters while disguised as Detective-Sergeant Hammell or consulting physician Dr. Stacey. Even police department medical examiner, Dr. Robert Dumarest, is a sardonic commentator on George Chance's double life. "You left a nice gentlemanly profession like magic to play in a slaughter house," he clucks.

To play in crime's slaughterhouse, handsome young George Chance routinely transforms himself into a ghastly apparition. "To create the character of the Ghost, I take small wire ovals and put them into my nose, tilting the tip and elongating the nostrils. For the somewhat ghastly effect proper to a ghost-character, I darken the inside of each nostril....Brown eyeshadow goes on to darken my eye pits. Pallor comes out of a powder box. I highlight my naturally prominent cheek bones. Over my own teeth I place shells the color of old ivory. After that, I have only to affect a fixed vacuity of expression and my face becomes something very much like a skull."

The shock effect of the Ghost's fright face was supplemented with a rollicking graveyard giggle and a suit full of secret pockets containing magical paraphernalia. As backup, his suit jacket concealed a double-edged throwing knife and a razor blade (handy for slicing bonds when tossed into a pool of hungry piranha). He also packed a flat automatic even though he admitted to being a rotten pistol shot.

But even originality has its drawbacks. While George Chance's leisurely first-person narrative gained the advantage of verisimilitude, it deprived readers of the knockabout pace and melodramtic violence that permeates the typical pulp hero novel. When sales figures proved less "Thrilling" than the publisher's colophon, Editorial Director Leo Margulies was quick to take action. With its fifth issue, *The Ghost Detective* (now re-named *The Green Ghost Detective*) dropped the George Chance by-line and gave credit to the series' real author. Along with the new credit was a return to the more comfortable third-person narrative.

Despite his pseudonymous-sounding by-line, G. T. Fleming-Roberts was the real name of a top notch pulpster who, as early as 1935, ghosted many of the better *Secret Agent X* novels and who, in 1949, created the final pulp hero, *Captain Zero*. Because characterization was a Fleming-Roberts specialty, his heroes were stigmatized by perversely human fallibilities: the Ghost carried a gun but couldn't shoot worth beans; and Captain Zero was just a little squirt, bland of personality and uncoordinated under stress. Some kind of hero, huh? But magic still persisted. He turned invisible every night at the stroke of midnight.

Fleming-Roberts' Green Ghost was essentially the old Ghost with the addition of a chemical vapor and a green light in his tie pin to turn his already ghastly head even more noxious. Unfortunately, plastic surgery wasn't enough to save the magazine. There were only two more issues, seven in all, then the character was retired to *Thrilling Mystery*, where he appeared in a further six short stories, all written by Fleming-Roberts. The demise of the Ghost/Green Ghost was unfortunate because, with the exception of Daniels' Black Bat, he was the most promising of Thrilling Publications' tryout titles.

If Ned Pines' "Thrilling" heroes of the forties failed to duplicate the impact of such rivals as the Spider and The Shadow, it really wasn't their fault. They were conceived as low-budget efforts from the beginning. Compared to such major pulp heroes as G-8 or Doc Savage, they were what B movies were to A movies--entertaining but routine. And, like those old B movies, they are enjoyable today as nostalgic whiffs of the past--pleasant reminders of those gloriously innocent years when a newspaperman or a pharmacist could don a little face mask and sally forth to rid the streets of crime.

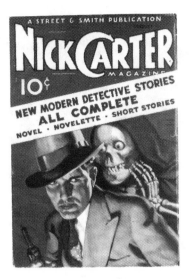

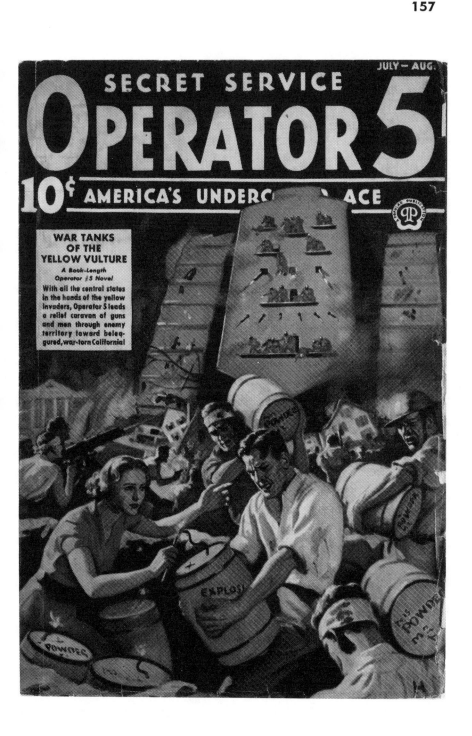

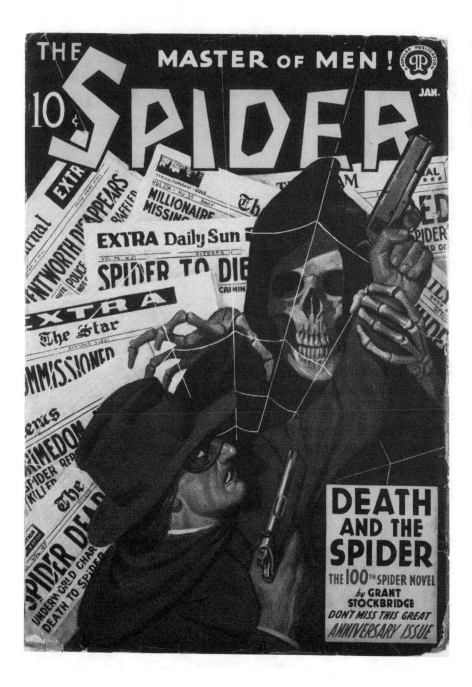

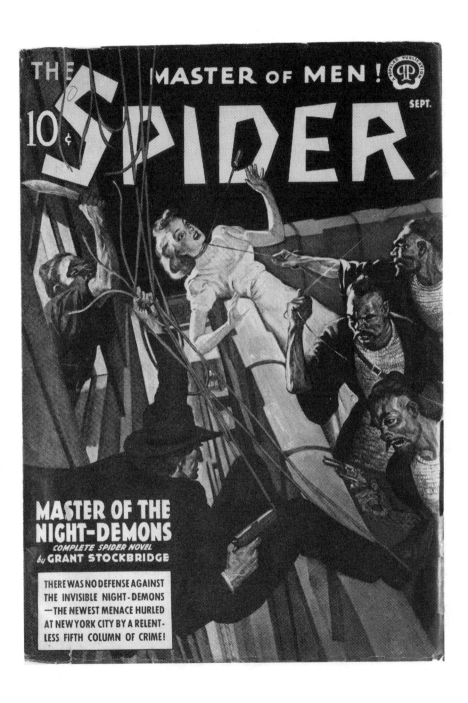

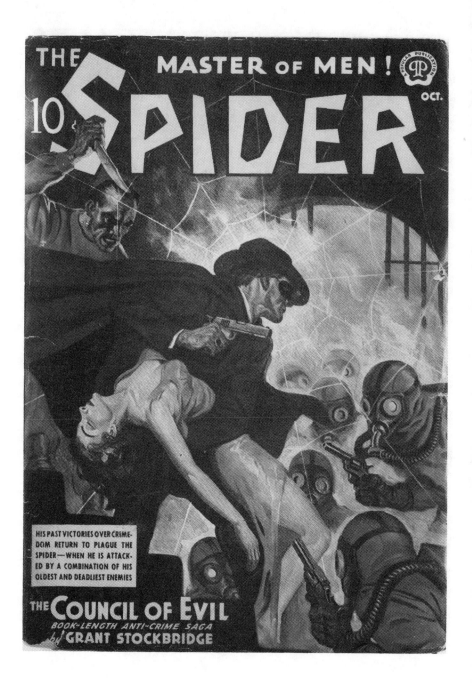

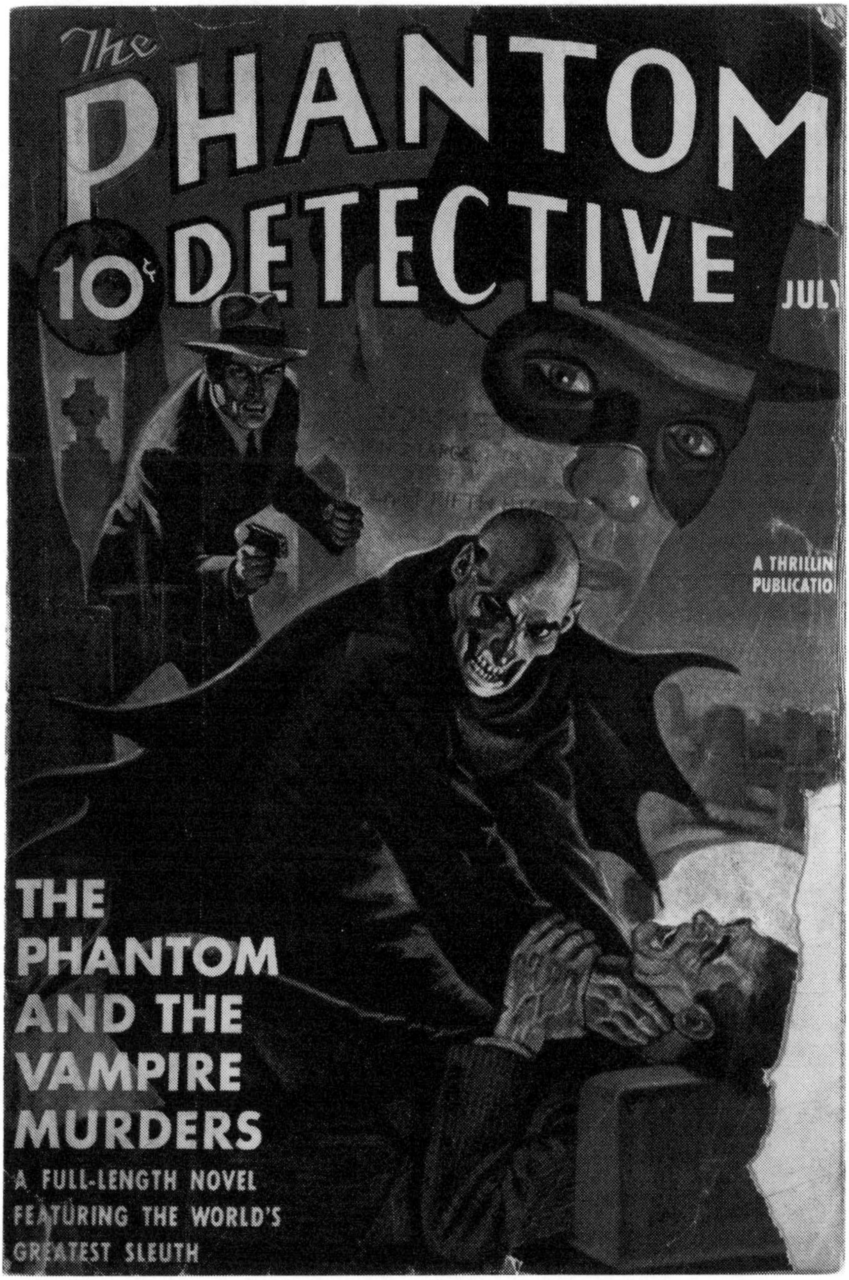
The
PHANTOM
10¢ DETECTIVE
JULY
A THRILLIN
PUBLICATIO
THE PHANTOM AND THE VAMPIRE MURDERS
A FULL-LENGTH NOVEL FEATURING THE WORLD'S GREATEST SLEUTH

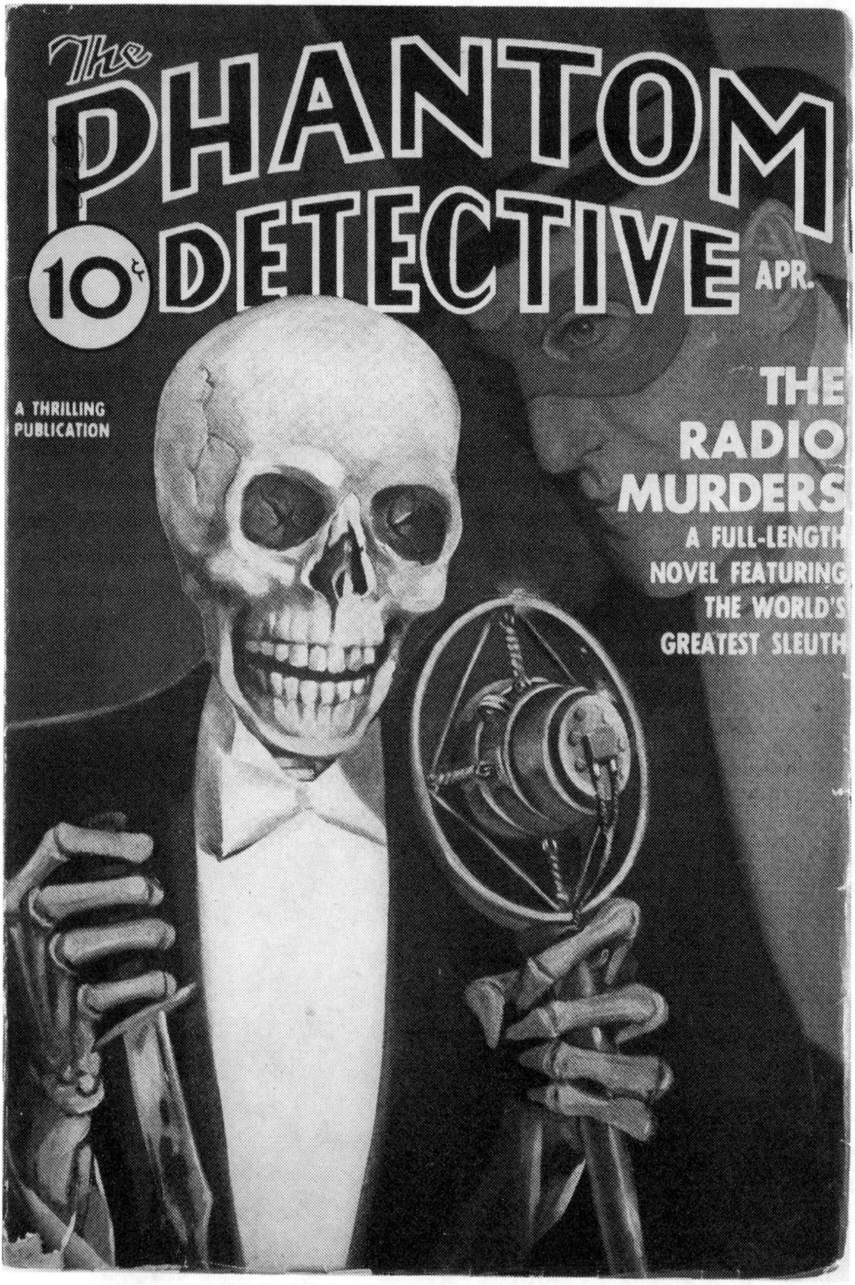
The
PHANTOM
DETECTIVE
10¢
APR.
A THRILLING
PUBLICATION
THE
RADIO
MURDERS
A FULL-LENGTH
NOVEL FEATURING
THE WORLD'S
GREATEST SLEUTH

10¢ BLACK BOOK DETECTIVE

JAN.

THE EYES OF THE BLIND

A Long Book-Length Novel Featuring Tony Quinn Masked Nemesis of Crime

$2.00 MYSTERY NOVEL EVERY ISSUE!

A THRILLING PUBLICATION

THE GREEN GHOST DETECTIVE

10¢

WINTER ISSUE

KILLER IN RED By MILTON LOWE

THE CASE OF THE FLAMING FIST
A Complete Novel Featuring
The Green Ghost, Magician Sleuth
By G. T. FLEMING-ROBERTS

A THRILLING PUBLICATION

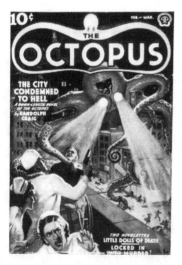

10¢

TRADE MARK APP. FOR

The WHISPERER

APRIL 1937

"THE RED HATCHETS" MENACE CHINATOWN

Mayor Calls on Police to Stop Spread of Mysterious Murders

"WHISPERER" RESPONSIBLE?

Is "The Whisperer" responsible for the spread of the Red Hatchet murders which have upset Chinatown, and which are now spreading to the exclusive parts of our city? That is the question which the Mayor wants settled, and he called upon Police Commissioner "Wildcat" Gordon to bring in the solution, or bring in his resignation! The city is alarmed over this new ace. Who is behind the mur-

CALLING CAPTAIN FUTURE

James Carthew went to the window and stepped out onto the little balcony. He looked up at the full moon that sailed in queenly splendor high above the soaring towers of nighted New York.

There was a look of desperation in the President's aging, haunted face as he gazed up at the shining white face of the lonely satellite.

Far out beyond New York's towers, the moon was declining from the zenith. They could see the distant rocket-flash of liners taking off from the spaceport for far Venus or Saturn or Pluto.

"Why doesn't Captain Future come?" North Bonnel burst out, unable to keep silent longer. "That ship of his can get from the moon to the Earth in a few hours--he should be here by now."

James Carthew's gray head lifted.
"He will be here. He's never yet failed
to answer our call."
"As a matter of fact, I'm here now, sir"
said a deep, laughing voice.
It came from the balcony outside the
window. A big, red-headed young man
had miraculously appeared there, as though
by magic.
"Curt Newton--Captain Future!" cried
the President eagerly.

Right. Captain Future it was. The smartest, hand-
somest, most daring good guy on all the nine planets.

A strapping red-haired scientific adventurer, Captain Future was the past's future crimefighter, an implac-
able nemesis of all oppressors and exploiters of the
System's planetary races. Whenever a menace threatened
to conquer, enslave, or destroy hapless mankind, President
Carthew had but to sent out a distress call to Cap's secret
base beneath Tycho crater on the moon (a kind of extended
bat-signal) and Captain Future would zoom out, proton
pistol in hand, to do battle with the wicked.

The good Captain was the titular star of his own
magazine (the only space opera character to be so honored)
which ran from early 1940 to 1944, as well as a series of
further adventures in *Startling Stories* which ran sporadi-
cally from 1945 to 1951.

There is little question that *Captain Future* is the one
magazine that apologists for pulp science fiction would
prefer to have forgotten. Both the magazine and its title
were unabashedly juvenile in tone--considered a joke or
even an insult by many sf fans of the day who foresaw
great possibilities in the nascent genre.

When the first issue of *Captain Future* burst forth,
the so-called Golden Age of science fiction--that memorable and to some almost legendary period--was just beginning. John Campbell was on his throne at *Astounding*

Science Fiction and he was developing new and exciting writers who would extend the horizons of the field. Many of the Campbell proteges-- Robert Heinlein, Theodore Sturgeon, Isaac Asimov, A. E. van Vogt--were soon to give it status as a mature and even thoughtful literature. By comparison, the advent of Captain Future must have seemed an ill-timed embarrassment.

Why then is Captain Future still remembered fondly as we reach the eve of the character's 56th birthday? The answer has to be in the story-telling magic of the writer hired to produce the series. His name was Edmond Hamilton.

Edmond Hamilton was born in Youngston, Ohio in 1904 and was raised on a nearby farm. When he was young the term science fiction did not exist--it had yet to be invented--but the precocious country boy devoured the scientific romances of H.G. Wells and Jules Verne and later snapped up copies of adventure pulps like *All-Story* and *Argosy* when they ran serials featuring lost races and pioneer interplanetary romances.

As Hamilton recalled it in an essay published in 1934: "I have been a strong science fiction fan since 1916, when I started in with the old *Argosy* tales of Burroughs, Julian Hawthorne and others. I had a newspaper route about that time and when Merritt's long-awaited sequel to "The Moon Pool" came out, I carried papers one night each week with the *All-Story Magazine* held three inches before my eyes, avoiding automobiles and street-cars by the grace of God and heaving every paper on the wrong porch."

At an early age he determined to become a professional writer and devote his own life to entertaining people, as he had been entertained, with yarns of derring-do on far planets and wondrous worlds. At the time of that momentous decision he had no idea that science fiction was about to become a category in its own right or that it would eventually encompass scores of magazines specializing in just that brand of fiction.

When Edmond Hamilton's first pulp yarn appeared in the August 1926 issue of *Weird Tales*, science fiction magazines were just five-months old (*Amazing Stories*, April 1926 was the genesis). Hamilton's initial venture into sf, bearing the simplistic title, "Across Space," was published only a month later. Within a short time he was routinely selling stories that took men out beyond the planets to the stars, then to other galaxies, and finally outside the known universe altogether.

Hamilton was almost the perfect pulpster. Working in the fabulist tradition of story telling, his wildly imaginative, action-packed space operas just about jumped off the page with writer-to-reader urgency. He once recalled how, in putting the finishing touches to an epic space battle, he became so excited that he punched his typewriter so hard that the machine "walked" over the surface of his old flat-topped desk--with the writer following it, banging away at it as he finished his climactic scene.

Such stuff wasn't great literature, nor was it meant to be. But his readers caught the excitement, and the Edmond Hamilton byline sold tons of magazines.

As a full-time pulpster Hamilton wrote under the pseudonyms Hugh Davidson, Robert Castle, and Robert Wentworth as well as the house names Brett Sterling and Will Garth. He also worked other fiction categories--mystery, detective, and even the supernatural--but he

| VOL. 3, NO. 2 | CONTENTS | FALL, 1941 |

A Complete Book-Length Scientifiction Novel

THE LOST WORLD
OF TIME

By
EDMOND HAMILTON

Thrilling Short Stories

Scientifiction Serial Novel

Special Features

Join THE FUTUREMEN, Our Great New Club for Readers!

thought of himself and was thought of as a science fiction writer.

Hamilton was a founding father of the sf pulps. His "Interstellar Patrol" stories (1928-1930) constituted the first space opera series, predating E.E. "Doc" Smith's more famous "Lensman" series by several years. The author of such archetypal yarns as "The Universe Wreckers," "Crashing Suns," and "Locked Worlds," his virile brand of far-out adventure stories soon earned him the sobriquet "World-Saver," or alternatively, "World-Wrecker" Hamilton due to his penchant for smashing worlds around like glass marbles.

If characterization was virtually nonexistent in Ed's early stories, he more than made up for it with his prodigal inventiveness, rocketing narrative drive, and deep-felt instinct for the heroic. He wrote about "the great booming suns of outer space"--and readers didn't stop to ponder whether suns could "boom" or not. It sounded just right.

As his career progressed, the old super-science melodramas were occasionally suplemented by more thoughtful stories in which depth of characterization and emotional drives became prominent. Hamilton proved he could write as sophisticated a story as the best of them and some of his short stories remain small masterpieces.

But we seldom get to choose our own epitaph. In 1940, when science fiction was just beginning to take itself seriously as a mature literary form, Edmond Hamilton was assigned the job of writing a series of book-length novels for a brand new magazine: *Captain Future*. The new title was designed to carry the breathless adventures of a futuristic Doc Savage-type superhero, aimed mainly at teenagers.

Legend has it that Hamilton was given the assignment for the series while attending the First World Science Fiction Convention in New York City, July 2, 1939. Leo Margulies that feisty little editorial director of Standard Magazines, was also at the convention and had been impressed by the enthusiasm of the early sf fans. Margulies announced on the spot that he planned to create a new pulp hero magazine aimed at younger readers in an effort to win them over to the new brand of future fiction. He reasoned that this innovation would do for science fiction what The Shadow had done for mystery and what Doc Savage had done for adventure.

The fact was that the Captain Future magazine had been planned some months before, and the World's first-ever sf convention had been deemed an appropriate place to announce the new title's imminent arrival.

Originally the new magazine was to be called *Mr. Future...Wizard of Science*. Hamilton was supplied a story and character outline by the publishers. In the publishers' scenario Curt Newton was not a man of heroic proportions but a biological mutant with a small body and big head, born of radioactive emanations, like some freak in a 1950's exploitation movie. His three companions were to be: an old man who was little more than a living memory bank, a telepathically controlled robot who served as a metallic Doppelganger for Mr. Future, and a crystalline warrior from Ganymede, who was to be a living jewel set in Future's ring. Hamilton found the outline and the characters unworkable and he was forced to go to New York and argue with Margulies and editor Mort Weisinger for days until the proposed set-up was changed to his liking. Eventually the character--now called Captain Future--emerged in a form acceptable to Hamilton, his new bosses, and their suitably impressed young readers.

In the freshly devised legend, Captain Future was really Curtis Newton, the son of a brilliant biologist who had established a secret base on the moon to escape an unscrupulous enemy. When the elder Newton is murdered by his old foe, young Curt Newton is raised by his father's three unhuman aides--the strangest trio of sidekicks in the annals of pulp literature.

Known as the Futuremen, Captain Future's three companions are:

The Brain--Simon Wright, who at one time had been Earth's greatest biologist. Faced with mortal death, the elderly Wright had proposed to Curt's father that his brain

The Rocketeers Blast Off on a Race Around the Sun

IN

STAR TRAIL TO GLORY

•

A Complete Book-Length Novel of the Trail-Blazers of the Spaceways
FEATURING CAPTAIN FUTURE

By EDMOND HAMILTON

COMING IN THE NEXT ISSUE

be transferred into a special serum-case in which it could live and think and work. Imprisoned forever within the transparent, indestructable case, the Brain's optic nerves are attached to artificial lens-eyes, while other nerves operate such apurtenances as microphone-ears, and the resonator by which he speaks. (At first the Brain could not move about by himself--one of the other Futuremen had to carry the serum-case by its attached handle--but Hamilton found this too hampering a restriction and eventually equipped his bizarre Futureman with tractor beams to supply locomotive powers.)

Otho, the android--is not human but a living man of synthetic flesh created in the moon laboratory by The Brain and Captain Future's father. Otho's hairless, streamlined body is many times stronger and more flexible than that of normal humans, enabling him to run faster, jump higher and move more quickly in an emergency than almost any other creature. By softening and resetting his synthetic skin Otho can disguise himself as almost anyone--or any *thing*--in the system.

Grag, the robot--is another creation of Curt's father. He towers over seven feet in height, a massive, manlike figure of gleaming "inert" metal. The robot was not designed to be merely an automaton but to have an intelligence and individuality of his own. The only thing not built into Grag was a sense of humor, as humans know it. The giant, naive robot would like nothing better than to be considered human. One of the running gags in the Captain Future novels is an ongoing battle between Grag and Otho (a la Monk and Ham in the Doc Savage series) as to which is the more "human" of Captain Future's unhuman pals.

Perhaps the Futuremen's only true human link is that of Curt Newton himself, the child they helped raise to manhood, a perfect specimen of mental and physical human superiority.

Not all of Curt's friends were unhuman. Romance entered the series in the person of Joan Randall, a young secret service agent of the Planet Police. She first met Captain Future in the Space Emperor mystery and then again when she was kidnapped by Doctor Zaro's Legion of Doom. Joan and grizzled Marshall Ezra Gurney, another friend of Curt's, are listed on "special detached service" with the Planet Police in order to hold themselves in readiness to aid Captain Future and his band when the occasion requires.

Almost as important as the cast of living characters was the Futuremen's cyclotron-powered space ship, the *Comet*--the flying laboratory of Captain Future and his roistering space soldiers. The *Comet* was designed like an elongated tear drop, a piece of Art Deco streamlining that would have no value in the resistanceless depths of deep space. It looked pretty, however, and must have impressed the natives of remote worlds as it zapped along their space trails.

The first issue of *Captain Future* appeared on the stands in late 1939, inexplicably cover-dated Winter 1940. The heroic cover painting featured Cap Future and his two mobile sidekicks, Grag and Otho. The Captain was decked out in a red spacesuit and bubble helmet, his proton blaster firing what appeared to be expanding Lifesaver mints, while Otho was pictured with tv antennas jutting from each of his dead white shoulders. (Simon Wright was to appear on only two of the series' covers, indicating a bias regarding the visual appeal of raw brains in see-thru boxes).

Hamilton called the first novel "The Horror on Jupiter," but that title was changed to "Captain Future and the Space Emperor," in order to capitalize on the Captain Future name.

Space Emperor was not an auspicous debut. It and a half dozen stories to follow read like first draft efforts (which they were) rushed out to meet deadlines. Five of the first seven stories were to feature the same basic plot, in which Captain Future--an amalgam of Doc Savage and the publisher's own Phantom Detective in a futuristic setting-- must catch and unmask a criminal in disguise who threatens Earth's solar system. None of the stories took place outside that system--a snug group of nine cozy planets with breathable atmospheres and native races of human descent. At this point the author was clearly working to restrictive and unadventurous guidelines.

"To tell the truth," Hamilton admitted, "so little was paid me for the early ones that they were all written first draft right out of the typewriter. After the first six, they paid me more, and I then did two drafts and they improved a lot."

To say that they improved was an understatement. In the first issue an anxious editorial had solicited advice: "Shall the scope of Captain Future's quests be limited to our Universe? Or shall his experiences plunge him into the fourth dimension--into the past, remote eons of time--or into the far-distant vistas of eternity a million years from today?" Reader response must have been positive because the editors finally allowed Hamilton to drop the "scientific detective" constraint. From that point on not even the sky was the limit in Captain Future's Universe. "World Saver" Hamilton had been unfettered.

In "The Lost World of Time," crime takes a holiday as Cap and his buddies travel a hundred million years back in time to an Earth where carboniferous plains are lit by flaring volcanoes and the silver glow of twin moons. In order to save the native inhabitants of Katain--the tenth planet which exploded aeons ago, forming the asteroids between Mercury and Jupiter--the Futuremen leap another three billion years backward still, only to find themselves stranded in an unthinkable time before the planets of our Solar System existed.

The following novel, "Quest Beyond The Stars," took the red-haired sojourner out of our Solar System altogether. In order to save the dying planet of Mercury the Futuremen traverse strange zones of space in which all ordinary scientific laws are overturned. They flash past alien suns, great meteor swarms, somber dark stars, and skirt the flaming coasts of gigantic nebulae of glowing gases. No piker when it came to travel, Hamilton brought his adventurers clear to the heart of the galactic core in search of the mysterious Birthplace of Matter.

In "The Comet Kings," Captain Future pursues disappearing space ships into the gaseous heart of Halley's Comet. He encounters a world of electrical splendor and terror, a race of glowing beings, and invaders from a four-dimensional region outside the universe. And that's just for starters.

"Planets In Peril," finds Curt Newton cast in a stellar role as the saviour of a dying island universe where the very stars are flickering out. He must battle the Cold Ones--living products of a disastrous chain of biological events that took place on the frozen planet of a long-dead star.

And so it went, with each new issue presenting breathless variations on a cosmic feast as "World Saver" Hamilton upped the fictional ante to become "Universe Saver." Then an upheaval occurred when Hamilton's name was dropped from the series.

"I wrote all the Captain Future novels until Pearl Harbor in December 1941," Hamilton explained. "As I was then a bachelor and figured I would soon be in the army,

I notified Leo that I wouldn't be able to write any more,
so he got two other writers and changed the authorship of
the magazine to the psudonym, 'Brett Sterling.' But, in
1942, the army ruled they would not accept men over
thirty-eight years old, so, on the verge of being inducted,
I was ruled out, and went back to writing Cap. Future
again. Some of my stories then appeared under the 'Brett
Sterling' byline, and others under my own name."

Seventeen issues of *Captain Future* were issued
between 1940 and 1944. Fifteen of the novels were written
by Hamilton, and two by William Morrison (pen name of
Brooklyn author Joseph Samachson). The Morrison stories, "Worlds to Come," and "Days of Creation" were more
than acceptable entries in the series, capitalizing on the
potential of Hamilton's freakish heroes.

"Star of Dread," a Brett Sterling byline penned by
Hamilton, continued to pursue Curt Newton's new destiny
as dedicated cosmic archaeologist. This was the story in
which the author went deeper into his consistently
developing "Past History" of the Solar System. On the
distant planet Deneb it is learned that our human race
came originally from another galaxy many millions of
years ago. Before they came, two non-human races held
sway in the galaxy--the protozoan Linids, whom our
ancestors conquered long ago, and the mysterious Kangas,
"the mighty lords of darkness who sailed the starways and
sucked power from the suns a billion years ago." It seems
that all of mankind has descended from the Denebians,

who terraformed and settled many of the other planets as well.

In William Morrison's "Days of Creation," it is revealed that Captain Future's beloved Solar System is bulging at the seams with population density. To solve matters, the ingenious super scientist proposes to do nothing less than create a brand new world between the orbits of Earth and Mars--the artificial planet Futuria. Create it he does. And Futuria becomes a decent enough answer to the housing shortage--if you have nothing against carniverous plants and Jovian flame breathers as neighbors.

"Worlds to Come," Morrison's second and final CF yarn, features a return trip to the Saggitarian System, the scene of Cap's previous epic voyage in search of the Birthplace of Matter. This time our adventurers lock in mortal combat with the deadly Sverds. The Sverds? Ah yes, the Sverds. Ten-foot high, green-gray dog-headed creatures half in and half out of another dimension. Upon the outcome of the cataclysmic battle hinges not just a single star system, but possibly the entire universe.

Despite apologists and critics, nearly all of the Captain Future novels were entertaining stories filled with color, excitement and fantastic adventure. Like all the hero pulps, the magazine had but one aim: to give the reader an hour or two of simple, infectious escape from life's hardships. The extent to which it succeeded was reflected in a fan letter in the Winter 1944 readers' column:

> *Dear (editor):*
> *If the paper shortage becomes so acute that you must cease publication of some of your magazines for the duration, may I suggest that you hang on to CAPTAIN FUTURE until the very last?*
> *I do the work of four or five people every day. I have an invalid father and an*

> *ailing mother to care for and it's up to me*
> *to look after everything besides perform-*
> *ing heavy manual labor every day six days*
> *a week on my railroad job. I'm so tired and*
> *exhausted that I almost collapse. So,*
> *occasionally, when I have an hour or so to*
> *spare, I treat myself to the super treat of*
> *treats--CAPTAIN FUTURE! That gives*
> *me the lift necessary to carry on. But*
> *without CAPTAIN FUTURE, my life*
> *would be dreary, gloomy and lonely in-*
> *deed.*

Despite editorial assurance that Captain Future was one of the lustiest of the science fictioneers, the lonely railroader must have been bitterly disappointed when no other issue of the magazine was ever produced. It had, indeed, been cancelled due to wartime paper shortage.

One consolation was that three additional Captain Future novels had already been written; these were published in *Startling Stories*, one of the publisher's companion magazines. The first of them, Hamilton's "Red Sun of Danger" sported a memorable cover painting of Grag the robot entwined in battle with a winged, fire-breathing "night dragon."

The final Captain Future novel, "The Solar Invasion," was ghosted by Manly Wade Wellman, a highly regarded American regional writer and fantasist. Unfortunately, science fiction was not Wellman's long suit, and his lack of enthusiasm for Captain Future's milieu resulted in an uninspired adventure for the rugged red-haired space hero.

While "The Solar Invasion" marked the end of the "book-length" novels, the character staged something of a comeback in 1950 with a series of seven "novelettes" (pulp euphemism for long short stories), all written by Hamilton. In this third phase, the mood changed from juvenile adventure to stories emphasizing atmosphere and characterization.

While even the longer novels were seldom as stereotyped as they have been depicted, the later Captain Future novelettes are excellent fiction by any standards. They are beautifully written stories revealing an unexpected sense of melancholy as the aging writer examined the brevity--and frailty--of human life set against the vastness of space and brooding eons of time.

Edmond Hamilton's final Captain Future story, "Birthplace of Creation," appeared in the May 1951 issue of *Startling Stories*. In it, a more sober Curtis Newton again travels beyond Sagittarious to the fount of the universe, the birthplace of material creation. There, in teeming star jungles ablaze with the glow of drowned and captured suns, he must wrestle with--and ultimately renounce--the opportunity of godhood. As a pulp hero's swan song, it was an ending that couldn't be topped.

While the Captain Future novels were aimed at a younger audience than most sf magazines, Hamilton's fecund imagination and zest for story telling insured that they were great fun to read. Who can say how many young readers were influenced by them and went on to shape the very future they dreamed about? There are no statistics on such things.

A few years before his death in 1977 Ed Hamilton and his wife Leigh Brackett (one of the great sf writers herself) were invited to sit in the reporters' press box at Cape Kennedy, and they watched Apollo 12 take off for the moon. Ed later wrote about his reactions to the launch:

"So as I watched Apollo 12 rise in flame and thunder, if anyone at that moment had asked me, 'Was it worthwhile to spend 44 years writing science fiction?' I would have unhesitatingly anwered 'Yes.' For I feel we had a part..a very tiny part..in this. We did not plan or build or launch this craft. We only dreamed about it. But perhaps the dreams helped a little to create a climate in which it could be planned and launched and built...

"Without a single exception all of my oldest friends, and some of them go back forty years, are science fictionists. Many others who were friends are now gone. And as the rocket soared up into the clouds, I found myself thinking of them all...looking back to the days when we were all looking forward, when we met in tiny groups and tried to peer into the future, discussed it, argued about it, and attempted awkwardly to put it into fiction. And it did not seem to me, with the thunder still echoing in my ears, that what we did or tried to do was completely unworthy."

Who is to say where imagination ends and reality begins?

CLOUDLAND CAVALIERS

Flying alone! A hundred miles, north,
south, east, west. Thirty thousand square
miles of unbroken cloud-plains! No trav-
eller in the desert, no pioneer to the Poles
had ever seen such an expanse of sand or
snow. Only the lonely threshers of the sky,
hidden from the earth, had gazed on it.
Only we who went up into the high places
under the shadow of wings!

Cecil Lewis

One of the great obsessions of the Depression years was with the romance of flying. Things were pretty rough down on the ground but they couldn't be rosier up there in the endless vista of the skies--or so it seemed when you were stuck hoplessly on the ground.

To weary job seekers and downtrodden laborers flying must have appeared a near miraculous escape from earthbound burdens, its practitioners akin to the gods as they rode the winds with white scarves fluttering in the slipstream. The trouble was that it cost a small fortune to actually own one of those crates. And you had to devote long hours achieving mechanical skill in order to fly them.

As usual, the pulps came up with a vicarious fix. Each month armchair aviators could take off from their corner newsstands with a choice of dozens of high-flying magazines, each promising delirious visions of winged glory. Although there were never as many air titles as detective, western, or even love, aviation fans remained a dedicated group of pulp consumers.

The magazine laying claim to being first off the ground was Fiction House's *Air Stories*, whose cover proclaimed itself "The First Air Story Magazine." On the other hand, Dell Publications' *War Birds* called itself "The Oldest Air War Magazine." Both were published within a short time of each other in 1927. A third magazine, *Wings*, zoomed out soon after, ultimately achieving some kind of record by being the last aviation magazine to to fold nearly thirty years later.

Most of the early stories were about air fighting in World War I, "the war to end all wars." The magazine logos reflected that fixation: *Flying Aces, Battle Birds, Dare-Devil Aces, War Aces, Sky Fighters*, and so on. Each was packed with romanticized epics featuring dashing Allied airmen and ruthless German foes locked in mortal combat above the clouds. Even the story titles soared: "Thundering Wings," " "Sky Graves for the Gallant," "Brothers of Aces," "Sky Rider's Reckoning."

Since all pulps were essentially hero oriented, it was inevitable that the aviation titles would come up with some recurring fictional characters. Although never as plentiful as detective mystery men, aerial series characters did prove popular. The most famous of these, G-8 (And His Battle Aces), has been discussed in Chapter Four. There were dozens of other daring young men in their flying machines. A few commanded their own magazine titles. Others were used to help boost the popularity of conventional aviation magazines.

And what names they had, those cavaliers in oval goggles! Speed Rossiter. Loop Murry. Coffin Kirk. Jinx Jones. Ace Dallas. Luke Lance. Buzz Travers. Ding Darley. There was even a flying jester named Phineas "Carbunkle" Pinkham, who didn't land planes--he crashed them.

Writer Arch Whitehouse, himself a Royal Flying Corps veteran with sixteen air victories, unleashed Larry Ledbeater and Todd Bancroft against the Japs. He wrote of Tug Hardwick and "Beansie" Baker in *Flying Aces*. Adventurous aircraft salesman Crash Carringer (reassuring name for a pilot!) appeared in the same magazine. Whitehouse also wrote a number of stories about "the Coffin Crew," pilots Armitage, Townsend, Ryan and Tate. Erle Stanley Gardner dreamed up a hyperactive flying detective named Speed Dash. And Doc Savage's Lester Dent wrote of Hair Noon, a Coast Guard pilot.

Most of the wind-bronzed highflyers were preposterously brave and handsome, with only their odd names to distinguish them. But a few stood out from the crowd.

A WWI series by Donald E. Keyhoe concerned the bizarre adventures of Philip Strange, "the phantom ace of G.2." Strange's exploits appeared in *Flying Aces*, a tripartite pulp which routinely mixed tales of Spads and Spandaus with factual articles and detailed model building instructions.

Although Strange pre-dated G-8 and shared similar characteristics, he never achieved G-8's popularity. Known as "the Brain Devil" because of his ESP and other near-occult mental powers, Strange was an ex child prodigy who had performed feats of magic, ventriloquism and hypnotism in showbiz. Like G-8, the Brain Devil was also an ace flier and Intelligence agent who used the art of disguise to confound the machinations of the Kaiser's evil scientists.

Philip Strange was the creation of Major Donald E. Keyhoe, who had flown in active service with the Marine Corps and had been an aide to Charles Lindbergh after his famous Paris flight. In later years he was to gain some fame and notoriety as the author who first brought UFOs to the attention of the public with five best-selling "fact" books including *The Flying Saucer Conspiracy* and *The Flying Saucers Are Real*. Critics of his UFO books often pointed out that he had once written masses of "far out" pulp fiction.

In the mid 30s Keyhoe sensed that youthful readers might be growing tired of beating the Boche. He developed a more contemporary barnstormer in Richard Knight, who was blind as a bat by day but eagle-eyed after dark. Not tied to the Western Front, Knight clocked considerably more miles than the WWI mental marvel, including flights to the Far East.

Flying Aces boasted other heroes of the crimson skies. Arch Whitehouse was responsible for Buzz Benson, an aviation reporter and undercover man for the Secret Service. The Benson plots usually involved peril to the US Fleet in the Pacific, with Buzz zooming in to wreck havoc on bands of international crooks and not-too-disguised Oriental aggressors.

Another Whitehouse character, the Griffon, was Kerry Keen, young millionaire layabout by day and flying avenger by night. Whenever stratospheric evil threatened, Keen would don a scarlet silk-and-rubber mask and zoom out in his supercharged plane, the Black Bullet, from an underground hangar on his Long Island estate. (Years later, radio's Green Hornet would use the same schtick in an earthbound format).

Flying series heroes became so popular at one point that prolific author Harold F. Cruickshank managed to maintain the monthly exploits of three different characters--Sky Wolf, Sky Devil and Red Eagle--in consecutive issues of three different Popular Publications titles.

One of the more unusual characters (by reason of sex) in the macho air pulps was Barbe Pivet, an aviatrix who appeared in a series written by Herman Petersen in *Air Stories* and later in *Wings*. A typical Pivet story, "Flaming Gas" (Wings Aug. 1928), has Barbe winging solo to the rescue and downing the villain's plane while her boyfriend watches helplessly on the ground.

And speaking of villains--Steve Fisher invented Mr. Death, a physically crippled Hun murder master who had "a face like powdered chalk." Death squared off with Yank flier Jed "Babyface" Garrett in a series of eight wild flights

Charger

Silver
Lancer

Scarlet
Stormer

BILL BARNES
Air Adventurer

in *Daredevil Aces*. These ran from March to November 1936, and terminated with Mr. Death and his black Fokker still terrorizing the Western Front.

Arthur J. Burks, Marine pilot and prolific pulpster, wrote of Jim Swain, an aerial Robin Hood in war ravaged China. Robert Burtt picked up the aerial mercenaries theme with his stories of "Battling Grogan and his Dragon Squadron" of China. And Frederick Nebel turned out a series in *Air Stories* concerning tramp flyers Gales and Mike McGill, who roistered through the mysterious skies of the Orient in the early '30s. In a companion magazine, *Wings*, Joel Rogers pulled the chocks with that amazing gentleman Captain Death--top-kick of the sky sleuths.

The instant success of Popuar Publications' G-8 magazine led a number of publishers to attempt single character air hero titles. As might be expected, Street & Smith's entry in the air race downplayed the flamboyant excesses of their rival's zombie-fighting Master Spy.

Bill Barnes, Air Adventurer began in early 1934 with a novel titled "Hawks of the Golden Crater." Compared to the likes of Coffin Kirk and Crash Carringer, Bill possessed the blandest of pulp hero monickers. The "Barnes" was meant to suggest "barnstormer"--in honor of those frolicsome gypsy fliers who found exhilarating freedom while courting aerial death. He even had a plane named the Stormer.

The initial Barnes novels were written by ex-cavalry officer Major Malcolm Wheeler-Nicholson, most of the others by Canadian-born writers Charles Spain Verral and Harold P. Montanye--all under the house name of George L. Eaton. The main plotline dealt with young flyer/designer Bill Barnes achieving fame and fortune as a daring air racer. With his prize money he assembles a gang of loyal aides and starts his own ultra-modern air field on Long Island.

One of the charms of the Bill Barnes stories is that he was a recognizably human character living in a recognizably real world. Many of his problems were financial (a

change from millionaire crimefighters) with Bill constantly running short of operating funds and desperately
trying to hold things together.

In his first adventure, Bill flew his self-designed
plane, a stubby little fighter called "the Bumblebee." It
featured rocket-assisted takeoff, folding wings and folding
rotors for vertical takeoff and landing. In his third issue,
he introduced "the Porpoise," a submerging seaplane-
submarine. As each of his super planes was shot down or
bombed in its hangar by various flying fiends, Bill was
forced back to the old drawing board to come up with new
ones. The "Scarlet Stormer" was a favorite for several
years, but it was eventually stolen and replaced by the
newer, faster "Silver Lancer." When even the Lancer came
a cropper (destroyed by a thermal bomb), it too was
replaced by the newer, more modern "Charger."

Even Bill's pals were fallible--the kind of people you
might really know. Sandy Sanders was a teenager who
could fly like a fool, but was just a kid like any other.
Others in the cast included Shorty Hassfurther, a stalky
little World War I ace; Bev Bates, a Bostonian; "Scotty"
MacCloskey, Bill's master mechanic; and Tony Lamport,
his ground radio operator. Occasionally an aide was
injured and remained out of action for a while. At least
three of his friends were killed outright, including close
pal, Texan Cy Hawkins, who was bumped off in a 1938
adventure.

Obviously Bill Barnes had to be on his guard; he
lived in the dangerously fragile world we all inhabit. At
the end of many of his exploits he sometimes realized that
he had worked his heart out, risked his life and those of
his associates--and all for nothing. Yet, like all pulp
heroes, he recognized adventure as an attitude toward
discomfort. If he and his pals came out of a story with their
lives, his blue eyes would brighten as he headed for home
and the prospect of another perilous venture.

One of the mainstays of the Bill Barnes magazine
was artist Frank Tinsley, brother of The Shadow ghost-

writer Theodore Tinsley. It's safe to say that the *Bill Barnes* pulp is collected today as much for Frank Tinsley's covers and interior illustrations as it is for the stories themselves. Tinsley dreamed up Bill's slightly futuristic air ships and even helped plot the stories. His intricate, painstaking drawings of the Bumblebee, the Stormer and the Lancer were complete down to every last rivet and bolt--so much so that few readers ever stopped to consider that Bill's advanced-design planes were really just imaginative fabrications. Even the Barnes Long Island airfield was portrayed in exact, unsparing detail in both the stories and in Tinsley's delightful interior sketches.

Unfortunately, after some twenty full-length novels, Bill Barnes suffered the ignominy of seeing his pulp refashioned into *Bill Barnes Air Trails*, a large-size semi-slick. Bill's own adventures were reduced in scope to accomodate articles and model building departments. Poor Bill. Eventually he was squeezed out of his own magazine altogether, winding up as a back-of-the-book character in *Doc Savage* magazine. Writer Verral and artist Tinsley stuck with Bill through his tribulations, but by the mid 1940s his glory days were clearly over.

One flying hero who commanded his own book without fear of eviction was John Masters, the Lone Eagle. Named in honor of Charles Lindbergh, The Lone Eagle first spread his wings in September of 1933--a month *before* the debut of *G-8 and his Battle Aces*. Although doomed to fly forever in G-8's propwash, he was the only air hero to last almost as long as the durable Master Spy--ten years and some seventy-six novel-length adventures.

Billed as "The World's Greatest Sky Fighter," the Lone Eagle was a legend of the Great War, a lone wolf ace of Yank Intelligence who appeared in the skies where the fighting was the toughest and under whose watchful eyes no Hun treachery could be perpetrated. But the man himself--John Masters--could not collect any of the glory which was his due.

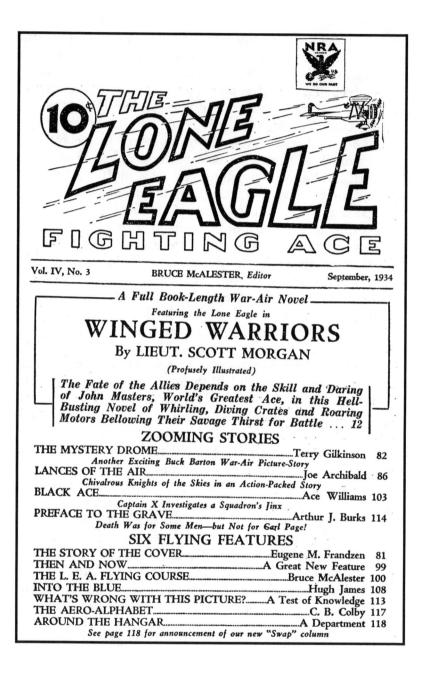

Vol. IV, No. 3   BRUCE McALESTER, Editor   September, 1934

—— *A Full Book-Length War-Air Novel* ——
Featuring the Lone Eagle in

WINGED WARRIORS
By LIEUT. SCOTT MORGAN
(Profusely Illustrated)

*The Fate of the Allies Depends on the Skill and Daring
of John Masters, World's Greatest Ace, in this Hell-
Busting Novel of Whirling, Diving Crates and Roaring
Motors Bellowing Their Savage Thirst for Battle ... 12*

ZOOMING STORIES

SIX FLYING FEATURES

See page 118 for announcement of our new "Swap" column

The moment he stepped out of his mottled Spad he ceased to be the Lone Eagle. Like a cloak he flung off that romantic personality and became merely John Masters, a man whose drab uniform bore neither insignia nor rank, and whose papers showed him to be a newspaper correspondent from Chicago.

In order to justify Masters' heroic nickname his writers made him a sharp-eyed hermit of the skies. He flew alone, fought alone, a free-lance dealer in death and destruction armed with apparently limitless ammunition. His only friends and confidantes were Colonel Tremaine, the paternal, grizzled chief of Yank Air Intelligence, and a fiery little French General, Viaud. There was no romance in his life, and only one woman of note--the seductive but deadly German undercover agent known as R-47.

Perhaps it was the Eagle's austere life that made him less exciting than G-8. Perhaps it was just the nature of his magazine to be less flamboyant and thus less attractive to jaded pulp readers. *The Lone Eagle* covers were technically good, but they featured routine air war paintings at a time when routine air war magazines were glutting the market. By comparison, the G-8 covers flypapered your eyes with bizarre compositions juxtaposing snarling Spads and Fokkers with skeleton men and giant vampire bats.

Although John Masters faced a few recurring villains (some masked suicide pilots known as the Lemmings, the dread organization of Boche spies called the Ring of the Nachrichtendienst, and the always provocative R-47) essentially the Lone Eagle stories were well-written, nononsense air war adventures.

What made the Eagle unique among pulp fliers was that he fought in two World Wars. In February, 1940, with "The Nazi Menace," he aged twenty years in one month as he jumped from the heart of World War I into the new conflict.

The character's updated legend had it that Masters had stood on the passenger deck of the Athenia and witnessed it shot from under him by a ruthless U-boat commander. He had been on his way home from Europe with the full intention of remaining a neutral. But the sight of innocent women and children struggling in the freezing waters of the Atlantic had turned him back with the determination that he would not head west again until Adolf Hitler had been personally destroyed.

Once again John Masters had thrown in with the Allies, on condition that he carry no rank and wear no uniform except when necessary. No mention is made of the age of the still virile Lone Eagle, but this time he is equipped with more youthful confidantes: Pierre Viaud, the son of old General Viaud, Chief of French Intelligence in WWI, and Henri Laval. Henri had been a Boy Scout back in those hectic days and is now a pilot in the French Air Service.

Even R-47, the Eagle's old nemesis, returns in the form of the German spy's own daughter. The new R-47 is beautiful, sinster and vicious--and she wears her mother's old perfume.

But something is missing in the "new" Lone Eagle-- a sense of innocent adventure perhaps. War is never fun. It can only appear so when distanced by time and memory. In the early and mid thirties it was easy to romanticize WWI flying spies, their planes slicing boldy through the clear winds high above the verminous trenches. By 1940 the reality of a new horror in Europe produced a more sober, oftentimes brooding fighting ace. Perhaps he was contemplating the fate of his magazine.

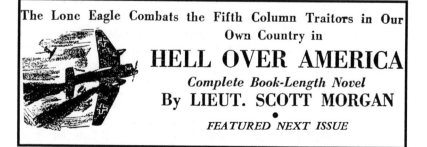

The Lone Eagle Combats the Fifth Column Traitors in Our Own Country in

HELL OVER AMERICA

Complete Book-Length Novel

By LIEUT. SCOTT MORGAN

•

FEATURED NEXT ISSUE

Hindsight indicates that Masters' abrupt switch from one war to another was a result of declining reader interest. The magazine's publication frequency had dropped from monthly to bi-monthly as early as 1937. It switched to quarterly in 1942. Even the name of the magazine was changed to *The American Eagle* and finally pluralized to *American Eagles* as poor old John Masters was pushed to the back of his own book for a final, ignominious adventure. The magazine folded with the Spring 1943 issue.

If the Lone Eagle never achieved the stratospheric success of other pulp heroes, he did remain a newsstand fixture for many years. Much of his popularity can be tied to the realistic details in his magazine's flying sequences. When the Lone Eagle vaults into his Spad, his feet "slam home in the rudder stirrups." He spots enemy planes by holding his thumb against the sun. And his wings "tilt in a split-S curve" when he turns to land. It all sounded just right because his writers had held their thumbs against the sun and had turned their fighting ships into split-S curves.

Most of the novels were ghosted by F.E. Reichnitzer and Robert Sidney Bowen, using the house name Lieut. Scott Morgan. Reichnitzer wrote the early stories. He had been an RAF Camel pilot in the Great War, had been shot down in Belgium while on a bombing mission and imprisoned at Rasstatt. Once he had been placed before a firing squad and saved only when the commandant had a last minute change of heart.

Robert Sidney Bowen had left high school when the war began and had lied about his age in order to join the Royal Flying Corps. The youngest member of the RFC, Bowen went to France as a scout pilot and shot down a number of German planes and balloons. Later he became a newspaperman, test pilot, editor of *Aviation Magazine* and finally a prolific fiction writer.

Bowen also created the Captain Danger character in *Air War* magazine, although the series was soon taken over by pulp hero specialist Norman Daniels. Beginning in 1940 and running through 1944, there were over a dozen Captain Allen Danger novels in all, with titles like "Captain Danger's Nazi Hunt," "Captain Danger's Blitz-krieg," and "Captain Danger over London."

Few of the World War II flying aces were as durable as their Great War counterparts. Two more "captains"--Captain Combat and Captain V--appeared briefly and then dropped from sight. Captain William Combat was the star of his own magazine, which lasted but three issues in 1940. A Yank-born RAF ace, Combat flew a Hawker Hurricane for the British 42nd Home Defense Squadron. Because of his mother's death at the hand of German flyers, the young American declared a personal war on the Nazi leader. A curiosity of the series is the publisher's reluctance to defame Adolf Hitler. In the novels the villainous Nazi leader is slightly disguised as Herr Gruber, a middle-aged man with a mustache and *a small Van Dyke beard*--and is so portrayed in the magazine's illustrations.

Captain V zoomed through seven short novels in *Battle Birds* from August 1942 to September 1943. Created from the flames of war, Captain V once had a name and a position as a minor attache to the pre-war Berlin Embassy. Indeed, the Gestapo had decided he was too well informed for the comfort of the Fuehrer, so they rigged a fiery plane crash in which he had come close to cremation. Declared officially dead--but reborn as the anonymous ace of American Intelligence--surgeons had given him a new, well-formed but masklike face. Returning to duty as Captain V, he worked in close contact with British Intelligence, and formed his own group of close-knit sky fighters--the V Aces. The V Aces had their own concrete underground hangar and their own Bell P-39 Airacorbras, each sleek plane carrying six machine guns and a 37 mm. cannon in the propeller hub.

Captain V was the creation of Ralph Oppenheim, a writer with no flying experience who had produced one of the first air series--the Three Mosquitoes--and, with Captain V, one of the last. It is an ironic fact that none of the flying pulp heroes survived the war they fought in. They flashed and flourished for a brief time between the wars. By 1943 they were hit a one-two blow by crippling paper shortages and a growing disdain for the glorification of fanciful characters supposedly taking part in a very real--and increasingly painful--war.

A slackening of interest in traditional air heroes had been felt almost a decade before, leading the ever alert Henry Steeger to revamp his mundane *Battle Aces* magazine into *G-8 and His Battle Aces*. In 1935 Steeger tried the same trick with the ailing *Battle Birds* when he transformed it into *Dusty Ayres and His Battle Birds*, a pulp hero magazine involving a fantasy war of the future, much in the style of his successful Operator #5.

Dusty Ayres was dreamed up over lunch--possibly a liquid one--at a 42nd Street restaurant by publisher Steeger and the ubiquitous Robert Sidney Bowen. Their protagonist would be a young man named Dusty Ayres and he would be instrumental in repulsing a future invasion of North America by a sinister foreign power.

The idea was to plunge the hero into a futuristic war using instruments and weapons still prototypal in the mid-thirties: radar, television, rockets, gas guns, and sleek futuristic aircraft that were sometimes bullet-proof and even fire-proof.

Dusty Ayres was designed as a pure adventure series, its "foreign" invaders carefully fabricated to avoid any realistic political implications. In fact, realism had little to do with the story line. Set in the near future (probably the 1940s) the background of the invaders and their curious leader was sketched in the opening paragraphs:

> *For three long years all Asia and Europe had been a seething inferno of war; a war started by one man, a man of mystery. Who he was, or from whence he*

came, no one knew. But like magic he had
risen up from an obscure part of Central
Asia and screamed his doctrine of eternal
vengeance for all forms of government
oppression.

    Nations tottered and fell, and were
swallowed up by the great black wave that
swept westward. The Black Invaders they
became known as, and the man of mystery
who commanded them they called "Fire-
Eyes," the Emperor of the World.

    The name was because of his eyes. They
were like blazing pools of flame that
looked out from behind a close-fitting
green mask...Yes, millions had seen him,
and even heard his harsh, cruel voice that
could speak every language on the face of
the globe, and speak it without a single
trace of any other language.

Old fire-Eyes was a hulking figure dressed in a black
form-fitting, bullet-proof uniform with snazzy gold shoulder straps. He wore black gauntlets and a black skull cap
that came down to cover the nape of his neck. Realizing
that he might not have the looks to win a democratic vote,
his aim was to take over the world by force.

    Not everybody was impressed. In the magazine's
editorial column, "Hanger Flying," one disgruntled reader
opined: "It's utterly impossible to think of a man like Fire-
Eyes even ruling Costa Rica, let alone Asia and Europe."

    Be that as it may, the masked invader and his black-
clad forces put up a pretty good show. Operating at first
from a base in Manitoba, they throw everything from
radio-controlled gas rockets to midget flame tanks at the
poor old U.S. And despite Dusty's heroic interventions,
cataclysmic events occur as his own Dayton Field is
destroyed and Atlanta and Roanoke are wiped off the map.

Throughout the series, young Dusty's perpetual eagerness for direct action lands him in hot water with his own superiors but has a telling effect on the flying killer hawks of the black-garbed invaders.

Dusty's perilous adventures were reminiscent of G-8's. Although they lacked the full-throttle horror aspects of the Flying Spy's more outrageous exploits, they had more than their share of exciting air action, captures, escapes, and cataclysmic cliffhangers. In addition, the covers by Frederick Blakeslee were some of the most arresting in the history of air magazines, all detailing futuristic planes and rocketships.

Blakeslee's cover for "The Red Destroyer" (December 1934) is classic. A massive crimson rocket slices through Manhattan skyscrapers. Up in the azure sky, bi-wing planes circle. Ant-sized figures race about on the roofs of buildings, their mouths open in silent screams as they run, trip, fall, plunge hopelessly down the yawning slopes of insubstantial towers slipping liquidly to ruin. It is a surrealistic daymare in vivid reds, blues and yellows. Pulp Armageddon. Who could resist?

Despite (or perhaps because of) such garnishments, the magazine failed to catch on. In hindsight it is easy to suggest that *Dusty Ayres* offered too much fantasy for air war fans but not enough for science fiction readers. Perhaps the masked Fire-Eyes was simply too absurd a menace to frighten readers already plagued by Depression and the threat of a real war in Europe. In addition, the nature of the series made it more of an ongoing serial, lacking the monthly change of venue afforded G-8 and other pulp heroes. For whatever reason, Dusty Ayres winged off into the sunset at the end of his twelfth issue.

If *Dusty Ayres and His Battle Birds* was an unusual air war magazine, Dell Publications came up with one that can only be described as absolutely loopy. *Terrence X. O'Leary's War Birds* was, in fact, so far out--even for the far out pulps--that it lasted but three short issues before it died of terminal strangeness.

Terrence X. ("sure and the X stands for 'xcillint'") O'Leary was the pugnacious Irish hero of several dozen novelettes that appeared in the late 1920s and early 1930s in Dell's *War Stories* and Fawcett's *Battle Stories* magazines--making him the only pulp hero to cross the loyalty line between rival publishers. Designed as a clone of that Irish scrapper of the movies, the late, great Victor McLaglen, O'Reilly traded bullets with the Boche and punches with his drinking buddy, one Peter Maher McGuffy.

O'Leary's creator, Arthur Guy Empey, was himself a colorful man of the times. Empey had served in the British Army in France during WWI and had been discharged on account of wounds received in the Battle of the Somme. Like his famous character, he also served in the U.S. Cavalry and the Tank Corps. *Over the Top*, a best-selling book based on his war experiences, brought him to Hollywood, where he wrote, produced, and even starred in numerous silent features. When he began writing for the pulps, he was billed as "the world's foremost author of war stories."

In such stories as "O'Leary's Rough Riders," and "That Fighting Irish Son-of-a-Gun," Empey's intrepid alter-ego (with his gang of cowboy "Kaiser hunters,") was sometimes a cavalryman and sometimes a member of the tank corps. In "O'Leary, Secret Service" (*War Stories*, June 1932) he even joined G-2 as an unlikely spy.

Such was the popularity of "the Mighty Mick" that Dell drafted him into the Air Corps in July of 1933, when he appeared in *War Birds* in a story titled "O'Leary, Sky Hawk." For some reason the double-fisted hero and his battling buddy, were even more popular in the air than they had been on the ground. In the new series, the two pals were both Air Force Captains, with O'Leary commonly known as Sky Hawk and McGuffey as Sky Rider.

In stories with titles like "Ghost of the Black Wings," "O'Leary Cracks the Crimson Legion" and "O'Leary, Zeppelin Killer," the indomitable warrior flew against such fearsome foes as The Scarlet Legion, The Black Eagle and The Black Roc. The O'Leary stories were so popular, in fact, that the publisher decided to let him take over the magazine. With the June 1935 issue *War Birds*, America's "oldest air war magazine," became *Terrence X. O'Leary's War Birds*.

It was a bit like allowing the monkeys to take over the zoo. O'Leary and his creator not only shanghied the magazine, but changed its nature entirely. For its brief three-issue run *Terrence X. O'Leary's War Birds* was to achieve dubious distinction as the most bizarre air war magazine ever published.

Gone were the Fokkers and Heinkels of earlier days. Gone too the Kaiser's pilots who flew them. As the new magazine's editorial so admirably phrased it: "We found that, to you, Terrence X. O'Leary represented the spirit of adventure, of dauntless, reckless, laughing courage. You wanted the Sky Hawk pitted against his natural foes--the evil, the scheming, and the vicious. You did not want him forever pitted against a nation with which we had ceased to be unfriendly."

Noble sentiments. Unfortunately, the characters recruited to replace the villainous Germans came straight from Cloud Cuckooland. The first of the new novels, "O'Leary Fights the Golden Ray," introduced Unuk, High Priest to the God of the Depths. Unuk is a mummified, half nude 500-year-old madman who, with an earless stooge named Alok, has seized control of Lataki, a hidden island in the South Pacific. With the help of various world scientists--captured and turned into zombie slaves--Unuk has devised fleets of air ships, death rays and other futuristic weapons with which he hopes to destroy a blissfully unprepared North America.

Before O'Leary thwarts his dastardly plans, Unuk does succeed in obliterating great gobs of the USA. The Statue of Liberty is demolished. Half of Cincinnati is laid waste. A large section of Washington is destroyed. Five battle cruisers are blasted into atoms. The Panama Canal is wrecked. Death and destruction rain down on Chicago, Minneapolis, El Paso, and Seattle. And that's just up to page 31!

In Empey's second superhero opus, "O'Leary, Dyno-Blaster, or Adventure of the Ageless Men," the vile whip-wielding Unuk returns again, this time armed with such wonders as "magic impello stratopedes"--produced by his brain-doctored scientist slaves. There is more destruction of American real estate, with O'Leary achieving a last-minute rescue of Washington after making mincemeat of his two hellish foes.

A third, and final, story ("The Purple Warriors of Neptunia") introduced no less a worthy than Umgoop the Horrible-- a shark-mouthed, indigo-hued, eight-foot-tall monster whose favorite sport is ripping arms and legs off hapless victims.

It seems that the bestial Umgoop is the High Priest of the sunken kingdom of Neptunia. Along with a wicked High Priestess called Satania, the horror's main goal is to copy the excellent ideas of Unuk and Alok before him, namely the utter destruction of the USA and the enslave-ment of the rest of the surface world.

To further his plans Umgoop even manages to restore Unuk and Alok back to life with the aid of a few drops of "cosmo-serafluo." Each drop of his restorative elixir is produced from the body parts of 1200 victims, hence the need for all those arms and legs. The Mighty Mick and his battling buddy are also killed and brought back to life in this one. ("I kid you not," as Jack Parr used to say).

If nothing else, *Terrence X. O'Leary's War Birds* did represent a unique--although misguided--attempt to come up with something a little different in air war fare. Unfortunately, the magazine's risible plots gave the word "juvenile" a bad name.

As for those fine boyos, O'Leary and McGuffy, they constantly converse in a brogue that went out with vaudeville. (In case I have inadvertently made *Terence X. O'Leary's War Birds* sound like a lot of fun, let me assure gentle readers that wading through 50,000 word novels filled with great globs of phoney blarney dialect is a bit like swimming upstream through underfed piranha. Each sentence takes a bite out of you.)

With the O'Leary experiment finished, *War Birds* reverted gratefully to its original format. There was one more Terrence X air story cleared from inventory, "The Sky Hawk Screams" (October 1935). After that, the amazingly adaptable warrior returned to his previous scenes of glory--back on terra firma--in both *Battle Stories* and Dell's second series of *War Stories*.

The Mighty Mick's final pulp battles were fought in 1936. This time he popped up in Ethiopia where, as a major in Haile Selassie's army, he again commanded a cavalry squadron and was known as "The Green Lion of Judah."

After O'Leary's delirious encounters in the stratosphere with Unuk and Alok and Umgoop, Ethiopia must have seemed a relief.

JUSTICE, INC.

The year was 1939. It was a history book year. War had been declared in Europe but, as troops gathered on the western front and fortifications were strengthened, a strange calm persisted in America.

On the literary front, Steinbeck's *Grapes of Wrath* first saw print, as did C. S. Forrestor's *Captain Horatio Hornblower* and James Joyce's monumental *Finnegan's Wake*.

On yet another literary front, youthful readers of Street & Smith's *Doc Savage* pulp magazine thrilled to a special announcement: a new periodical was soon to be published. It was called *The Avenger*--the very name held a ring of excitement!--and the stories were to be written by none other than Kenneth Robeson, "the famous creator of Doc Savage." The new magazine would appear on newsstands August 2nd.

For most of Doc's fans the wait must have seemed interminable. Finally, the first issue of *The Avenger*, dated September 1939, was dropped in wire-wrapped bundles from distributors' trucks all across the continent.

On the cover, a giant, dead face with colorless eyes like ice in a polar dawn stared balefully down at a group of puny humans cupped within the figure's Brobdingnagian hands. It was all the fans could have desired. An inset box announced the title of the lead novel, "Justice, Inc."

The editorial column proclaimed: "We give you all the best that is in Kenneth Robeson's magic writing ability; and we give you a character that is the result of long and careful research and study, and not the result of a snap judgment. We have used the experience gained in making Doc Savage so successful, and feel that this new character will be of even more interest to you."

It was not pointed out, but the interior art was handled by Paul Orban, who was well known for his similar work on both Doc Savage and The Shadow.

There were other echoes of the publisher's dynamic duo. While Doc was known as The Man of Bronze, The Avenger became The Man of Steel. The Shadow had often been called The Master Avenger; Richard Henry Benson was simply The Avenger--a mysterious being with a terrifying countenance, "dead as wax, motionless as gray steel." Much had been made of The Shadow's "burning eyes"; The Avenger's were described as "colorless, marksman's eyes, as brilliant as moonstones with a light behind them."

It appears safe to assume that the cancellation of several of Street & Smith's single character pulp magazines and the announcement of The Avenger's birth was no accident. The Skipper, Bill Barnes and The Whisperer had all failed to capture the audience loyalty generated by their block-busters, Doc Savage and The Shadow. The Avenger was clearly an effort to form a hybrid of the company's more successful creations.

The magazine had much to recommend it. The "Kenneth Robeson" by-line was a strong plus factor, and with it The Avenger made an auspicious debut.

While the publishers exploited the Robeson name to the hilt, the stories were not actually written by "Kenneth

Robeson" nor even by Lester Dent, his tireless alter-ego. They were the product of still another well-known pulpster, Paul Frederick Ernst.

Born in 1902, Ernst had taken up fiction writing in his early twenties. Like many of his pulp confreres he was a prolific manufacturer of potboilers-made-to-order; he frequently employed smooth writing techniques combined with a fine story sense to bring new life to tired themes. Many of his stories in the early science fiction and fantasy magazines (*Astounding Stories, Strange Tales, Amazing*) were of high quality, and he was the author of the famous Doctor Satan series in *Weird Tales* (see chapter twelve). Later, when pulp magazine markets dried up, Ernst made a painless transition into the more prestigious "slick" magazines, where his skill with words earned him higher financial rewards.

Writing under the Robeson pseudonym, Ernst put real effort into The Avenger stories. The yarns were well plotted, characterizations were good, and there was an unusual amount of attention paid to detail, at least by prevailing pulp standards.

Nevertheless, few derivatives engender strong reader support. The most popular of pulp characters--Doc Savage, the Spider, G-8, The Shadow, Operator #5, the Phantom-- were all original creations. The novelty of their concepts, the youthful dreams they evoked, were rightfully stronger than the quality of writing that chronicled their fabulous exploits.

But, if The Avenger was a failure as an amalgam, he was at the very least an interesting failure and can perhaps be considered the last of the great pulp heroes.

His real name was Richard Henry Benson. He had made his millions by professional adventuring in the days when he was a warm, normal human being, before a traumatic criminal tragedy had transformed him into the dread Avenger.

In his teens Benson had spotted rubber in South American jungles, led native armies in Java, made aerial maps in the Congo. In his twenties he had mined amethysts in Australia and emeralds in Brazil, found gold in Alaska and diamonds in the Transvaal. He had done these things so successfully that while still a young man he was very wealthy. As noted before, wealth was almost a prerequisite for pulp heroes, despite (or perhaps because of) the fact that they were all children of the Great Depression. Whatever the sociological implications, there were obvious pragmatic factors: it took real bread to support such crime-fighting appurtenances as souped-up roadsters and high- speed autogyros.

In the first Avenger story, "Justice, Inc.," Richard Benson, now a world-renowned industrial engineer, boards a Montreal-bound airplane with his wife Alicia and their small daughter, Alice. While still over Lake Ontario, Benson returns from a trip to the lavatory to find that his wife and daughter have both vanished. Worse still, no one on the plane will admit to having even seen them previously. When the plane lands, Benson is alone.

In subsequent investigations Benson finds that both his loved ones have been dropped through a trap door into the icy waters of the lake--victims of a dreadful criminal error. The shock of his loss and the macabre nature of the tragedy combine to paralyze Benson's features, leaving his face as static as a wax mold, white, terrifying, never again to express emotion. Only his eyes could indicate that, "the glints in their colorless depths gleaming like ice under moonlight."

Much was made of The Avenger's unique physiognomy. In "The Smiling Dogs," Ernst/Robeson wrote: "His face was dead, like something dug out of a cemetery. The muscles were paralyzed so that never, under any circumstances, could they move in an expression. This dead, weird face was as white as snow--as white, in a word, as you'd expect any dead flesh to be! In the glacial expanse of the face were set eyes so light-gray as to seem absolutely colorless. They were like deep slitted holes into which you could peer and get a half glimpse of a world of fog and ice and personal despair."

Benson's extreme personal misfortune was probably the strongest motivation accorded any of the great pulp heroes. His was a death in life, without the wife and daughter crime had taken from him. Strong-willed, powerful, he is a Man of Destiny, stalking relentlessly through a desolate world, avenging but never replacing that which had been taken from him.

There is an archetypal scene at the end of "The Frosted Death," in which The Avenger stares emptily at the raging inferno of a shed into which he has lured his foes:

> *The fire lit up his wax-dead face and white hair. Fire that was saving nations from immediate war. The Avenger had succeeded in the greatest venture yet. But as always, success brought no content to his pale and awful eyes. He did not work for content. He knew that was impossible. He worked only to avenge the memory of his wife and daughter, killed by such scum as these--and for whose deaths all other scum should pay.*

The Avenger stories were well-plotted mysteries with mild science-fictional extrapolations. As in many of Street & Smith's pulps, the stories often seemed bland when compared to the wildly extravagant melodramas of rival publications. While The Man of Steel could (and often did) save the world from various Napoleons of crime, there was little of the incredible spectacle and macabre variations of such pulp giants as the Spider and Operator #5.

Eschewing the Spider's frenzied carnage, Dick Benson played it his own way--cooly and intellectuallly. He was the master of the last-minute escape, falling in and out of traps with consumate ease. He made it a policy, as a matter of fact, to allow himself to be trapped as often as possible, this being his unique way of finding out just what the heck was going on.

Mentally Benson was the equal of Doc Savage--a fellow expert in almost all fields of endeavor, with a mind that was a combination of camera and filing cabinet.

He differed from other superheroes in his physical make-up. Benson was but an average-sized man, just five-foot-eight and weighing barely 165 pounds. Needless to say, each of those pounds packed superb muscle quality, as demonstrated in most of the stories.

Another of his unique accomplishments related to the tremendous nervous shock that had paralyzed his face. The trauma had left his face in a curiously plastic state. The features could not move of themselves but under prodding fingers they could be molded into any shape desired--and would stay that way until they were carefully put back into place. Hence, The Avenger also became known as Man of a Thousand Faces.

Like most blessings, The Avenger's chameleon-like countenance was not without its drawbacks. His face could never express emotion; and, if pressed out of shape, it stayed that way--a constant menace to him when he went disguised.

If comic buffs believe that Stan Lee was the first to invent superguys with hangups, they are simply unaware of such pulp stalwarts as Dick Benson. In one of his adventures, while in disguise, a blow to his jaw flattened and distorted the dead flesh around his mouth. And the flesh simply stayed that way, like putty! A disconcerting phenomenon to be sure.

Nor was The Avenger immune to common errors in judgment.

Once, while disguised as a crew member of a hostile submarine, he was accosted by an old friend of the man whose role he was playing:

> *"Do you remember, Molan,"* the man
> asked, *"the time in Kolmogne when we*
> *went swimming and you saved my life?"*
> *A trap likely. If Benson said yes, the*

> man was apt to say there had been no such
> occurrence.
> "I'm afraid I do not," Benson said. "In
> fact, I do not remember ever having been
> in Kilmogne--"
> "Seize him!" the man screamed. "Brocker
> has a twitching of his right cheek muscles.
> This man has not. And he does not
> remember our childhood in Kolmogne."
> The Avenger had overestimated his
> man. The question had been a straight one
> and not a trick.
> The crew leaped toward him.

Following Doc Savage's lead, Benson's adventures were never solo performances; he became the leader of a small coterie of people known as Justice, Inc.--a group of people whose lives had been irreparably damaged by crime.

While still tracking down the murderers of his wife and child, The Man of Steel picked up two helpers. First assistance came from a dour Scots chemist named Fergus MacMurdie. MacMurdie's bleak, hard eyes reflected a tragedy similar to that of Benson's; he too had lost his family when protection racketeers bombed one of his drugstores. Like Benson, Mac's tragedy had left him indifferent to the threat of personal death, and he was eager to join The Avenger in a campaign against the scum who prey on innocent people.

Algernon Heathcote Smith--or just plain Smitty--was a Hercules. He stood six-foot-nine, weighed two hunded and eighty-five pounds, and wore a size nineteen collar. Smitty was an electrical engineer who had been framed and unjustly sent to prison for a year. He joined Justice, Inc. after nearly killing Benson in their first encounter, believing that The Avenger had come to arrest him on a false kidnapping charge.

Richard Henry Benson &
Algernon Heathcote Smith

In "The Yellow Hoard," the avenging trio met blonde diminuitive Nellie Gray, who quickly became a member of their group. Nellie was the Emma Peel of her day; a blonde grenade of a girl, barely five feet tall with soft blue eyes, she could fling herself like a dainty projectile, scattering men like Indian clubs. She joined Justice, Inc. after Benson and his aides solved the murder of her archaeologist father, saving the old man's cache of buried Aztec gold in the process. Though the treasure was in Nellie's name, it became the equivalent of Doc Savage's hoarde of inexhaustible Mayan gold.

Josh and Rosabel Newton joined the group next when Justice, Inc. rescued them from assassins in the mystery of "The Sky Walker." The Newtons were a black couple, unique in fiction of the time in that there was little trace of condescension in Ernst's portrayal of them. An honor graduate of Tuskegee Institute, Josh was often described as a "lithe, black panther" but he feigned Stepin Fetchit docility when it served his purposes. Josh's "protective coloration" was an ironic comment on the image of the black man in the films and fiction of the day.

In later issues, still another member joined the group in the person of Cole Wilson, a young mechanical engineer "with a streak of Robin Hood in him," but the character made less impact.

Headquarters for Justice, Inc. was located on Bleek Street, a short block in New York City. The street was unique in that it was entirely owned by Richard Henry Benson. Three brick buildings opposite a block-square warehouse had been thrown into one, to house his complete laboratory, office and living accommodations.

Over the entrance was a small sign:

JUSTICE, INC.

The many windows in the enormous room on the top floor of headquarters seemed to have Venetian blinds over them. But the slats were not wooden strips and could not be tilted. They were strips of nickel-steel, set at a forty-five degree angle so no bullet could penetrate the windows. Their ends were embedded in the masonry of the building.

The reason for such paranoid fortifications was that Bleek Street knew few unmotivated wayfarers. Quite often the street's only inhabitants were the ubiquitous baddies who made frequent sallies against The Avenger's fortress.

A closed-circuit television system linked the Bleek Street headquarters with a certain drugstore at Wayverly Place and Sixth Avenue. This was the store owned by Fergus MacMurdie and was perhaps the strangest drugstore in America.

The rear was twice as big as the front and was locked off from the store by a heavy iron door. In this big back room was a double laboratory. Along one side ran all the paraphernalia used by an expert chemist, which modestly described MacMurdie's abilities. Along the other was all the equipment needed by a first rank electrical engineer; and this was used by Smitty.

It was in these locations that Benson, aided by Mac and Smitty, invented and fabricated the scientific equipment and weapons used in their endeavors.

An entire article could be devoted to The Avenger's crime- fighting gadgets. They included: tiny, two-way belt radios (shades of Dick Tracy); bulletproof garments fashioned of special woven, transparent plastic that would turn anything up to a .50 calibre machine-gun bullet; and glass pellets containing a gas with such affinity for oxygen that it volatized instantly, spreading a black, impenetrable pall like instant night. The Avenger could touch a certain spot on his collar and, through the knot of his tie, spout this same inky pall, much the same as an octopus attempting to camouflage its hasty retreat.

The Avenger's automobile deserves special mention. It wasn't much to look at, being a rather dull 1935 model of a well- known inexpensive make. But it was the favorite automobile of Richard Benson who was rich enough to have ordered Rolls Royces in six-packs. It had a top speed of a hundred and thirty miles an hour--and don't think for a minute *that* wasn't science fiction. It was bullet-proofed throughout and equipped with devices and special little inventions for offense and defense that would have made an army tank officer gasp in disbelief.

When the vehicle was fired upon, powerful springs could ram bullet-proof windows into place instantly. A small tube opening just under the breather-cap on the radiator would retaliate with miniature torpedoes of potent knock-out gas.

Other more personal tools in The Avenger's arsenal included a pair of weapons that he kept strapped in slim sheaths on right and left calf, below the knee. He called one Mike and the other Ike. Mike was a special .22 revolver--so streamlined that it appeared to be a length of blue pipe--with a tiny cylinder holding only four cartridges and with a specially devised silencer on it. Ike was a needle-pointed throwing knife with a hollow tube for a handle, with which Benson could hit a fly-speck from twenty feet.

He tried not to kill, but went to elaborate lengths to ensure that criminals would destroy themselves in traps of their own devising. Whatever the merits of such moralistic hair-splitting, The Avenger's machinations did allow Paul Ernst to fashion some fascinating, albeit elaborate plot structures. If the plots creaked and groaned at times readers seldom complained, thanks to the magic secret of pulp fiction writing: pace, pace, pace. Action was spooned out in great dollops. Fans had no time to stop and ponder.

Despite strong action plots and sympathetic characters, the adventures or Richard Henry Benson lasted but some twenty-four issues in his own magazine. For a short time there was an Avenger comic strip running in Street & Smith's *Shadow Comics* and even an Avenger radio serial carried by Station WHN in New York City and syndicated to other parts of the country.

The magazine had begun with high hopes in September of 1939, but at a time when other pulps were beginning to lose some of their vast audience to the lure of radio, motion pictures and the new breed of superhero comic book. It started as a monthly and ran that way for eleven issues, through July 1940. Thirteen more issues were pubished bi-monthly

In its brief lifetime, the series spanned two distinct eras. Volumes I and II followed the adventures of Dick Benson while his face was still paralyzed from his personal ordeal. This era featured the ominous cover portraits of H. W. Scott--covers that combined foreground action with the brooding face of a giant Avenger.

Beginning with volume III, Dick Benson suffered "a nerve shock of a different sort," regaining his normal appearance. The covers also became more mundane in aspect. These were executed with routine competence by Graves Gladney, Lenosci, and Leslie Ross.

The changes in Benson's physical appearance augured worse things to come. With its third anniversary issue, September 1942, came the sad announcement that the magazine was folding and that the stories would be continued as novelettes in *Clues Detective* magazine. This was the kiss of death that had been accorded such other Street & Smith heroes as Bill Barnes and The Whisperer.

Emile C. Tepperman, pulpdom's favorite take-over specialist was assigned the continuation of the series in short story form. Five of these truncated Avengers appeared in *Clues*, with a sixth and final one popping up in the back pages of *The Shadow*. Unlike Paul Ernst's concept, Tepperman's Avenger was a more violent character, shooting to kill rather than incapacitate.

The Street & Smith company was an old family firm first founded in 1855. Over several generations they had promoted such characters as Jesse James, Buffalo Bill Cody, Frank Merriwell and Horation Alger, Jr. into household names. In the early 1930s, with The Shadow and Doc Savage, they literally invented the superhero.

The Avenger was clearly another attempt to produce a national institution. What had gone wrong? The answer lay in the history of the pulp hero mystique.

During the "roaring twenties" and early thirties in America, organized crime went unchecked. The average man felt helpless. When The Shadow entered the scene in 1931, that same average guy was in the mood for instant justice. The Shadow meted it out with blazing .45s and chilling laughter. When Doc Savage arrived, he carried the fight to global proportions. The Spider started off still another playboy detective but quickly became enshrined as a ferocious national savior. By the time Operator #5 entered the picture, the North American continent required monthly salvation from incalculable armies of fiendish invaders. Still more demigods rose to join the fray: Secret Agent X, The Whisperer, The Phantom, The Secret Six. Tens of millions of readers thrilled to their exploits. Entire forests were levelled to spread the word. The law may have been helpless, institutions trampled and broken, but this secret army of incorruptible champions would arise--often with only minutes to spare--to restore order and sanity to a universe threatened by madness.

The truth was that by the time The Avenger made his entrance in 1939, he was simply an unnecessary commodity. Because he was second best he had tried harder. But the timing was all wrong.

The world did not require another good ten-cent hero.

MASTERS OF MENACE

Everybody loves a bad guy.

...Not in everyday life perhaps, but in the larger-than-life world of vicarious thrills and adventure.

The great heroes of the pulp magazines could never have existed without an unceasing flow of enthusiastic foes. There were hundreds of pulp villains--thousands of them--cackling, scheming, dreaming. And barely a dull or uninteresting personality in the lot. Each month a plethora of magazines shrilled news of their bizarre affronts:

> *From out of the East swings the Oriental mastermind, Shiwan Khan, into New York in another attempt at world domination! The mysterious power of the Orient against The Shadow's automatics as Shiwan Khan attempts to rule the world!*
> (Shiwan Khan returns--*The Shadow*
> magazine, December 1939)

*Over New York fell the murderous spell
of Death's burning stare--and men died in
the throes of some terrible, secret, inner
fire! Richard Wentworth, alone, as THE
SPIDER, dared challenge this astounding attack by a modern Genghis Khan
gone mad...this new and fearful crime
master who had blanketed Manhattan in
the human ashes of his helpless victims!*
(Blight of the Blazing Eye--
The Spider magazine,April 1939)

*He came from the very fires of Hell to
blight the living, and he cared not for the
cost of his lust! It was G-8 who had to
meet this living scourge and match with
his human courage and brains a Lust and
a Hate and a Scorn for Life such as The
Earth Had Never Known!*
(Scourge of the Steel Mask--*G-8 And
His Battle Aces*, January 1937)

If the bad guys were almost as popular as the good
guys in the hero magazines, it seems inevitable that
sooner or later someone should have thought of starring
a super-villain in his very own magazine. Oddly enough,
that was not to happen until given the sales impetus of an
entire new breed of magazine: the weird menace pulp.

The so-called weird menace field was conceived in
1933 when Popular Publications' Henry Steeger decided to
revamp the ailing *Dime Mystery* magazine. He used as his
inspiration the nineteenth-century Gothic romances of
Horace Walpole and Ann Radcliffe combined with the
visceral appeal of the legendary Grand Guignol of Paris,
a theatrical company that specialized in the realistic
depiction of scenes of torture, horror and bloodshed.

Infused with new blood (literally), *Dime Mystery*
emerged as one of the best-selling titles in the pulp field.

Under the canny editorship of Rogers Terrill, the new/old magazine was so successful that Popular soon issued two more titles in a sanguinary vein: *Terror Tales* and *Horror Stories*. Rival publishers soon trailed with *Thrilling Mystery*, *Eerie Mysteries*, *Uncanny*, and *Sinister Stories* among others.

Mild by the unshockable standards of the 1990s, the weird menace pulps were considered pretty racy stuff in their day; their stories flirted with sado-sexual themes and their covers usually portrayed young women in bras and panties (and sometimes less) at the mercies of slavering nogoodnicks.

Even though the stories were seldom as salacious as the covers promised, these few magazines were largely responsible for the low opinion many people held (and still hold) of the entire pulp fiction field. Many dealers sold them under the counter, and New York's Mayor Fiorello La Guardia singled them out when he warned the pulp publishers to clean up their act--or get out of town.

The weird menace yarns usually stuck to twentieth century settings but paid due homage to such trappings of Gothicism as: threatened heroines, storm-lashed nights, dank castles, Stygian caves, secret passages, and purple prose. Many of the top pulp fiction writers (Hugh B. Cave, Ray Cummings, Arthur Leo Zagat, and Norvell Page) churned out stories for this sub-genre. The writing was formula stuff, similar in many ways to the Gothic romance market of today, although decidedly more colorful.

The covers were great, though--especially if you have a taste for the preposterous; and who could resist such titles as "The Corpse Wants Your Widow," "Our Host, The Madman," "Mate For the Thing in the Box," "The Werewolf of Wall Street," and--my favorite--"The Corpses' Christmas Party"?

It was only a matter of time before someone came up with the idea of combining the appeal of the single character pulp hero genre with the weird-horror pulps. The first such hybrid burbled out of its cauldron in February of 1935.

It's name was *Doctor Death*.

In fact Doctor Death had been previewed a year earlier in a series of four novellas by Edward P. Norris in Dell Publishing Company's *All Detective*. With the February 1935 number, *All Detective* became *Doctor Death*, thus inaugurating pulpdom's first full-fledged villain magazine.

Like all of the single character villain pulps to follow, *Doctor Death* failed to capture readers' fancies and the magazine lasted only three short issues. But what issues they were!

The first full-length Doc Death novel was called "Twelve Must Die" and it was credited to a writer with the single cognomen of Zorro--who was not Johnston McCulley's famed Robin Hood of California, but simply the penname of a pulpster with the unprepossessing name of Harold Ward. Ward, who died in 1950, was a newspaperman, song writer and theatrical press agent, who had achieved some success in the early pulps. He was one of the mainstays of the legendary *Black Mask* when it began its life in 1920, and was a regular in the equally legendary *Weird Tales* magazine prior to his work on Doctor Death.

Ward was never a full-time fiction writer but wrote nights, after work, typing rapidly with two fingers. Unlike many pulp pros, he never submitted first draft material, preferring to rework patiently until he was satisfied. It is amusing to think that the man would write such terror-filled manuscripts as "The Shrivellng Murders" and "The Gray Creatures" was also the author of some two-hundred Tin Pan Alley songs of the soft, mushy, sentimental variety--the kind wherein the singer informs his beloved that "Under a moon is a good place to spoon some night in June," etc. Who knows? Doctor Death may have been Ward's revenge on the public that lapped up such stuff.

The character of Doctor Death as expounded by Ward in "12 Must Die" is certainly one of the wackiest, most entertaining villainous creations in the history of the pulps.

The world's greatest occultist, ex-Dean of Psychology at Yale, Doctor Death (or Doctor Rance Mandarin as he was once known) is described as a white-thatched, cadaverous figure with a thin face, hooked nose and weirdly-glaring, deep-set eyes. If a movie had been made of Doctor Death back in the 1930s the part could have been played to perfection by Ernest Thesiger, the late, great character actor who portrayed the wonderfully nutty Dr. Pretorius in Universal's *Bride of Frankenstein*.

A habitue of caves and underground places, the old man is a human fungus who appears to have an affinity with the earth itself. It is this affinity perhaps that makes him one of the world's leading but most misguided amateur ecologists. Despite the author's assurance that "maggots of madness" are chiseling into the old man's brain like feasting woodpeckers, Death is portrayed almost sympathetically as a half-crazed old dotard who, deprived of his Messianic tendencies, would probably be content to while away his days, and especially nights, in his gloomy caves, caring for his fungi. His one fatal flaw is that he is sincere--a sincere fanatic that is.

Like John Brown, he believed that he had a mission-- that an all-seeing Creator had placed him on this earth to accomplish certain goals, and that the mantle of sanctification made it impossible for him to commit a wrong. (Perhaps no one is a villain to himself. Mob boss Al Capone once bragged that all he wanted to do was bring a little happiness into the world).

In the name of righteousness Dr. Death had made himself master of the black arts: necromancy, sorcery, metemsphychosis, demonology, divination--you name it. Backed up by regiments of zombie stooges, dissolution rays, anti-gravity flying machines, and gelatinous, vermin-gray primal earth forces, the dedicated doctor waged a concerted attack upon 4000 years of civilization.

In order to destroy the plutocracy of science and hopefully return everything to a virginal state, Death selects as his target the world's leading scientists and begins to destroy them one by one. Using methods both weird and singular, he delivers his ulatimatum to a reeling society:

"The wheels of industry must stop. Scientists must cease their work. All patents in the United States Patent office must be destroyed. The cities must be emptied and men must return to the soil. Eventually I intend to wipe out all cities as I have destroyed the aircraft plant of the men who disobeyed my commands. To do so now would cause the deaths of many innocent people, and I have no quarrel with the common man. I intend, therefore, to give the cities time to purge themelves before I blast them to dust.

"Two weeks from today, on August 24th, unless I see that steps have been taken to carry out my commands, I strike again. The national capital will be crumpled into dust and the dust scattered to the four winds of heaven. Following that, another respite of two weeks will be given. Then I strike for the last time. When I finish, not a plant of any consequence, not a machine, not a building of importance will be left in the hemisphere."

Tough talk! But old Doc Death had the wherewithal to back it up.

Arrayed against him in his fight for the Good Life were a handful of recurring characters, principal among them being Jimmy Holm, the ostensible hero of the piece. Jimmy's biography was true to the great pulp hero tradition. Orphaned at an early age, his guardianship had been placed in the hands of the man who later became mayor of the great city. A millionaire many times over,

Jimmy distinguished himself by his studies in chemistry, psychology and the occult, and later, after traveling extensively, had surprised his guardian by requesting a position in the city's detective bureau.

Jimmy's friend and superior was Detective Inspector John Ricks, a grizzled, honest "copper" who had clubbed and fought his way from a routine beat to the position of the head of the greatest detective force in the world.

Ricks and Jimmy are joined in their battle against Death by Nina Fererra, Mandarin's own beautiful niece who comes to recognize the extent of her uncle's madness.

Later, in a remarkable secret meeting held in a small town on the east coast, Franklin D. Roosevelt himself forms an organization known as the Secret Twelve--a dozen influential figures all concerted in their fight to curb Dr. Death's exaggerated Socialistic tendencies--headed by the President of the United States and with Jimmy Holm as his managing director.

In the meantime, the object of the Secret Twelve's vigilante justice was operating from a hideout only a quarter of a mile from Lake View cemetery, connected to it by a cavern once used as a burial ground by the ancient Mound Builders. A perfect spot for Death to function. It was here that the old fiend collected and stacked like cordwood hundreds of dead bodies in his recruitment drives for zombie armies.

"I am anticipating the future," he bragged to Jimmy Holm. "When the time comes that all mechanical activity ceases, there will be a need for additional labor. It will be hard for man to adjust to changing conditions. Nor is it the Creator's desire that humanity should become a race of slaves. These Zombies, then, must do the drudgery."

Like many of pulpdom's mad villains, Dr. Death had the natural pride of an originator. It was his fatal flaw. Over and over again, just when he should be concentrating on the primary task of eliminating his chief antagonist, he takes time out to justify his actions or to brag about his genius. The consequences of such foolish technique is that

"12 Must Die" ends happily for society with Death temporarily routed, his headquarters--and with it all his infernal apparati--burned to the ground. Nina is awarded The Congressional Medal by a grateful President and she and Jimmy announce their wedding plans.

But wait. One of the President's secretaries hands a wire to Jimmy, who glances at it and then passes it on to the President to read aloud.

CONGRATULATIONS ON YOUR APPROACHING WEDDING. TAKE WARNING: GOD GAVE ME THE RIGHT TO DESTROY AND THE WEAPONS WITH WHICH TO WORK. THE WORLD MUST BE SAVED FROM ITSELF AND I AM THE INSTRUMENT. I GO, BUT SOON I WILL RETURN.

--DOCTOR DEATH

Return he did, and only a month later, in a story called "The Gray Creatures." That one began with Death's kidnaping of Nina and his consequent flight to Egypt in a scheme designed to bring civilization to its knees through instant overpopulation. Aware of the countless millions of Egyptians buried in the past whose bodies had been preserved through mumification, the diabolical doctor envisioned bringing to life hordes of men and women who had walked the earth thousands of years before Christ. He pictured a world inundated by living corpses, every spot as thickly settled as New York City.

Needless to report, he was eventually foiled in his scheme-- but only after a dozen cliffhanger scenes of chills and thrills. The novel ended with Death crushed beneath an avalanche of rock in far-off Egypt.

Death epic number three, "The Shriveling Murders," began with a remarkable scene in which President Roosevelt called together a special meeting of the Secret Twelve. With trembling fingers, the President removed from his briefcase a small shoe box done up in brown wrapping paper.

> *"This arrived at the White House by*
> *special delivery late this afternoon," the*
> *President whispered. "Look!"*
> *He lifted the lid. In the box was the tiny*
> *figure of a man, perfect in every detail, yet*
> *smaller than a new born infant.*
> *It was the body of the Vice-President of*
> *the United States.*

But that was only the beginning. The President proclaims a State of Dictatorship. More great men shrink right out of their clothes. There is a lovely but sadistic Egyptian princess; voodoo rites in the Louisiana outback; horrific doings beneath an asylum for the homicidally insane; poisoned postage stamps; the theft of Cagliostro's secrets from the Library of Congress; and last but not least, Death's final confrontation in the gloomy caverns on the little island in the middle of his beloved swampland.

Meanwhile, over at *Weird Tales*, the legendary magazine (under the editorship of the equally legendary Farnsworth Wright) was undergoing some lean days. Circulation was down--despite its fame, the magazine at the best of times was seldom far out of the red--and Wright was concerned that the new weird menace pulps, *Terror Tales* and *Horror Stories*, might be draining off some of his old-time readers. In retrospect it seems doubtful that this was so, due to the fact that *Weird Tales* had long established its reputation as a quality vehicle for literate tales of imagination and the supernatural. The weird menace pulps, on the other hand, appealed blatantly to less sophisticated readers who did not demand writing above a cliche level and who, in fact, preferred mundane explanations for supernatural trappings.

Wright attempted to appeal to both factions when in August of 1935 he introduced a new series character to the pages of "the Unique Magazine." That character, Doctor Satan, is included within the scope of this investigation not because he was ever honored with his own magazine but because he was an obvious blood kin to Doctor Death (they may have attended the same medical school) and because he was linked to the supervillains yet to come.

Loyal *Weird Tales* readers must have been startled when they witnessed Margaret Brundage's cover for that landmark issue. Her painting featured a masked figure dressed in an outlandish devil's costume complete with horns and a scarlet cape. The cover blurb announced: "Meet the sinister and mysterious Doctor Satan--the world's weirdest criminal."

If the character on the cover appeared to be dressed somewhat ludicrously, it was not because Ms. Brundage embroidered the author's initial description of Satan's habiliment: "The figure looked like one robed for a costume ball, save that in every line of it was a deadliness that robbed it of all suggestions of anything humorous or social.

"Tall and spare, it was covered by a blood-red robe. Red rubber gloves swathed the hands. The face was concealed behind a red mask that curtained it from forehead to chin with only two black eyes, like living coals, showing through the eye-holes.

"Lucifer! And to complete the medieval portrait of the Archfiend, two horned red projections showed above the red skullcap that hid the man's hair."

While Doc Satan may not have looked like your average pulp maniac, his actions certainly qualified him for that elite brotherhood.

In the editorial pages of that debut issue, Wright somewhat nervously announced: "We await with eager interest your verdict on the stories about Dr. Satan, the first of which is published in this issue...To those of you who are afraid that *Weird Tales* will degenerate into just another detective magazine, we definitely promise that it will not do so...If the stories about Dr. Satan and Ascott Keane--the world's greatest criminal and strangest criminologist--are ordinary detective stories, then we do not know a weird story when we see one."

There was little danger of the astute editor not recognizing a weird tale when he saw one. In the first story, titled simply "Doctor Satan," sides are drawn. The hero of the piece is a criminal investigator named Ascott Keane (love that name!), a man who has "raised a hobby of criminology into an art that passes genius." Keane is clearly patterned after Sherlock Holmes, that Victorian archetype whose hawk-visaged face and steel-trap mind were seminal influences on many a pulp hero.

The investigator is accompanied by his "secretary and companion" beautiful Beatrice Dale, while Satan is backed up by a monkey-like man named Girf and a legless giant named Bostiff, proving once again that a man can be judged by the company he keeps.

In the first story, hints are given as to Satan's real identity: that of a rich man, still young, with a family name known to everyone in America, a man jaded with purchased thrills who has made a study of super science and the occult in order to become the world's leading criminal.

Satan makes his criminal debut with the aid of a little science and more than a soupcon of the occult. He begins by blackmailing and then destroying millionaires by his unsettling use of a species of Australian thornbush. Altered by the malefic doctor's botanical skills, the thornbush seed, a tiny thing that floats in the air, is first inhaled by the victim and then roosts itself in his brain before flowering a mere hour or two later.

When the doctor finds his scheme threatened by criminologist Keane, he trots out his second little surprise: a destroying voodoo flame first compounded in temples along the Nile some 5000 years ago. Keene counteracts with the green paste which the old priests used against the consuming flame of their enemies.

"I'll not underestimate you a second time," Doctor Satan warns. "The death shrub--the blue flame--you are armed against those. But I have other weapons."

The Mephistophelian inventor unleashed his other

weapons in the string of seven novelettes that followed: "The Man Who Chained The Lightning," "Hollywood Horror," "The Consuming Flame," "Horror Insured," "Beyond Death's Gateway," "The Devil's Double," and "Mask of Death."

Satan's arsenal included: static electricity bombs, Cretan voodoo dolls, a time diverter, occult dragons, and a deadly crystalline lightning tube. One of the arch-fiends choicest pieces of blackmail machinery involved an atomic ray which he used to realign the molecular stucture of skin. Beaming the ray from a movie studio light, he was able to change the world-famous faces of Hollywood stars into grinning skulls--and right in the middle of a take.

As the series progressed Ascott Keane followed Dr. Satan right into the realm of death itself, discovered that there was an actual hell...and had cause to wonder if his red-cloaked foe was in fact the incarnation of Old Scratch himself.

The Dr. Satan stories were all turned out by Paul Ernst, a popular and prolific writer whose name was a staple in the weird menace sub-genre, and who later wrote the Avenger novels under the famous Kenneth Robeson by-line. In addition, Ernst was already well known in the pages of the Unique Magazine. One of his non-Doctor Satan stories, "The Way Home" (*Weird Tales*, November 1935) is considered a near-classic in the field. Ernst's Satan yarns were all competently written and are still fun to read, but it soon became evident that loyal *Weird Tales* readers wanted no part of the formula.

"Glad you left out Dr. Satan," one indignant fan wrote in the magazine's letter column. "We readers can struggle along very nicely without him. A super detective against a super crook has no place in a magazine devoted to Weird Tales."

Fearful that more old readers would be repelled than new readers attracted, Wright could only concur and the series was peremptorily dropped.

Stimulated by the advent of the Doctors Death and Satan, the folks at Popular Publications (who started the whole thing when they revamped *Dime Mystery*) decided to come up with a villain magazine of their own. They used as their model Sax Rohmer's immensely successful creation, Dr. Fu Manchu.

Entire books could, and should, be written about the Yellow Peril theme which was prevalent in the literature and theater of the West in the first half of this century. No matter what depths of ignorance and paranoia it sprang from, the menace of the Yellow Peril certainly added thrills and chills to literally thousands of motion pictures, plays, books, magazines and even comics. Today it is a quaint footnote in the history of pop literature--an era of adventurous menace that a more tolerant and more sophisticated society can no longer endorse.

Sax Rohmer more than any other writer brought world fame to London's Chinatown in the East End Limehouse District. In Rohmer's day the area was a badly-lit maze of alleyways where opium dens actually flourished and cutthroats really stalked. It was there, in 1911, that young Arthur Henry Ward recorded his first glimpse of "Mr. King," Chinatown's uncrowned ruler of crime.

"I knew that I had seen Dr. Fu Manchu!" Ward said. "His face was the living embodiment of Satan." That same year, Ward, writing under the pseudonym Sax Rohmer, finished the first of the Fu Manchu thrillers that would bring him lasting fame and would influence the entire body of popular literature for years to come.

Rohmer was not the first to exploit the Yellow Peril theme (a good decade earlier some of M.P. Shiel's novels were of the Oriental-hordes-invading-the-West type), but he certainly did it with more style and with decidedly more impact on the mass collective unconscious. Furthermore he added his own wrinkle: not just an individual menace, but a secret international organization consisting of criminous types representing all races and countries.

Small wonder that Popular's first all-villain pulp should be titled *The Mysterious Wu Fang*. In 1935, when the Wu Fang magazine made its debut, the name of Fu Manchu was already a household word; the Fu Manchu books were best-sellers and they were usually serialized in such prestigious slick magazines as *Colliers* and *Liberty*. If the public confused one character with the other the confusion could only aid the sales of the humble pulp magazine.

Oddly enough, the name Wu Fang was in itself not completely unknown at the time of his pulp magazine debut. As early as 1915 Arthur K. Reeve, creator of Craig Kennedy the Scientific Detective, had featured an Oriental mastermind of that name in his Kennedy novel, *The Romance of Elaine*. The villainous creation was carried over into the Pathe serial version starring serial queen Pearl White.

Silent movie audiences must have responded to the thrill of the Yellow Peril because Wu Fang became Miss White's own saffron menace in a number of early chapter plays. In one such thriller, *The Lightning Raider* (1919), he was portrayed by Warner Oland, a Swedish actor who later graduated to playing Fu Manchu himself as well as the decidedly non-villainous Charlie Chan.

For a few years there was even a British Wu Fang; his adventures as related by Roland Daniel appeared first in *The Thriller* and in such books as *Wu Fang* (1929), *Wu Fang's Revenge* (1934), *The Son of Wu Fang* (1935), and *The Return of Wu Fang* (1937).

The character Wu Fang also turned up in comic strips (notably *Dan Dunn, Secret Operator 48*) and in comic books as well. Unlike Sax Rohmer's menace, old Wu seems to have been in the public domain, a sort of unlicensed yellow terror.

Doing their best to add to the identity crisis, the publishers of Wu Fang obtained the services of illustrator John Richard Flanagan, a fine commercial artist who had illustrated all of Sax Rohmer's stories in *Colliers* from

1929 to 1935 as well as the American book edition of *The Mask of Fu Manchu.*

Known alternatively as the Emperor of Death and the Yellow Dragon Lord of Crime, the mysterious Wu Fang was described as a tall, gaunt figure with sloping shoulders; his mouth was pinched and narrow, but the upper part of his face above the hideously gleaming green eyes widened to a forehead of great brain capacity. He usually wore a yellow silk robe embroidered across the front with a dragon--and was thus depicted in Jerome Rozen's excellent cover paintings.

Rozen's depictions were true to the mood of the Wu Fang stories, which in turn reflected the entire Rohmerian netherworld of secret passages, dank caves, trap doors, Egyptian tombs, poisonous creepy-crawlies, and the ubiquitous hordes of leering acolytes.

When publisher Henry Steeger first decided to do a Fu Manchu type magazine he chose as his writer Robert J. Hogan of *G-8 and His Battle Aces* fame. Hogan was no stranger to themes of Oriental menace, having successfuly transplanted a Chinese villain--the infamous warlord, Chu Lung--into The Master Spy's adventures on the Western Front during World War One. Editorship of Wu Fang was handed over to young and pretty Edythe Seims, who was also a veteran of the G-8 magazine.

Under Hogan's guidance Wu Fang emerged as a worthy godson of the notorious Devil Doctor. Like his prototype, he operated at first from Limehouse London but the ever-lasting contest between Wu Fang and his heroic adversaries soon spread around the world.

Playing the Nayland Smith to Wu's Fu Manchu was Val Kildare, former number one investigator of the United States Secret Serice.

The hero of the original Fu Manchu books, Nayland Smith, was British through and through--a character based, in turn, on Conan Doyle's Sherlock Holmes. Val is, of course, American but on occasion he reveals his literary ancestry with such Anglicized exclamations as "Jove, what a pity."

One of the Wu Fang magazine editorials even went so far as to compare Val directly to the Great Detective of Baker Street: "Out of sheer modesty we concede that Mr. Kildare has not yet attained the prominence of Sherlock Holmes. But being younger, we are convinced that he can not only think as clearly, but can run faster and fight harder than the distinguished gentleman from Scotland Yard (sic)."

Aiding Kildare in his battle against the sinister symbol of the night is young Jerry Hazard, a newspaper reporter. Jerry is eventually crippled and retires voluntarily from the fray in favor of a two-fisted explorer and archeologist named Rod Carson.

Their wily nemesis played it safe by employing hundreds of helpers, although he preferred the company of female slaves. Old Wu was unlucky in love, however--he thought that whips made up for caresses. As was often the case in pulp melodrama, his number one aide, a beautiful young lady named Mohra, fell in love and ran off with Jerry Hazard. Later still, Wu's tall, blonde helper, Tanya, began making eyes at Rod Carson. No wonder Wu was mad.

Ever faithful to him were such staunch buddies as Zaru the beast man, who was part ape, and Djigas, who was described as being the most repulsive of Wu's agents. Djigas was keeper of the Death Beasts--a poisonous menagerie of vipers, spiders, bats, and scaly mini-monsters that combined the worst features of the lizard, the toad, and the rat.

Wu employed these and other little pets throughout a series of seven fast-paced novels beginning with "The Case of the Six Coffins." He was killed off in his sixth caper ("The Case of he Black Lotus") but the following month saw him resurrected from his glass sarcophogus. That particular yarn ("The Case of the Hidden Scourge") sent the saffron scourge packing off to Bagdad hot on the trail of electrical secrets first developed by Nebuchadnezzar when he illuminated the ancient hanging gardens.

Nebuchadnezzar's secret suggested a plan whereby one man (guess who?) could fry every person on earth who uses electricity.

True to format, the Hidden Scourge ended with wily Wu once again in shackles, his shocking schemes short-circuited.

"It is written," Wu Fang cooed through his thin, cruel lips, "that defeat is often nearest when victory appears to come."

The Dragon Lord of Crime was to have the last word. His statement was the last one uttered in the final issue of the magazine.

It is not certain whether the Wu Fang title was discontinued because of poor sales or because Sax Rohmer may have finally balked at the use of a name so close to that of his famous creation. In any case, the folks at Popular Publications must have retained faith in the idea of an Oriental menace magazine; after a mere two month breather they introduced a similar title--*Dr. Yen Sin.*

Yen Sin as portrayed on Jerome Rozen's cover looked suspiciously like his predecessor, Wu Fang. In fact the cover was commissioned for the eighth Wu Fang novel, "The Case of the Living Poison," which was announced but never issued. It seemed to matter little since both characters were based on the identical model--Fu Manchu.

The editor of the new magazine was Ken White. Interior illustrations were handled by Ralph Carlson, and the novels themselves were written by pulp writer Donald E. Keyhoe--the same man who as Major Donald E. Keyhoe was to become well known as the author of five best-selling "fact" books on UFOs.

Keyhoe shifted the scene from London's Limehouse to Washington, D.C. It is a Washington that must have seemed foreign to Americans of the year 1936: fog-shrouded, mysterious, deadly, with dark doings in places both high and low. (Think of it... this is forty years before the Watergate conspiracy; Yen Sin probably ranks as the most prophetic pulp to precede John Campbell's *Astounding Science Fiction*).

Fog, like a sinister cloak, had swept in from the Potomac, enshrouding Washington in its clammy folds. By nine o'clock, the Capital lay buried under an ocean of drifting mist, the light of Pennysylvania Avenue only blurred yellow spots in the almost impenetrable gloom.

Unseen cars crawled along the famous thoroughfare, the hoarse blasts of their horns muffled in the evil-smelling murk. Shadowy forms moved like phantoms in the fog.

But there was one shadow that did not move.

Almost invisible in the blackness of a shop entry, stood a motionless figure. Except for its low, harsh breathing, it might have been a dummy--a wooden figure placed there to draw attention to the trinkets in the window. But the window was dark, and the shop was closed.

Minutes passed, and still the shadow did not move. There was something more than ominous about that crouching form. It was as though Death itself lurked there in the fog, inexorably waiting.

Just once, the man's arm lifted. For an instant, blurred light from the nearby restaurant fell on a dark-skinned hand, on a curious silken noose gripped between powerful fingers. Then the hand was jerked back, and the strangler's cord was swiftly hidden from view...

From those opening paragraphs we are plunged into an unrelenting world of night, a universe dominated by mystery and murder...and even worse. Burmese blow guns poke from raised coffin lids. Innocent-seeming chair covers conceal Dacoit stranglers. Beams of emerald flame cut through walls and windows. Torture chambers beneath the Potomac. Tibetan Corpse- flowers. Mummies that sing. Corpses with their heads sewn on backwards. It's the formula as before, straight from the special world of magic and menace that only Sax Rohmer could have inspired.

Dr. Yen Sin, also known as the Crime Emperor and the Invisible Peril, was more or less interchangeable with other Oriental menaces (one can postulate a medical college somewhere in Kwangchow that specialized in graduating Evil Doctors *magna cum laude*). His eyes were a de rigeur green, although sometimes his pupils enlarged like hypnotic black pools--bottomless, malignant. Yen's symbol was a cobra. He was taller than most Chinese--an expert might have traced the Manchurian blood which coursed in his veins--and his feline grace was accentuated by the silken folds of his mandarin costume.

Fortunately, the good guy of the piece, Michael Traile, was considerably more interesting than most. Traile was known as The Man Who Never Slept, pre-dating Lawrence Block's Evan Tanner, "The Thief Who Never Slept," by several decades.

Traile had been the youthful victim of a hasty brain operation by a Hindu surgeon. His horrified parents had discovered after the operation that the surgeon had damaged the lobes of the brain controlling the function of sleep. An Indian Yogi had saved his life by teaching him the art of relaxing his body completely, even though his mind would ever be awake.

"That's the reason for my hobbies--my studies--my eternally keeping busy," Traile once confided to his adventurous side-kick, Eric Gordon. "Be thankful that you can lie down--close your eyes, and shut out the world for a few blessed hours. I have never known a single instant of forgetfulness--in twenty-seven years!"

Traile's functional apartment contained no bedroom, thus frustrating Yen Sin who, like Fu Manchu, made a habit of springing surprises on sleeping adversaries. Instead, the apartment was a maze of exotic weapons, gun cases, lamps, sword, carvings and curios from scores of countries. The objects were like monuments down the long vista of sleepless years, even to the language books on his table--reminders of Traile's endless search for new challenges to ward off the desolation of endless nights.

While most of us would consider his affliction a blessing--he had his nights free to read and bone up on all the world's knowledge--Traile himself considered it his Achilles heel. He had an imperative need for recharging his vitality by frequent rest periods; prolonged action without a yoga-like relaxation would bring on a state of exhaustion terrifying in its sudden effect. He knew that not even sheer agony, not a stunning blow, could blot out his wakeful brain. Death was the only sleep he would ever know.

Despite this intriguing hero-with-a-hangup, the new magazine was even less successful than its predecessor. The career of the Crime Emperor was terminated after three brief forays into print. (Sales were not the only reason; publisher Steeger has since related that he yanked the magazine off the stands when someone pointed out that Yen Sin sounded like a sexual reference in Hebrew).

As in all the super-villain magazines, the series had no resolution. At the end of the third novel, Dr. Yen Sin remained still at large. Somewhere in the Valhalla of pulp villains, Wu Fang and Yen Sin must still exist, plotting their evil schemes, dreaming their insane dreams.

Two of the strangest and most puzzling of all pulp magazines were *The Octopus* and *The Scorpion*. The magazines lasted but one issue each and one was really a follow-up to the other. For years pulp historians believed that both issues were written by Norvel W. Page (under the pseudonym Randolph Craig), the super- imaginative chronicler of the Spider's turbulent tribulations. Small wonder since both *The Octopus* and *The Scorpion* race with Page's brand of manic invention and overheated melodrama. But researcher Robert Weinberg has since revealed that payment checks for both stories were made out to the husband-and-wife team of Ejler and Edith Jacobson, Page's fellow specialists in the weird menace field. If Page did write both novels, it's possible that the Jacobsons were paid to retool his Octopus character into the equally sinister Scorpion--surely the most bizarre mutation in fictional history.

The first and only issue of *The Octopus* (listed on the contents page as Volume I, Number 4 for reasons that only pulp publisher's accountants understood) contained an editorial feature that attempted to explain something of the magazine's new slant on villainy.

> *The pages of man's history are crowded with strange and awesome legends," the editorial began, "weird, unauthenticated tales of monstrous beings and eerie happenings. Of them all, perhaps the most fantastically grewsome (sic) is the little-known legend of the 'Purple Eye'. All the evils of mankind (so runs this legend) can be blamed upon the men with purple eyes. During every great social catastrophe in history, purple eyes have made their appearance as harbingers of destruction.....Randolph Craig--an author of national reputation who has assumed this non de plume for the purpose of this series--has, in the pages which follow, revived this figure out of ancient legend. He has made of him a modern super-criminal who, for protective purposes, has assumed the name of the Octopus. And he has given him all those truly weird and terrifying powers which modern science can bestow upon a great intellect.*

Other than that outre historical footnote, there is no more attempt to explain who the Octopus is, or what fuels his insane range. He is the consummate, interchangeable master villain: a madman willing to destroy human society in order to dominate it.

Physically the Octopus would draw second-takes in any crowd, even in today's liberated milieu. He is described as a weird sea-green thing with four suction-cupped weaving tentacles above hideously malformed legs. He wears a small, pointed mask; beneath the mask a purple light glows and behind the light--two gigantic luminous eyes.

If the Octopus himself was a little strange, he was hardly more so than his chief antagonist. The hero of the book was a young millionaire philanthropist named Jeffrey Fairchild. Like many another pulp hero, and especially those created by Norvell Page, Fairchild is not content with one simple identity. In fact not even two distinct identities are good enough for him. Within a few pages of the story opening Jeffrey is revealed in a weird triptychal personality split.

At least part of the time he is Jeffrey Fairchild, son of the late Dr. Henry Fairchild, who had achieved medical fame and a sizable fortune before his death. Jeffrey, as administrator of his father's estate, had been instrumental in the erection of the Mid-City Hospital and in the further allowance of the large sums necessary for the hospital's upkeep.

Jeffrey's own younger brother, Robert Fairchild, was a long-time patient in Mid-City Hospital; the youth's body had been permanently crippled by ruthless criminals. It was from that traumatic incident that Jeff's interest in crime fighting had started.

His brother's illness, both physical and mental, had taught Jeff that healing must go deeper than he had imagined. With the use of a gray wig and make-up in order to pose as the trusted old Dr. Skull, he sometimes had been able to fight more battles for the poor in his slum neighborhood than confining his skill solely to the struggle against disease.

It was Jeff's third identity tht leads the reader to suspect the lad's own sanity, for in an even greater effort to root out the malignant growth of crime in the community body he assumed the role of the dreaded Skull Killer.

The legend of the Skull Killer had flared to life when three insurance policy racketeers were found one by one, in various lonely corners of New York, with raw outlines of skulls burned into their foreheads. The weapon used had been a metal stamp fashioned in the shape of a skull; in the middle of the stamp: a single steel spike. The tooth of the skull had been used like the exacting thunderbolt of an ancient god, and when the victim fell he bore the Mark of the Skull as a death sign.

In the underworld, the Skull Killer--like the Spider before him--was a dread legend, and the Mark of the Skull was known as a declaration of war to the death. Among the police he was regarded benevolently, although each fresh killing brought assurances from the Commissioner's office that the Skull Killer would shortly be brought to justice.

As a man trained to heal rather than injure, Jeffrey was aware that his work as the Skull Killer was violent medicine, but he also believed that there were times when nothing short of radical surgery could keep the patient alive--the patient in this case being society itself.

This theme of ruthless vigilante justice was a popular one in the pulp magazines of the 1930s (and no one was more skillful in its employ than Norvell Page). It was a theme that popular entertainment would return to with the advent of such controversial films as *Death Wish* and *Dirty Harry*, and in a rash of pulp-inspired paperback novels along the lines of Don Pendleton's best-selling "Executioner" books.

What made the 1930s' stories drastically different from their modern counterparts was the imaginative scope of their plots, inspired no doubt by the flagrant schemes of their larger- than-life villains.

The Octopus, for instance, was clearly no semi-sympathetic Sicilian father figure. Instead, he was the genuine article: a real honest-to-god pulp fiction maniac.

Consider as evidence this opening vignette in "The City Condemned to Hell." Gentle old Dr. Skull (Jeffrey Fairchild) has taken in a woman who has been found battered and half crazed, the victim of an inexplicable assault that left her almost drained of blood. Then the good doctor discovers--to his horror--that his patient has no pulse or heartbeat, and that her blood is of the temperature and approximate consistency of sea-water! And she moans repeatedly something about an octopus....

The scene in question begins when Dr. Skull hears a scuffle behind the curtains which veil Mrs. Purvins from the rest of Ward Seven. He brushes past the curtain and finds--

> *Mrs. Purvins' mouth was fastened like a suction pump on the nurse's bosom, and in the staring grey eyes there was stark, maddened hunger!*
>
> *Dr. Skull seized his patient's shoulders, his muscular fingers pulled against that sucking, intractable force even as he gasped at the hideous strength of those hungry lips.....Then, with a soft woosh, he pulled her clear.*
>
> *The nurse dropped like a dead weight, with a three-inch circle of raw muscle bleeding over her heart, and even more terrifying in its implications, he saw the shredded torn remnants of part of her uniform on the floor!*
>
> *The thing that had been his patient turned its shining unhuman eyes on the doctor. Suddenly it reared--not on it legs,*

but with a swift upward surge that seemed to involve every molecule of matter in its body. He felt the white surgeon's jacket torn from him as though it were cheese-cloth and suddenly he understood why the nurse had been unable to give alarm when she had been attacked.

The thing's clammy hand slapped against his mouth, jammed into his throat, nearly suffocating him, while with the swiftness of a striking snake, that terrible mouth fastened on his shoulder, its suction rending his skin, tearing with intolerable pain at the muscular flesh beneath.

He lunged desperately with arms and legs--felt himself free, and gasped for air. He cried out then, trying to call for help as his staring eyes saw his erstwhile patient rear up at the window, and with a peculiarly undulating movement slip outside. He staggered after it, his fingers clutching the sill as the Thing descended the fire escape with unbelievable rapidity...And then he saw something else that momentarily caused him to forget his pain, and his horror.

As the Thing passed the third floor, a snakily prehensile arm whirled a net from a window, trapped the creature that had been Mrs. Purvins and pulled her back inside the hospital.

And that, he knew, was one of the windows opening from the maternity ward!

What in the name of reason is going on here? Well, it seems that our friend the Octopus has created

an army of atavisms--once ordinary men and women who
have had millions and millions of years of evolution lobbed
off their heritage. They have suffered some kind of
dreadful sea change. And now, as the city sleeps, they come
crawling from their subteranean sanctuaries to perform
the tasks set out by their octopod mentor.

Entrenched in the very heart of Manhattan, in a new
skyscraper citadel aptly called the Victory Building, the
Octopus beams out a purple arm of death--an ultra-violet
ray--to sweep away his enemies. Each night a dreadful
cavalcade--malformed creatures that once were human--
pour forth from their secret places as if summoned by the
awful beam.

New York City is in a state of siege, the first pawn
in a master plan for world conquest.

As in most pulp character novels, things get a lot
worse before they get better. The Octopus beams in on
Jeff's beloved Mid-City Hospital, demolishing the building
entirely. Within a few lightning-paced chapters, some
eight million innocent victims have been destroyed (you
got a lot of spectacle for your dime in those days). What's
worse, Jeff's alter-ego, Dr. Skull, is condemned as their
murderer.

All's well that ends well, however--as another famous
hack writer once said. By the time page 63 rolls around a
bewildering array of plot complexities have been resolved,
the Octopus and his fishy minions have been routed, and
Jeff takes over as the new owner of the once infamous
Victory Building. He plans to turn the edifice into a haven
for the sick and injured, a logical substitute for his
devastated Mid-City Hospital. Considering the numer of
sick and injured by this point, one can only hope that it's
a mighty BIG structure.

> But the Octopus--that incredibly evil
> personality who had been the skycraper's
> first master--would his presence really be
> gone forever from the place he lorded?

*Jeffrey recalled those old legends of the
Deathless One, and he couldn't swear that
the man was dead. It had been impossible
to identify all the mangled bodies after
that dreadful revenge.*

*Jeffrey sighed. He had done his part in
the freeing of this city; he could only
continue to do his part in the interests of
its welfare. If sometime in the unpredict-
able future that esence of evil threatened
once more to test its malignant, deadly
powers, the new owner of the Victory
Building would have to do his part
again...*

Poor Jeff didn't have long to wait. Precisely two
months later his specialized services were required once
again in what appeared to be a new magazine--*The
Scorpion.*

Despite the magazine's disclaimer, the Scorpion was
really our old friend the Octopus wearing a new fright
mask. The lead novel, "Satan's Incubator," was an obvious
rewrite of what was to have been the second Octopus story,
with all references to the Octopus altered to that of the
Scorpion. All of the other major characters remained the
same.

Physically, the cowled figure of the Scorpion appeared to be more human than the tentacle-waving
Octopus--if it hadn't been for a birthmark extending from
his forehead to his chin. Black and as clearly outlined as
a shadow at noon, the disfigurement is the exact replica
of a scorpion.

While the super fiend's stigmata is less grotesque
than in his previous incarnation, his brain is honed to even
greater nastiness.

This time the chastened but wily madman has
discovered the benefits of working within the Establishment. Operating through the city administration itself, he

has somehow fashioned a huge base beneath Manhattan, the symbolic entrance to which is the city's main garbage incinerator. A fleet of Scorpion-controlled garbage trucks rumble out into the city's streets each night, each one equipped with the latest in hellish gadgetry: hypnotic brain rotors capable of turning ordinary citizens into packs of murder-maniacs.

"Last week," announces a Scorpion henchman at a secret council meeting, "we had three trucks making rounds in the city, equipped with four brain rotors each. Even with that meager equipment we were able to bring several score new subjects a day to the Scorpion. Now, we have fifty trucks ready to start as soon as the new rotors are put in. Six of them will be equipped with one multiple brain rotor capable off transforming twice as many subjects as the old-type engine, in one-tenth the time."

American know-how in action! Furthermore, the Scorpion has the ruthlessness to see that his new-found slaves stay in line. You think you're familiar with nastiness? Witness this scene in the

master fiend's incinerator headquarters; the Scorpion is addressing his lieutenants:

"What you are about to witness will sharpen your faculties immensely," he promises. "You, Gordon, you were a veterinarian once. I want you to perform an operation on this man Dugan. Take him into the inner room and amputate his legs. Be careful about it--I want him to stay alive and in good appetite. When he comes to, if he requires a fluid diet, offer him broth brewed from his own legs. Nothing else. As soon as he can stand it, take off the arms. Those four chunks of meat should have enough nourishment to last him a week. If he wants something solid, fry him a piece of his own ham."

How's that for nasty?

Fortunately for the citizens of Fun City, Jeff Fairchild is around in his guise as the villain-hating Skull Killer. As in the previous Octopus novel, the plot of "Satan's Incubator" contained enough elements for a dozen normal stories. It combined an outrageous sense of melodrama with the pulp writers' knack of making the preposterous believable. Well...almost believable.

Suffice it to say that by the time the final chapter rolled around much of New York City was in ruins (again), and the good guys were about to pull themselves phoenix-like from the Scorpion's funeral pyre.

> *The city would be as it had been before except for a thousand empty places that had been filled before these two days of horror. How long would it be that way? No man could have survived who remained below ground during that terrific explosion--but was the Scorpion a man, and no more? For the leader of the Purple Eyes could not die, the old legend had stated-- and everything else in the legend had proven true.*

> *Jeffrey touched the Stamp of the Skull*
> *Killer in his pocket. If the city were*
> *attacked some time in the future, that ws*
> *the only answer he knew.*

The stamp of the Skull Killer was to remain in Jeff's pocket because no other issue of *The Scorpion* ever appeared. Perhaps the bizarre two-faced villain and his tripartite protagonist were too far-out even for the wild and wooly pulps.

Perhaps readers simply did not take to magazines that honored criminals in their titles.

In any case, the quick death of the Octopus/Scorpion brought an end to the all-villain pulp magazines. It was the bad guy's last hurrah.

Today these magazines are among the scarcest of all pulps. They fetch inflated prices from collectors--anywhere from fifty to three hundred dollars a copy, depending on title and condition--an interesting fact when you consider what must have been reader resistance to laying out the original cover price: a modest ten cents.

Not counting the Dr. Satan stories in *Weird Tales*, there were only five pulp villain titles ever published--fifteen novels in all. The entire sub-genre came into existence and perished forever with those fifteen issues.

Various arch-fiends would continue plaguing the great pulp heroes right up until the final gasp of the pulps themselves. But never again would a villain have a magazine all to his very own.

The publishers had learned the bitter lesson which their readers already knew:

Crime Does Not Pay.

LOST CITIES AND HIDDEN JUNGLES

Imagine a world in which Tarzan of the Apes had never existed. Even if you could, who would want to live in such a dreary place?

Of all the great pulp heroes, Tarzan is incontestably the most universally renowned, even among those who have never read a book of any kind.

In the mid 1940s, in the lingering summer dusk, there was barely a street in our neighborhood that was not punctuated by sudden falsetto impressions of Johnny Weissmuller's fearsome jungle yodel. Known to youthful literati as "the Victory Cry of the Bull Ape," it was a sound effect as familiar to my generation of kids as a mother's call to dinner.

Like Dodge City, Pacific battlegounds, and the red planet Mars, Tarzan's jungle was never far from us. We swung on ropes, pretending they were vines, and loped down city laneways grunting "UNGAWA!" to faithful elephants, just out of sight. And in the steamy summer evenings, we tossed in crumpled sheets, imagining ourselves in jungle tents.

What fabled riches, lost races, and bizarre life forms inhabit such uncharted regions of the earth? That's a question that causes few to lose much sleep nowadays. The jungles of the world, a luxurious girdle around the equator, are themselves threatened by man's desire to turn everything into parking lots as he steadily forecloses on his own future.

Happily, it was not always so.

One of the joys of reading pulp fiction is to be able to take a time trip back to a more innocent age (was it *only* a mere half century ago?) when the world seemed still unformed and we could imagine vast miasmic places untramelled by camera-wielding tourists and hard-eyed men in business suits--places suffocating with impenetrable vines and parasitic creepers masking cities of stone and ancient civilizations. If our view of native races was naive and even ignorant, so was our comforting vision of a natural world too immense to be plundered, too remote for all its mysteries to be revealed.

This was the untamed jungle of the imagination that a failed businessman named Edgar Rice Burroughs liked to dream of at the end of vexing days. Stuck in sweltering Chicago traffic, Burroughs comforted himself with visions of a splendid alter-ego who did not have to cope with crowds, clients, or the problems of raising a family. Dressed only in a loin cloth and with a knife between his teeth, he could zip his way from one end of Africa to the other without even touching the ground. He'd swing on vines. What a way to go!

Not being a business success, Burroughs began to put his dreams to paper. "Most of the stories I wrote," he later admitted, "were the stories I told myself just before I went to sleep."

Such a story was Tarzan of the Apes, scribbled in longhand on scraps of paper left over from the author's failed mail order schemes.

"I did not think it was a very good story," he confessed years later, "and doubted if it would sell."

He was wrong. ERB (as he would become known to his legions of admirers) sold his jungle yarn to Munsey's *The All-Story Magazine*. Subtitled "A Romance of the Jungle," it was published complete in the October 1912 issue, where it caused an immediate sensation. A hardcover version, published two years later, sold over a million copies, not counting later reprint editions. A torrent of novels followed: stories about Mars, Venus, Apaches, detectives, tales of the Moon and of Pellucidar at the earth's core--nearly seventy books in all, published in 31 languages--an impressive 322 pulp magazine credits. But it was Tarzan who would remain ERB's most famous creation--one of the indelible figures in the history of popular literature.

Edgar Rice Burroughs

Burroughs published 23 more Tarzan books in his lifetime, most of them appearing first in such top adventure pulps as *Argosy, All-Story Weekly,* and *Blue Book.* None of the novels were stylistic masterpieces but Tarzan himself achieved a literary permanence because he tapped a universal human myth, that of the Noble Savage, Rousseau's "natural man" personified.

Following the runaway success of the Tarzan books, movies, comics, and radio shows, producing Tarzan-type characters became a growth industry in the pulps. Otis Adelbert Kline, a Chicago-based writer long considered Burrough's chief rival and slickest imitator (exluding Burroughs himself), came up with Tam, Son of the Tiger for *Weird Tales,* Jan of the Jungle, and Jan In India for *Argosy,* all take-offs on Tarzan. Kline's Jan of the Jungle was raised as a chimpanzee-boy--in Florida, of all places-- but did his Tarzan thing in the jungles of South America and India in order not to clash with the Ape Man's African franchise.

There was talk of a Burroughs-Kline feud, but little substantiation. The truth is that imitation is the sincerest form of flattery and Kline was an acknowledged fan of Burroughs. Besides, wasn't Tarzan himself a derivation of Kipling's Mowgli, transported holus-bolus from India to Africa? (Although a magnificent tale spinner, ERB didn't know squat about the Dark Continent, managing to relocate one of Kipling's Indian tigers in the process).

While he was the greatest of the great pulp heroes in terms of worldwide fame, Tarzan never did achieve his own magazine. That honor would be left to a mere four of the Jungle Lord's brusquely-named competitors: Matalaa, Ka-Zar, Ki-Gor and the lovely--but even more unlikely-- Sheena, Queen of the Jungle. Before these swingers arrived on the scene there were any number of less prominent tryouts.

While manufacturing Tarzan clones, writers strained to come up with exotic locations that would not impinge on Burroughs' Congo. Morgo the Mighty appeared in a serial of that name in *The Popular Magazine,* beginning in August 1930. Morgo was a Tarzan type who inhabited bizarre caverns in the bowels of the Himalayas. Morgo's author, one "Sean O'Larkin," supplied his hero with jungles of fungus and an army of flying bat men companions named Bakketes.

Not to be undone, Walter A. Tompkins (writing as Valentine Wood) produced Ozar the Aztec, who appeared in a number of stories ("Ozar and the Jade Altar" "Death Drums of Ozar," "Ozar and the Plumed Serpent," etc.) in Street & Smith's *Top Notch* in 1933. Known as the sky king of the Aztecs, Ozar was really Larry Sterling, captured as an infant in the mountains of Mexico by a "lost" tribe of Aztec Sun God worshipers.

William L. Chester's Kioga, the Snow Hawk, was a popular staple in *Blue Book* from 1935 to 1938. Kioga did his treeswinging as far from Tarzan's turf as could be imagined--marooned as a youth in a strange land north of the Arctic Circle. Called Nato'wa by the ancestors of the American Indians who still lived there, the island was made habitable by warm ocean currents and a ring of still active volcanoes. His parents killed by savages (a sacrificial prerequisite in the jungle god business), young Kioga is raised by their Indian friend, Mokuyi, from whom he learns the English of his fathers as well as the Indian arts of hunting and fighting. He is joined in his subsequent adventures by a pet bear, Aki, and a silver-coated puma, Mika.

Kioga's similarity to Tarzan was enhanced by the fact that *Blue Book* illustrator Herbert Morton Stoops was assigned to delineate both characters for the magazine. A further Kioga/Tarzan connection was introduced in 1938 when Republic Pictures produced a 12 chapter serial based on the initial Kioga novel, *Hawk of the Wilderness.* A first-rate production, the chapter play starred a leanly muscled Olymic athlete named Herman Brix, ERB's own choice as the ideal Tarzan type.

The jungles of the Malay Peninsula were the setting for "Sangroo the Sun God," who appeared in the first issue of Clayton's short-lived *Jungle Stories* in August 1931. The character, written by J. Irving Crump, appeared in at least one other story, "The Trumpeting Herd," which was featured in the October 1931 number. Crump left the pulp field shortly after to write daily radio dramas for the late-afternoon cereal set. (Both he and the legendary Talbot Mundy worked on Jack Armstrong, the All-American Boy, that national institution sponsored by Wheaties, "breakfast of champions.")

Kwa of the Jungle, raised among apes in Africa, proved to be an an uninspired Tarzan copy. He appeared in a half dozen stories in Standard's *Thrilling Adventure* in 1932 and 1933, but gathered no fan club. The same might be said for the likes of Avar (*Fantastic Adventures*), Tharn (*Amazing Stories*)and Toka (*Fantastic Adventures*). These three, along with Manly Wade Wellman's Hok (*Amazing Stories*) were part of a phalanx of Cro-Magnon Tarzans nurtured by editor Raymond Palmer of Ziff-Davis Publications, who had a thing about cavemen. What attracted him to them was that they sold magazines--especially when those magazines bore covers painted by J. Allen St. John, the master artist most closely associated with Tarzan himself.

Robert Moore Williams' Jongor ("Jongor of Lost Land," "The Return of Jongor," "Jongor Fights Back") also appeared in *Fantastic Adventures*, but proved a cut above the rest, if only because of his interesting milieu--a modern-day dinosaur-infested land in the middle of Australia's great desert.

Jongor's Lost Land was a world that was not only lost to map makers but lost to time as well. Here a gray-eyed young giant rode out on dinosaurs, fought leather-winged pterodactyls, and waged war on the Murians--a lost colony of degenerate monkey-men from ancient Mu. Because anything that ever existed on earth might still exist in Lost Land, it was a premise open to endless variations.

Even so, only three Jongor stories were ever published, and these over a ten year period.

One of the irksome factors in the jungle Adonis image was that the hero invariably had the wherewithal to battle bull apes but appeared to lack the testosterone sufficient to raise a five o'clock shadow. Robert Moore Williams dismissed this anomoly with a brief mention of Jongor's "bearded face." Even so, the illustrators continued to depict his cheeks as bereft of fuzz as a granite statue.

One of the Jongor illustrators was the aforementioned J. Allen St. John, whose striking cover for the first Jongor novel has been credited with setting new sales records for Ziff-Davis, thereby saving *Fantastic Adventures* from threatened cancellation. Most of the caveman stories that appeared in Jongor's wake were created specifically to encourage new Tarzan-like paintings from the estimable Mr. St. John.

Not surprisingly, the Tarzan myth became a merchandising craze in the gray days of the Great Depression when Americans' need to escape reality increased and their faith in the "benefits" of civilization decreased. It seemed inevitable that some enterprising publisher would finally offer a Tarzan type in his own magazine. The first of these, Bob Byrd's Ka-Zar, not only achieved his own title, but had it named after him.

Ka-Zar was introduced in October 1936 in a novel titled "King of Fang and Claw." The story was well crafted but hewed tediously close to Burroughs' initial concept. A ritualized child-of-the-jungle origin was dusted off: John Rand, his wife Constance and infant son, David, crash in a light plane in the heart of the Congo two degrees south of the Equator. Mother dies (to no reader's surprise) and father becomes mentally unbalanced when conked on the head by a falling tree.

Raised in the wilderness by a lunatic father, young David realizes that a kid has to have some kind of pals, so he makes friends of the jungle beasts. On one occasion he saves Zar the lion from a treacherous bed of quicksand.

When young David's father dies in his arms from a murderer's bullet, the mighty lion adopts the grief-stricken boy and takes him to his own jungle lair. There a pact of brotherhood is sworn. The boy ceases to be David Rand and becomes instead Ka-Zar, brother of Zar the lion. He even learns to speak the universal language of the beasts, a kind of jungle Esperanto.

In his second adventure, "Roar of the Jungle," Ka-Zar encounters the opposite sex in the person of beautiful Claudette, slave to a banished Indian rajah who has set up a kingdom (complete with harem) in the Congo. Ka-Zar saves Claudette from the rajah's Fate Worse Than Death but, in an ironic twist, loses the girl because he is unable to communicate with her. He speaks only the language of the beasts.

While ostensibly a bi-monthly, the third (and final) issue, retitled *Ka-Zar the Great*, did not appear until June of '37. It was an improvement on the first two plots in that it dealt with that reliable theme beloved by both H. Rider Haggard and ERB, "The Lost Empire." In this case the "lost" people are descendants of ancient Egyptians who rule an inaccessible valley in the manner of their ancestors. The citizens of Khalli must have picked up something from the Romans as well since there is one scene in which Ka-Zar is is tied to a block in an arena to be fed to a wild lion. The lion turns out to be our old friend Zar, who gives his jungle "brother" an affectionate greeting, much to the crowd's disdain.

While Ka-Zar lasted only three issues as a pulp hero, he had a longer life in the comics. In 1939, Ka-Zar pulp publisher Martin Goodman produced a comic book titled *Marvel Comics*, after his sf pulp *Marvel Stories*. Kazar and his faithful beast brother popped up in Goodman's comic as back-up acts to the likes of the Human Torch. They were reinstated in 1965 in the Marvel Comics line as jungle peacekeepers in a sort of Antarctic Pellucidar.

Matalaa, the White Savage, appeared in the lead novel spot in each issue of *Red Star Adventures* magazine.

While not strictly a jungle swinger, he fulfilled the pseudo-
Tarzan image by sticking to Burroughs' tried-and-true
"noble savage" formula. Christened Warren Steele, Jr., he
was orphaned when shipwrecked with his parents on a reef
off a tiny South Pacific island. Raised by natives, and re-
named Matalaa, or "Eye of the Sun," because of his red-
gold hair, the youth was taken under the wing of an old
witch doctor, Poi Uto, who instructed him in things no
other white man had ever learned. Matalaa fought evil
Asiatics, renegade whites (usually Dutchmen), pearl
poachers and even a typhoon, but was downed by his own
publisher when his magazine was cancelled in 1940 after
a mere four issues.

In truth there was only one pulp jungle hero who
would prove as popular as Tarzan--at least in number of
return engagements. His name was Ki-Gor, known to
friends and crocodiles alike as the White Jungle Lord.

Ki-Gor swung along the arboreal routes in every
issue of Fiction House's *Jungle Stories* (no relation to
Clayton's earlier title). The new *Jungle Stories* maintained quarterly publication from Winter 1939 to Spring
1954, producing 59 Ki-Gor novels in all--a respectable
record for any vine crawler.

Because he wasn't the first jungle kid on the block,
Ki-Gor had to try harder. Most of his adventures bore titles
of undisciplined invention: "Cobra Queen of the Congo
Legions," "Safari of the Serpent Slaves," "Monkey-Men of
Loba-Gola," "Voodoo Slaves of the Devil's Daughter,"
"Warrior Queen of Attila's Lost Legion," "The Beast Gods
of Atlantis," "Slave Brides for the Dawn Men," and so on.

Flamboyance was the norm in T.T. Scott's Fiction
House publications. But when it came to their pulp and
comic magazine logos, the company favored bare bones
titles: *Action Stories, Fight Stories, Frontier Stories, Planet
Stories, Wings*. They couldn't afford the best stories or the
top writers, so they concentrated on other features. The
action-packed Fiction House covers (identified by a colophon inset in a bulls-eye target) invariably exhibited

lightly-draped females in attitudes of peril. Those parts of the covers not taken up with sexually-tinged violence (admittedly a miser's portion) were overprinted with manic titles designed to reach out and punch the newsstand browser.

Even the story blurbs crackled:

> *The jungle seethed with terror. Devilish rumors flew the vine-route: Ki-Gor was doomed! The vile Wandarobo, hordes of stunted beast-men, had trapped the blond stalker....And copper-haired Helene, the tree-telegraph whispered, would die beneath the cannibal moon!*

> *Into the soulless domain of the gray apes; into the jungle city of Dargh-Abar-- where man was slave and beast was king--stormed a wrathful Ki-Gor to pit muscle and guile against the brute strength and simian cunning of a power-mad ape army.*

> *In the heart of the juju forest...in an island city...the strange V'Lorians murdered in the night. Ony Ki-Gor, great White Lord of the Jungle, could face that unworldly horde and hope to win. Yet within his heart was not the will to fight-- for Helene, his golden mate, was no longer at his side. She was among the living dead in an unmarked grave.*

From the foregoing hyperbole, astute readers will note that Ki-Gor was (a) blond (b) married to a red head named Helene (c) kept busy rescuing said Helene from menaces ranging from giant snakes to pygmy cannibals.

Ki-Gor was the son of a Scots missionary, Robert Kilgour, who was killed by natives so that his son could grow up lion-thewed and command his own pulp magazine. This happened off-stage in the first Jungle Lord story, "King of the Jungle."

In the best pulp tradition, author John Murray Reynolds began that introductory story in the middle of cliffhanger action. Helene Vaughn, a 25-year-old "society aviatrix" is winging her way across equatorial Africa when the engine of her small plane splutters and dies, and she is forced to crash land in a patch of open grassland.

> Suddenly from just behind her, very close and somehow threatening came a soft sinister rustle of leaves. Quickly she turned her head, and the warm blood in her veins turned cold. Not more than a dozen paces away was a great sable jungle cat. A black panther, sleek and cruel.

But, hey, this is Ki-Gor country. A naked brown form shoots from the trees directly onto the panther's back. One of the jungle man's arms slides around the panther's neck, the other stabs a long bladed knife between the beast's ribs. This is the dynamic scene that top pulp artist Norman Saunders portrayed on the historic cover. Helene was portrayed in full flying suit with aviator's cap and goggles--the last time she would appear clothed in public.

That first Ki-Gor story was not very long, only 22 pages, but it set the stage for future action. In it Ki-Gor not only meets the woman who will become his mate but gets some worthwhile on-the-job training while rescuing her from native tribes, a giant ape, and Arab slave traders. As in all subsequent issues, *Jungle Stories* delivered what it promised: a magazine packed with stories about the jungle. Its back pages would be routinely filled with yarns about treasure hunters, witch doctors, explorers and headhunters, along with copious supplies of treacherous jungle bullies. The magazine's publication would be sporadic--mostly a quarterly, occasionally bi-monthly, and sometimes skipping an issue altogether--but for sixteen years it would remain a jungle fan's cornucopia.

So why did Ki-Gor succeed when dozens of Tarzan types did not? Despite those wild covers and even wilder story blurbs, the answer lies in the stories themselves and in the fact that there were so many of them. What Tarzan fans wanted was not variations on a theme, but more Tarzan adventures--and lots of them. Ki-Gor was not a dawn world cave man or a modern day Arctic Indian. To all intents and purposes, Ki-Gor *was* Tarzan--an amalgam of Burrough's literary creation with the more familiar (and comfortably simplistic) movie version.

In order to set up Ki-Gor as a surrogate for fans who couldn't get enough of Tarzan, a hefty amount of detail was lifted from ERB's own books. Like Tarzan, Ki-Gor was a man who moved backwards on the bitter trail of evolution. King of the predatory jungle, he fought crocodiles and apes, befriended elephants, and ruled the jungle with his mate like Adam and Eve before the fall. While Ki-Gor's eyes were a blazing blue in his origin story, they soon turned gray--a shade Ki-Gor's pseudonymous authors no doubt picked up while cribbing from The Master.

Like most nostalgiacs, Burroughs was fond of ancient civilizations. In order to keep the Tarzan stew bubbling he had his hero mix it up with a lost colony of Atlanteans, various cities inhabited by the descendants of Amazons, ancient Romans, and even a lost race of Mayans in the Pacific. Ki-Gor's scribes took ERB's fantastic elements to their limits with stories not only of lost cities and civilizations but horrendous battles with prehistoric thunder-dragons, ant-men, talking apes, zombies, sea serpents, stunted beast-men, and humans turned into gigantic monsters.

The surprise in all this is not that so many of the stories are repetitious and hackneyed but that so many of them are energetic and entertainingly preposterous in the best pulp hero tradition.

Today *Jungle Stories* is considered one of the more collectible of pulp hero magazines, a feat made compli-cated by the magazine's bewildering inconsistencies. There are three pairs of issues bearing the same cover but different novels inside; six other pairs of issues share the same cover and identical titles, but the stories are all different; two other novels, "Ki-Gor and the Gorilla Men" and "Nirvana of the Seven Voodoos," although bearing different titles, covers and interior illustrations, are identical stories. If this isn't confusing enough, many of the stories have little connection to their titles, including one listed as "Cromba Has a Thousand Spears," on the cover and "Zomba Has a Thousand Spears" inside. In addition, dates and volume numbers on the spines often do not correspond to similar information on the contents pages.

Editors responsible for this jungle-style stew included Malcolm Reiss (sometimes labeled as General Manager), W. Scott Peacock, Jerome Bixby and Jack O'Sullivan. Authors of the Ki-Gor series are harder to pin down. John Murray Reynolds wrote only the first story, the one with his name on it. Writers who labored under the subsequent John Peter Drummond house name included Stanley Mullin, Dan Cushman, and top mystery writer Robert Turner (who wrote the Feb. 1943 novel, but not the Fall 1950 story, which had the same title and cover). Fiction House artist Murphy Anderson believes that Scott

Peacock was alternating on the novels with an unnamed Florida writer. When Peacock became editor (Summer 1944) he wrote all of the lead novels until he left the editorial post the following year.

The White Jungle Lord's writers may appear guilty at best of a condescending attitude toward native Africans, but the truth is that they were reflecting a stigmatization of racial types long accepted in popular literature, both in and out of the pulps. To Ki-Gor's credit, his two closest jungle pals were both black--N'Geeso, Chief of the Kamazila pygmy tribe, and the giant Tembu George--once known as George Spelvin of Cincinnati, U.S.A.--a former Pullman porter and ship's cook, who had become a Masai chief in the M'balla tribe of the East Congo. Both men are portrayed as intelligent, brave, humorous, and ferociously effective in battle. They are the "Monk and Ham" to Ki-Gor's "Doc."

While both Ki-Gor and Tembu (meaning elephant) George were usually armed with shovel-bladed Masai spears and little N'Geeso with a darkly-polished blowgun, the giant George was known to go into battle packing a .45 automatic "equalizer" in a holster on his waist.

Like Tarzan and Jane before them, Ki-Gor and Helene were married with official church blessing ("Ki Gor and the Cannibal Kingdom," Summer 1940). In the course of the series, the Jungle Lord's blue-blooded mate gradually developed from a spoiled social butterfly into a pelt-draped equal of the Jungle Lord. One of the later stories enthuses: "Helene Vaughn had been a beautiful woman when she first came to the jungle--but now, after many moons of the swift, yet simple life in the island home, of chase and tree-top travel through the wide bush, of the freedom of a scanty two-piece leopard-skin garment, she was more than just beautiful. She was lithe and strong now, although completely a woman. She curved in the right places; her legs were long and clean and her bosom was evident, shapely and firm."

Talk about redundant! All you had to do was glance
at one of those cover paintings and you knew that such
descriptions were superflous. As some have pointed out,
the covers of Fiction House magazines were often the best
part. The company continued this tradition when they
entered the comic book field in 1938. Ki-Gor and Helene
were carried over into *Jungle Comics* in January of 1940,
but their names were changed to Kaanga and Ann for
reasons unexplained. All else was identical, including a
pygmy friend named N'Geeso.

Another Fiction House comic, *Jumbo Comics*, featured the exploits of a she-Tarzan named Sheena. Although it is true that Fiction House created hundreds of
characters for their long-running comic line, none made
the impact that Sheena did. Because she was better
looking, sexier and tougher than her competition, she
appeared in 18 issues of her own magazine, one 3-D comic,
and all 167 issues of *Jumbo Comics*. Small wonder that
the company decided to try her out in her own pulp title
in 1951. Alas, her comic fame did not carry over to a pulp
audience and her book died with that single issue. A final
Sheena story was carried in the last issue of *Jungle Stories*,
but it was a case of too little too late. Although the single
issue of her magazine is considered eminently collectible,
the leopard-skinned Sheena and her jungle consort, Bob,
did not have a significant role to play in pulpwood history.

The final issue of *Jungle Stories* was dated Spring
1954. Before his magazine disappeared Ki-Gor was alone
among the great pulp heroes, the last of his fictional breed.
Perhaps he outlived his rivals because of the enduring
legacy of his literary precursor, the immortal Tarzan. Ki-
Gor, like dozens of Tarzan acts before him, had been an
idealized identity figure for any reader who ever answered
Sir Arthur Conan Doyle's classic description of "the boy
who's half a man or the man who's half a boy."

Edgar Rice Burroughs, the man who practically
invented jungles, died in his sleep in 1950 at the age of
seventy-four. Newspapers all over the world reported his

passing and millions of readers felt the loss as if they had known him. Not only did Burroughs make the grade from pulp magazines to books, but he had become one of the most influential authors of all time, thanks to his enthralling daydream of a youth raised in the jungle by apes.

"The power of imagination is all that differentiates the human mind from that of brute creation," ERB once wrote in defense of so-called pulp literature. "Without imagination there is no power to visualize what we have never experienced and without that power there can be no progress."

THE ROAD TO ZERO

The great pulp heroes were a phenomenon of the Great Depression. During the giddy thirties every pulp publisher had at least one superguy among his titles. But for every Doc Savage or Spider there were hundreds of hungry wanabees--masked and muscled symbols of hard times and youthful expectations, all reaching for the brass ring of popular adulation.

Some characters achieved the dignity of their own magazines, their names slashed across covers in vivid reds and yellows. But for every hero with a title of his own there were hundreds of other characters--often more unusual-- who helped fill the short-story quotas. Some series ran for years, although not always in the same magazine. Others appeared briefly and were dismissed.

The detective pulps alone featured uncounted numbers of idiosyncratic oddballs and also-rans. Robert Leslie Bellem's private eye, Dan Turner, who operated out of *Spicy Detective* (renamed *Hollywood Detective*), was once burlesqued by the famous humorist S.J. Perelman, but Turner's own adventures were parody enough. Dan spent most of his time either bashing someone or getting bashed, and he had a colorful way of describing things. (The guns in his yarns never barked or even spat--they sneezed: *Ka-chow!*)

While Dan is best described as the stereotypic private eye, dozens of other detectives and their writers took pains to be different. Street & Smith's *Detective Story* was the home of Thubway Tham, a lithping (pardon: lisping) pickpocket who preyed on those in need of a little humility. *Detective Story* also harbored The Crimson Clown, another street-wise Robin Hood. The clown stole from rich baddies in order to give handouts to the poor--minus his commissions of course--while "disguised" in the full regalia of a circus clown.

Thubway Tham and The Crimson Clown were but two of the mystery men invented by the prodigious hero-maker, Johnston McCulley. Over three decades, McCulley introduced a host of roguish pulp characters, including The Thunderbolt, The Man in Purple, Black Star, Captain Fly-by-Night, Don Renegade, The Whirlwind, and even an early version of The Green Ghost. His most famous creation, of course, was Zorro, that dashing caballero from L.A., who was first introduced to the pulp world as early as 1919. In the 1940s and early '50s McCulley was still cranking out Zorro stories for the magazine *West*. To prove he was a bonafide pulp hero and not some movie dandy, the magazine Zorro wasn't content to scratch his famous "Z" trademark on furniture and costumes--he slashed it on startled faces with three incisive sword strokes.

The Western pulps alone were clotted with hundreds of barb-wire-tough town tamers. Riders of the purple prose ranged from owlhoots with colorful names like Warwhoop Wilson and Guncat Bodman to such recognizable waddies as Hopalong Cassidy and The Lone Ranger. Despite his radio and comic strip fame, *The Lone Ranger* lasted but eight issues, while his pulp clone, *The Masked Rider*, galloped on for over one hundred numbers, from April of 1934 into the 1950s. Go figure.

There were, of course, hordes of other characters who rose to challenge the rule of the great pulp heroes. Some of the challengers commanded their own titles, along with their own devout fans, before succumbing to the ruthless odds against them.

The venerable Nick Carter left dime novels for the pulps back in 1915, when he appeared in the premier issue of *Street & Smith's Detective Story Magazine*. He graduated to his own magazine in 1933, which ran for three years until June of 1936. But old Nick couldn't compete with his publisher's own dynamic duo--The Shadow and Doc Savage.

Doc and The Shadow were tough acts to copy. Even their own publisher bombed out trying. Street & Smith's Cap Fury was a sea-faring roughneck groomed to be a tougher, sexier version of Doc. He appeared in his own short-lived title, *The Skipper*, and then was relegated to the back pages of Doc's own magazine, where he continued doing battle with pirates and other aquatic scum.

The Whisperer was designed to be a Shadow type but also experienced a short run. He wound up as an addendum back in the final folios of the magazine he sought to imitate. He was an interesting character, though. A brash and stocky police commissioner with a taste for violently clashing clothes, James "Wildcat" Gordon assumed the strange gray guise of The Whisperer in order to deal brutal justice to criminals the law could not touch. The colorful Wildcat made his transition into The Whisperer with the aid of a drab gray outfit and a pair of odd dental plates which, when inserted, lengthened his upper lip and made his jaw freakishly pointed. The plates also caused him to speak in a low, weird whisper. His publishers must have liked the bizarre Whisperer because they revived his magazine three years after its original cancellation, and it ran for another ten issues before becoming yet another victim of wartime paper shortages.

The only successful single-character title published by A.A. Wynn's "Ace" magazines was *Secret Agent X*, which enjoyed a healthy run of 41 issues over five years, beginning in 1934. Agent X was another disguise whiz who, unlike the Phantom, had no identity of his own. Faced with a hero sans personality, the stories tried harder to excite. Bearing such titles as "Legion of the Living Dead," "Brand of the Metal Maiden," "Claws of the Corpse Cult," and "Hand of Horror," X's adventures were certainly titillating enough, even if his authors were guilty of formula filching from more successful rivals like the Spider and Operator #5. Amid an atmosphere rife with monstrous crimes and grim death devices, the only humor to be found in *Secret Agent X* was the publisher's blatant invention of the name Brant House as a 'house name' to mask the magazine's true authors.

And so it went. Through the pages of the pulps the garish parade flowed: hordes of masked, cowled, caped, and variously disguised crime-fighting geniuses dedicated to bringing law, order and tranquility to the land, even if they did leave the streets corpse-littered in their wake.

But every parade must have an end.

While the pulps enjoyed unprecedented profits during World War II, the growing cost of wood-pulp paper combined with the gradual erosion of their entertainment market by comic books, paperbacks, radio, the movies, and later, television, conspired against them. The hero pulps took the first blows when wartime readers began rejecting their brand of outright fantasy in favor of stories reflecting a world closer to the one they lived in. The more extravagant pulp icons either disappeared or lost much of their superhuman powers, elbowed out by the relatively mundane figures of the coming TV age: private eyes, G-Men, cops and cowboys. As their sales softened, the watered-down heroes remaining saw their monthly exploits slip back to bi-monthly and even quarterly issuance. Only a few of the character pulps limped on through the late '40s and into the final days of the pulps themselves. They were increasingly out of place in a literature turned slavishly realistic.

Harry Steeger, who had created the Spider, G-8, and Operator #5 back in the glory days, made a nostalgic bid to extend pulp heroism a little longer when he brought out the *Captain Zero* magazine in late 1949. The initial cover promised much, from its dramatic logo to a lead story titled "City of Dreadful Sleep."

Even the story blurb rang with the zest of halcyon days: *Three sinister slay-rides turned a giant metropolis into a city patrolled by terror...helpless, save for one man-- the fabulous Master of Midnight, whose strange cloak of invisibility was, at the same time, a gift of the gods--and a curse of the Devil!*

The only problem was that the "Master of Midnight" really was a zero. His name was Lee Allyn--not too impressive compared to such bell-ringing monickers as Richard Wentworth, Lamont Cranston, and Richard Curtis Van Loan. Even worse, Lee was just a little squirt--only five-feet-four--bland of personality, uncoordinated under stress, and blind as a bat without his glasses. If he'd been forced to fill out a pulp hero job application form, he surely would have flunked the test.

What happened was that editor Alden Norton had instructed author G.T. Fleming-Roberts to produce a pulp character with more human characteristics. Earlier, Fleming-Roberts had brought a sense of sophistication and humor to the adventures of his magician sleuth The Ghost. With Captain Zero he turned the conventional pulp hero upside down. Because of an atomic experiment gone wrong, Lee Allyn becomes invisible every night at midnight and snaps back to visibility each morning at dawn. But he has no control over it. It just happens. "It's an affliction--not an asset," the poor guy points out.

As Captain Zero, Lee really tries to be a good crime fighter but he lacks the expertise that came so naturally to the superguys of the 1930s. His author has trapped him in the real world--our world--where nothing goes smoothly. Wherever he walks, someone is always noticing his footprints from depressions in the grass or carpets. He can't carry a weapon because weapons aren't invisible. Because his eyeglasses would also reveal his presence, he substitues contact lenses; but the light keeps striking them, alerting cops and crooks to his presence. He even has to bum rides, because how long would a driverless car go unnoticed? And since he's on the job all night as Captain Zero, he barely drags himself to work each day.

It sounds like parody, but with Fleming-Roberts it was just good-natured fun. The Captain Zero novels all had busy, intricate story lines featuring suspense, realistic action, good characterization and a terse writing style. But old-time pulp readers, perhaps anticipating a return to the imaginative mayhem of The Shadow or the Spider, were less than enthusiastic about the new brand of realism. And more sophisticated types were put off by cover depictions of The Master of Midnight as a giant robed figure with electrical discharges sizzling from his fingers. For whatever reason, the *Captain Zero* magazine was terminated with its third issue. With it died pulp fiction's Heroic Age--not with a bang, but a whimper.

When the pulps perished of neglect in the mid 1950s, it was the end of a way of writing and a way of dreaming. Many pulpsters never escaped from their penny-a-word ghetto. Some of the old-timers graduated into the 'slicks' or family magazines. Others found work in comic books, and many, like John D. MacDonald, Elmore Leonard, and Louis L'Amour, emigrated to the paperback field where publishers welcomed their hard-earned ability to tell a good story and make the story *move*. Still others drifted out to Hollywood to work in movies and TV. Ironically, they were fueling the very mediums that had killed the pulps by imitation--the sincerest form of flattery.

In their variety, the pulps attempted to supply something for almost every age and taste. While such quality titles as *Argosy,* and *Blue Book* commanded the loyalty of mature readers, the demographics for *Captain Future* and *Operator #5* were weighted heavily with the male youths who answered all those back-of-the-book ads for acne relief and Charles Atlas's body-building secrets. Author Will Murray once pointed out that it is an axiom of popular literature that if you write for the young and touch their young lives, they will never forget you. Perhaps this is why the single-character pulp hero magazines are the most warmly remembered today and the most avidly pursued by collectors of yesterday's ephemeral treasures.

Time is taking its inevitable toll on the crude paper, glue and staples that bound together those summer-sweet dreams of masked phantoms and bronzed geniuses. But, to their once-youthful readers, the great pulp heroes live on in the theatre of the mind, where nothing once loved is ever forgotten. It is there where bronzed Doc's trilling whistle still echoes through impossible green jungles; it is where the Spider and The Shadow--midnight's twins--still perch on timeless skyscraper eyries, black cloaks billowing like giant wings, their chilling laughter even yet filling the mind's ear with mystery and excitement.

Thanks for the memories, superguys.

Québec, Canada
1998